Humans of Magic

Humans of Magic

Interviews with
the Game's Greatest Minds

—

JAMES HSU

For Donna and Julian

Table of Contents

Foreword

Things have changed a lot for *Magic: The Gathering* in the last couple of years. One of the more fascinating changes is the increased focus on Magic players as personalities. We have a window into their passions and lives as never before. The growth of Magic on Twitch is one example of this. Another is the increasingly popular events run by Wizards of the Coast and other Magic organisers – Fandom Legends, for example. Every World Champion from last year onwards will receive their likeness on a card to celebrate their success. Seeing the first entrant, Javier Dominguez, show up on the card Fervent Champion was a delight. The most dramatic example is the creation of the Magic Pro League and the Rivals League – via which Wizards of the Coast is building the brands of individual players and engaging viewers with their personalities.

In this new, ever-changing world, James Hsu's *Humans of Magic* podcast was ahead of its time in connecting the players with the greatest minds in Magic. This sense of connection is the key to make broadcasting high-level Magic events successful. Cedric Phillips, one of the masterminds behind the current coverage at Star City Games, has said that, "The stars sell the cards." You can see this on the coverage of Star City Games events where a lot of effort is put in to help players build their own personal brands. Player-focused interviews and deck techs are the go-to between-round content, and getting your face printed on a token is one of the rewards for taking down their most prestigious events or becoming a content producer for their website.

People want to feel some level of connection with the individuals they see and hear on screen. Whilst it's certainly true that many people watch coverage just to see games of Magic, for me, whoever is commentating is a huge part of my enjoyment. The best commentators give you that feeling of hanging out with friends. And nothing will make me drop everything to turn on coverage like hearing Aaron Barich, Allison Warfield or Dominic Harvey are battling. When I'm rooting for a player the stakes feel higher, viewing the match feels more intense, and the joy of seeing them succeed is all the more rewarding.

This is no small part of the success of Magic streams on Twitch, too. The feeling that by watching someone's stream you can hang out in their company, experience their personality, maybe learn a little about their lives. This isn't the appeal of streams for everyone, but it's no coincidence that the platform via which you can directly communicate with the person entertaining you has become so popular. People crave that sense of connection.

With Magic going through such a big cultural shift in this regard, towards one where the players that you watch are people that you connect with, there could not possibly be a better time for this book, collecting some of the most enjoyable, revealing interviews held on the *Humans of Magic* podcast. I hope that it will help us both remember and better know some of the great players and stunning minds that accompanied the game's journey to this point, whilst also preparing us for the exciting future the game is moving towards.

Autumn Burchett

Introduction

All competitive *Magic: The Gathering* players share one thing in common, and that is the mental battle with oneself. This mental battle is all-encompassing. It is the challenge of trying to be the best one can be while attempting to master a highly complex and evolving game.

Magic deeply resonates with players on a global scale – some have called it *The Greatest Game Ever Made* – but perfect mastery is impossible. The road to self-improvement and growth is filled with epic disappointments and cruel, tournament-ending misplays.

Being a great player takes drive, humility, and self-reflection. The tenacious players experience failures and pick themselves back up, ready to face the next challenge.

Naturally, achievements and actions say a lot about a player's pedigree. Jon Finkel has the most top eight Pro Tour finishes of any player in the game's history. As a result, he is widely considered to be the best Magic player of all time.

Gerry Thompson won a Pro Tour in 2017 and has been a popular voice in the community due to his willingness to stand up for players' rights.

Noah Walker has four Grand Prix top eight finishes and two Star City Games Open wins – and he's barely old enough to drink.

Achievements are the bottom line and the shortcut to understanding a player's body of work. But what mental obstacles did these players conquer to reach the highest pinnacles of peak performance?

Resource management is often described in Magic as the art of effectively managing the in-game resources available to a player. Allocation of resources on different axes of play – life totals, mana, creatures, spells, and so forth.

A big part of that equation, however, includes *emotional management*. Players need to keep their frustrations in check, take things one turn (or game) at a time, and reflect carefully on short- and long-term discoveries.

The *Humans of Magic* project was created to address these questions about self-growth and managing the mental battle. The goal is to highlight each guest's competitive mindset and journey on this long and winding road. Each conversation with a guest is an opportunity for me to converse with top Magic talent and give them a forum to share their experiences.

This book is a "greatest hits" compilation of the podcast. Twelve of the best conversations have been picked and edited for brevity and readability. Key themes are highlighted, such as the power of community, key friendships/rivalries, tips for leveling up, and dealing with adversity. I have added introductions to the chapters that serve as player introductions, as well as explaining my personal connections to them.

Highlighting the personal journey of players is critical given the arrival of a new era of Magic. In this new timeline, Magic is being heavily pushed as an esport in terms of audience, presentation, and future growth.

The guests in this book are featured front and center in live broadcasts and social media. In this climate, the personalities behind the game – who they are, and what they say – resonate more than ever.

This book serves as a reminder that there is so much more to the great Magic players than meets the eye. Each person started from the bottom and worked their way up the ranks.

They worked on their games for years, usually decades – and it never stops. The grind never stops.

This book is dedicated to the brilliant people around the world who play this wonderful yet cruel game. Enjoy.

James Hsu

Regarding Terminology

Magic: The Gathering has a rich and illustrious 25-year history. Many concepts and references have been created in that time span. As such, there are Magic terms thrown about in this book that can be difficult for non-players, and even long-time players, to comprehend.

The goal of this book is to preserve the voice of the original interviews without removing the in-game lingo. It is, after all, the authentic language of the game.

To mitigate this, I have created a glossary located at the end of the book. The glossary contains explanations of commonly used Magic terms and phrases.

The glossary will tell you what a "top eight" is, and what separates "Caw-Blade" from "Czech Pile." (No, I'm not joking.)

Where references are made to specific Magic cards, I have opted not to create glossary entries for each. Instead, all 20,000+ cards can be found at https://gatherer.wizards.com.

Happy reading!

"*Generally, Magic players tend to be bright and interesting people, and have good, useful ways to view and understand the world. So we wanted to step in and do something to help out a little bit there. And so, we had the idea to start Gamers Helping Gamers.*"

—*Jon Finkel*

CHAPTER 1

JON FINKEL

I'm a bit of a late bloomer when it comes to competitive Magic. I started playing the game in the early 90s with my younger brother, but did not play in any tournaments until 2008.

As I didn't follow the competitive scene, I completely missed out on Jon Finkel's ascent as the most dominant Magic player in the game's history. Jon made his first Magic Pro Tour appearance in 1996, and then went on to have an unbelievable career, making the top eight of sixteen Pro Tour events – and outright winning three of them. He's also held the title of World Champion and played on the US National Team. That team won the event, too, for good measure.

Jon was one of the first players inducted into the Magic Hall of Fame, and for good reason – he's definitely the Michael Jordan of Magic. The Greatest of All Time (GOAT), as his overwhelming dominance and unbreakable records within the game can attest to.

Funnily enough, Jon didn't come across my radar until he was featured in an article that a pop culture journalist wrote about him in 2011. In a piece titled "My Brief OkCupid Affair With a World Champion *Magic: The Gathering* Player," Jon's date described the perils of not Googling him ahead of time, and being very surprised that he had a Magic card illustrated in his likeness. All very cool stuff, actually, if you were a Magic player reading about these revelations for the first time.

Being the late bloomer I was, I went back to the archives to learn a *lot* more about Jon. I found out that he had an entire book written about him, called *Jonny Magic & the Card Shark Kids*. I bought the book and devoured it within a few days. After that, the legend of "Jonny Magic" was forever captured in my imagination.

Fast forward several years later, and I happened to meet Jon's college roommate Brian while he visited China. Imagine my surprise, and sheer delight, when I made the connection to Jon Finkel from this fortuitous encounter.

I must have asked Brian to ask Jon to do a podcast recording with me about fifteen times that night. Brian, being the nice guy that he was, told me he'd try but that he couldn't make any promises.

After all, Jon was a busy man. He still plays Magic competitively, but that's in addition to his day job running a hedge fund. These days, he's using his intellect to figure out how to make his fund a lot of money. He's also sponsoring young Magic players and helping them with their college tuition, which is a noble and awesome gesture.

Fortunately, Jon accepted my interview request. I think it was because Brian and Jon were both huge basketball fans, and I happened to chat Brian's ear off that night with hoops talk. I even played pickup ball with Brian that week to prove my love for the game.

Hey, sometimes common ground matters. I'm just glad I had the chance to talk to the GOAT.

Interview recorded in July 2018.

James: How long have you been living in Tribeca?[1]

Jon: Two months. Before this, I lived in Soho, which stands for South of Houston, in the Southern end,

---

[1] A neighborhood in Lower Manhattan, New York City.

which is just right north of Tribeca. So it's about an eight-minute walk from where I am here.

James: I remember my only trip to New York a few years back. I tried to ask a nice lady, "Where can I find *Hues-ton*?" She corrected me on the spot. Just cut me off and said, "No, it's *House-ton*."

Jon: Yeah, it's named after a Revolutionary War hero. [William] Houston. So yes, that's the pronunciation. And Houston is actually zero street. If the numbers continued on down, and then Soho goes down to Canal Street, which is effectively "negative Fifth Street". I'd be at roughly "negative Eighth Street" or so.

James: Have you mostly been living in this area, or have you lived elsewhere in the United States?

Jon: I've been in either New York City or New Jersey for almost my entire life. Specifically, the North part of New Jersey. I was born in upstate New York but moved to New Jersey as far back as I can remember. I was about a year old. And when I was in high school for my first three years, my father's company transferred to England.

I lived in a town called Woking, about 25 miles south of London, from the ages of fourteen to seventeen. But besides that, it's been North New Jersey and then New York for about the last fifteen years.

James: And what were those three years like in Woking? Did you pick up a British accent or get indoctrinated into the culture there?

Jon: I did not pick up a British accent. In fact, I still can't do one. There's a lot that I picked up that I found very interesting. It was so long ago and it almost seems like a different world. That is where I started to play Magic, though. That ended up becoming quite relevant. Although I suspect that if I had not moved there, I would have probably ended up playing Magic somehow, anyway.

James: It's just one of those things that's destined for you, it seems.

Jon: Yeah. Given the universe that I was in and my interest, it seemed very likely.

James: I'm guessing that you had always been into gaming and competitive gaming, or some mixture of the two.

Jon: Yeah. I always liked to game, and I always had a bit of a competitive streak. I don't think I ever did any activity before Magic that was really considered competitive gaming. Certainly not anything on an organized scale. But I also started playing Magic when I was fourteen years old, so there wasn't that much other room. Maybe I could have played chess. I played some chess casually with my parents and a couple of friends, but no real competitive gaming endeavors before that.

James: How did you get introduced into Magic?

Jon: Within Woking, there's Horsell Park, which is famous because that's where the aliens landed in *The War of the Worlds*. Both the book and the radio broadcast depicted that about 80 years ago. And there's a game store downtown that was pretty close to the train station.

I'd always been interested in Dungeons and Dragons, and I played the computer role playing games that were single player. I read a lot of fantasy and science fiction. I read a lot of the Dungeons and

Dragons world books, especially the ones by Weis and Hickman [The Dragonlance Chronicles].

My dad played a ton of games as well. And so one day, I decided to stop by the store to check the scene out. I was interested in the idea of playing some role-playing games, which I had never done live. And there were some people there playing Magic. They offered to show me how, and they did.

And I ended up getting some commons and started to play some Magic. I was hooked pretty quickly. And here I am now, twenty-five years later.

James: Do you remember some of the earliest cards, or decks, that you played?

Jon: I do. And I want to say I figured it out. I was actually fifteen years old. I did a little math in my head.

James: It was a long time ago, yeah. No worries.

Jon: When you get to my age—I think you're probably a little bit younger than I am, but I recently turned forty—you look back in time and think, "Yeah, I don't remember exactly when that was." And then you have to do some math to figure it out.

But yeah, I always liked the control decks. The decks that I would build were similar in style to "The Deck." [Weissman's classic control deck] Although they were not as well-tuned. It was more of a casual local store environment. I might have attended one or two tournaments in the early days, but that was about it.

James: How long did it take you to realize that there were specific Magic strategies like control and aggro? Did you pick up the concepts fairly quickly?

Jon: I don't know exactly how these concepts were discussed or thought about. But immediately, I loved playing blue. It was not only my favorite color, but clearly the best color. I liked to play Counterspell decks, decks that were—if not creature-less, very close to creature-less. I don't know if we used the term control decks or not back then, but that's definitely what they were.

James: You talked about growing up in England and in the US. You must have travelled quite a lot as a Magic player. How many countries in total have you visited?

Jon: I think it's in the neighborhood of 40 or so countries. Maybe a bit more. I played Magic in at least 30 of them.

James: Do you have a specific memory of playing Magic on the road that you're particularly fond of?

Jon: I don't really have a ton of memories of specific matches, or specific top eights. After a while, they all blend together. My brain tends to remember the lessons in terms of playing the game. But a lot of the specifics and the details—I don't remember those.

Obviously, I remember playing Bob Maher in the 2000 World Championships, which I won. Although to be honest, it's hard to know how much of my memories from that are *my* memories, and how much of it comes from online archive videos. I guess there was no VHS video, so it must have been ESPN. I've probably seen the match a dozen times afterwards.

I do remember winning the World Championships. I also remember being in Chicago, in '97, when I made my first top eight. That was probably the one I was happiest about because I had four top sixteen finishes before that.

I also remember some of my more recent tournaments. But it's not like anything specific really stands out. When you've played for as long as I have, everything has happened to you already both in good and bad ways.

James: A lot of your Magic memories...do they feel more important in retrospect, or do you have a pretty good memory of how things went at the time?

Jon: I think this is mostly an impossible question for people to answer. I think most people will give an answer and they'll probably be pretty confident in it. I think in practice it is very difficult for people to really know the difference in how their memory has shifted, or how much of what they remember was *what actually happened*.

I don't know if you have any siblings. But I have a sister, and sometimes we'll talk about things from when we were kids and we'll have wildly different recollections. Who the story happened to, where it was, and so forth. It's interesting when you have a memory that you feel is real and you feel very confident about it. And then somebody else has one that they feel just as strongly about, that's totally different, but it's obviously pointing at the same event.

So you know that at least one of you has to be wrong. And you know that in some of these instances, the one that's wrong has to be you. It definitely makes you aware of the imperfections of memory.

James: I've had that happen, and not just with my younger brother. But just in general, there are things...sometimes they're minor, but sometimes they shatter your world. Because you've been operating on this assumption for many, many years, and you realize it was all falsely constructed.

Jon: Exactly.

James: Are there moments that stand out to you, when you look back?

Jon: Most of what I remember—and I probably remember more from the recent years—is just spending time with my teammates, and playing Magic with my teammates. We'd often rent out houses or places to stay, all over the world.

And I definitely have my memory of those times and those places, and playing Magic with my team. More than the actual tournament itself. After being inducted into the Hall of Fame, I've made six top eights and I have some vague recollections about that. But nothing more strongly than a mental image of what I think the venue looked like, or one or two other things. And this is common for me when it comes to playing Magic tournaments.

James: Has there ever been anything memorable, in terms of something crazy that's happened to you on the road?

Jon: Maybe it's just that I'm older, but I don't tend to—I tend to view a much smaller percentage of things as crazy or weird than I used to. And I don't even know exactly what qualifies. I know that the few times I've gone to Grand Prix events in Latin American countries, I end up taking so many photographs and signing so many playmats and cards.

When I was in Costa Rica a few years ago, I honestly took over five hundred photographs and signed over five hundred cards. Part of me likes and enjoys that, but it can also get pretty tiring. I don't know if that really counts as something crazy.

In Belgium, we stayed at this sort of old farmhouse, but it was several centuries old. And it was in the middle of nowhere. I do remember that there was a supermarket ten minutes down the block that had some of the best croissants I've ever had—and they were supermarket croissants. Maybe that's an indictment of croissants in the United States, I don't know.

We stayed on Bondi Beach in Australia, which was really nice. We also stayed in a castle in Ireland. They called it a castle. Maybe it was slightly generous to call it that. But it was big, made of stone, and really old. So we stayed in a lot of interesting places like that.

When we were in Valencia, Spain, we rented out this house that was a little bit out of town. And this happens a fair bit because if you want to get a lot of people into one space, sometimes you end up going a little bit out of town. We were in this place and it was kind of nice, but there was a problem with their sewage system. Their toilet just backed up and all the sewage started coming out of the toilet. And it was pretty nuts.

I remember the owner taking our security deposit because of that. Even though there was no way we could have made the entire sewage system back up through their toilet. It flooded the house, which was really bad for us. I don't know what service we were using, but it was one of those systems where it was very difficult to get your money back. The owner was making some claims, and the service really didn't want to get involved.

And then I remember a few years later, the owner friended me on LinkedIn. And I'm like, "dude." I'm sure the LinkedIn request was automated. But I was like, "Are you for real?" I thought that in my head, but I didn't bother writing to him. At that point, what are you gonna do?

James: Right. Not only could you not use the toilet, but you were scammed out of the money.

Jon: Yeah. There was also a portion of the house that was not usable. So, not great. But if that was the worst thing that happened to me that month, then it was still a pretty good month.

James: I'd like to talk a little bit about the pro team that you're currently part of, the Ultimate Guard Pro Team. Who else is on the team?

Jon: The team contains William Jensen, who is the current Magic World Champion. Then we have Reid Duke, who might even be the top-ranked player based on the current player ranking system.

           It's hard to pin down exactly the ranking of these players. But it's a reasonable claim that [we have some of the] best Magic players in the world right now.

           And then we also have two other excellent players in Paul Reitzl and Andrew Cuneo.

James: How long have you been with this team? How did you initially get involved?

Jon: It's a group of people that I've played with for a long time. I started playing some tournaments again at the end of 2011, and there was a group of people that I ended up playing with. Over time, the groups change. Some people stop coming and others join us.

Reid [Duke] was with us from the beginning, Andrew [Cuneo] has been with us for a really long time. Paul [Reitzl] has come and gone. He's been with us again for a while.

William Jensen joined us and started to play with us after being elected to the Hall of Fame in 2013. It might have been 2012. I knew William from years ago, before I took a break from Magic. He's probably five years younger than me and we had a friendly relationship. It wasn't like we hung out all the time, but I always really liked him, and had a ton of respect for him as a Magic player. Even when he was fourteen or fifteen, he was obviously really good.

There's also a bunch of other people we played with for extended periods of time, but pro teams cut off at six people. We've tested with Gabriel Nassif, Jelger Wiegersma, and Ben Rubin. Sometimes Kai Budde plays with us, and he's obviously very well known. Shahar Shenhar plays with us. Brock Parker, too. There's a decent number of well-known people.

James: So it's a core team of six people, but there are other players that practice with you as well.

Jon: Yeah. We used to have a playtest group that was larger than that. But for the team series competition, it's the six of us together. Obviously, the other players play on some of their own teams, too.

James: What kinds of things have you learned from the other team members? Are there specific things that you may have learned—in terms of helping your Magic game?

Jon: The answer is definitely yes. The biggest benefit that I've gotten from the team is that they help me with information. I have a full-time job so I don't necessarily play a ton between Pro Tours. And I can get out of practice, which really matters. When I show up a week and a half before the Pro Tour and put in a lot of playtesting, that makes a huge difference to my game. The team gives me constructive preparation in all of these areas, including the metagame.

Of course, there's also a lot of Limited play for each new set. We talk about strategies a lot, and we draft as a group against each other. We'll also draft together on Magic Online and discuss picks. I'm sure I've learned things from everybody in terms of drafting, because there is so much to learn about formats in general. Different people have different experiences with cards, and getting their perspectives is important.

James: It sounds like you're less day-to-day throughout the course of the year with the Magic sets and the cards. But when the Pro Tours come together, that's when you get the crash course.

Jon: If I was playing all the time, I would certainly be better than I am when I show up at the Pro Tour. But with the amount that I'm able to play, I can get to maybe ninety to ninety-five percent of where I could be. And like a lot of other things, it's easier to get up to ninety percent, than it is to go from ninety percent to a hundred percent.

James: Have you learned to think about Magic differently, as a result of working with these guys?

Jon: I don't know how much of it comes from being with these guys, versus the fact that Magic has just changed as a game. The biggest change now is that the preparation process in Constructed has moved away from finding something new in order to break the format. Rather, it's about trying to figure out which of the expected decks is going to be the best, and finding the optimal build based on what other people are playing. How to tune it and have a deep understanding of the deck.

That's not to say that occasionally you can't go ahead and find something brand new. And I still try to do that. But usually that's not the case, and that's fine. You shouldn't knock yourself out trying to invent a better wheel. A lot of the time, in these Magic formats, breaking the format simply doesn't exist because of the speed in which the information is disseminated. Someone probably would have already found a way.

James: So you're saying it's become an optimization problem, because of the availability of the information out there. Are there other factors as well?

Jon: I think it's also the way they've been building the cards. They made a concerted effort a number of years ago to make the threats stronger and more powerful than the answers. And they also made an effort to make the more expensive cards—the ones that cost four, five, or six mana—much stronger.

Then they countered that by making a lot of the really cheap and aggressive cards even more powerful. You end up in a situation where you have really strong cards like Teferi, Hero of Dominaria. They balanced that by having really strong cards, like a bunch of cheap aggressive red creatures. It really tends to put a lot of constraints on the format in terms of what you can realistically try to do.

You end up in a lot of situations where the aggressive decks are so strong, and they have to do like that if they're going to make the dragons that show on the booster box really powerful as well. You end up in a situation where a little bit of inconsistency can make the game almost unwinnable.

If you play against these red decks and you miss a few of your land drops, or if you happen to play some lands that come into play tapped at the wrong time, you almost can't win. So the game today rewards more focused and linear decks. And that will then narrow the range of reasonable decks that could be successful in any given Standard format.

James: Do you have any feelings about how things are today, compared to how they were in the past?

Jon: I think Constructed is much worse and not particularly fun in any of the formats. I don't know how much of it is the desire of the people who make the cards to have the rare cards be a lot better than the other cards, and to have aggressive cards and threats be a much bigger deal. And to have the game revolve around big haymakers.

Back when I played, there was a lot more of an incremental advantage and you gained a little edge here and there. Which is different from the very cheap, very good cards that kill you fast—pitted against the more expensive but really powerful haymakers.

It also felt like there used to be a lot more weird ways that you could attack the game. You're not just trying to build some on-board advantage, where you kill all their creatures or they kill all of yours. I mean, think about all the old combo decks of old,

[like] Illusions-Donate decks. You had High Tide-Time Spiral [and other similar decks.]

And I'm not saying that you are always going to have decks like that, that are dominating. But it felt like there were a lot of different ways you could attack the game.

Now, all that being said, it might be the case that the information distribution was so much slower back then. Although the Internet was around, it just wasn't like it is today. Maybe if we had the way things are today and went back to those years, it would be even worse than things are today. The formats would get solved much more quickly. The things that I found really interesting might not exist, what with the scrutiny of the players and all the brainpower that's going into it today.

James: I think it also goes back to what we discussed earlier, which is the concept of memory. I wonder sometimes if we're just very nostalgic and look back on things with rose-colored glasses.

Jon: It might be. To be honest, I was never a huge fan of Constructed. I always found Limited Magic to be much more interesting. Constructed felt more like doing your homework and doing a lot of similar things over and over again, and trying to change one thing, and then seeing what happens, and then changing another thing. I always preferred to draft.

I went to multiple Constructed Pro Tours—back when Constructed and Limited formats were separate—without ever having done a ton of testing. That was also true for some of the Limited Pro Tours, including a couple I made top eight in. But mostly, I thought Draft was a much more interesting format to play, and a lot more skill testing because there were so many more decisions. It wasn't a matter of you playing this one deck over and over again, in order to learn all the different situations.

James: Do top-level players just gravitate towards Limited?

Jon: If you asked the top one hundred Magic players in the world about their favorite format, seventy-five of them would say Limited. The reality, of course, is that Limited coverage doesn't sell as many cards.

Wizards has something they call the New World Order.[2] They really try to optimize Magic in a way to sell as many cards as possible, which is often related to having the best game, but not always. When they want to make the big threats better, they never want a card like Counterspell for two blue mana. They want all the big dragons and things to be good.

Then there's planeswalker cards, which I think was just an enormous design mistake. I think they made Magic into a much worse game.

They also made a concerted effort to move the cards that were going to be Constructed playable into the rare and mythic slots. In order to make a competitive deck, you had to purchase a lot more cards. A much higher percentage of the cards will be mythic or rare, as opposed to common and uncommon.

James: Have you, or other pro players you know, talked to Wizards and given them this feedback?

---

[2] A deliberate decision by Magic Research & Development to design cards with reduced complexity as a way to make the game more accessible to newer players. For more details, see: https://magic.wizards.com/en/articles/archive/making-magic/new-world-order-2011-12-05

Jon: Yeah. I know a lot of people who work there. They're aware and they make some arguments the other way, which is fine. They say, "Well, we're trying to make it the best game for *everybody*, not just for the pro players." And of course, I understand that. That's more of an argument around making the big dragons good, and not having a game where it's more about small edges.

Look, the Pro Tour is—I don't want to say it's an afterthought, but it's a secondary concern. The Pro Tour is there to help them sell cards. It's a marketing device. And their primary interest is in selling cards.

So if you say, "Hey, you guys are making the mythics and the rares a lot better, and that means we need to have decks that are made out of all those cards." Well, that's kind of the entire point. And these decisions aren't coming from R&D per se, but those are the constraints within which they operate.

I think it's a pretty good business decision. I'm not sure if it necessarily leads to the best game, but in terms of the tension between those two goals, it makes sense.

James: I'm not sure I buy that. Let's take an analogy like basketball, where you have Steph Curry shooting thirty-five footers. He is doing things in order to win and to maximize his chance of winning, and then guess what? Casual basketball players, they imitate that. They're going to imitate whatever the top players do.

So if the Pro players actually started winning again with Recurring Nightmare and whatnot, you can bet the casual players, tournament players, and Friday Night Magic players will be trying to do the same as well.

Jon: I think this is certainly true to some extent. Obviously, this is a bit orthogonal to the question of what rarity to print the good cards at. But even back in the day, there's an old joke that people would play online with certain conditions. When you were looking for an opponent, they'd say: "No counters and no land destruction."

Wizards made it so that there would never be a good land destruction deck again. That's what they want, and that's been eliminated from the universe. People don't like Counterspells, they don't like land destruction, they don't really like this card, they don't like it when their opponents combo off. And so, these things have been intentionally shuttered to be less good strategies in general.

It would be like if people didn't like shooting three-pointers in basketball. If people used the same distance three-point line in casual games as they did in the NBA, the NBA would move the line farther back three feet. It would then make it much harder to shoot and make three-pointers. It probably wouldn't affect Steph Curry, though, because he's an otherworldly shooting talent.

James: Right. Let's talk about Limited for a second. You mentioned that you feel confident about your Limited game. When it comes to Pro Tours, what is your preparation process for that?

Jon: We play a lot of Magic Online. There was also a time when you weren't able to draft on Magic Online until a few days before the Pro Tour. You basically had to get together with people and play in person. So we do a lot of that. We keep records, we see how we're doing with different archetypes and colors. And I'm sure other people do this.

But people really need to be wary of trying to make conclusions from small sample sizes. You may even have some things that appear to be statistically significant, but when you think about the number of different things you're analyzing, some of them will be outliers. You have to consider and think through that.

For example, we analyzed a pretty substantive number of matches or games involving mulligans. In our data, mulliganing on the play was six percent better than mulliganing on the draw. Even after you corrected for the difference in the win rates overall between those scenarios, there was a point where it was definitely at least two, if not three, standard deviations different.

But given the amount that we played and general understanding of it, mulliganing is going to hurt you more on the play than on the draw because you're effectively losing a higher percentage of your total resources. Drawing six cards from seven cards is better than drawing from seven cards to eight cards. It's almost certainly illusory and not really predictive. You have to be aware of all these things when you're keeping stats, and then try to find some insight from those.

James: Maybe it's the way you're describing it—or maybe it's the fact that I know you work for a hedge fund—but I get the feeling that you have a better nose for these types of statistical analyses. Is that something that you've tried to tell your team about, as a unique way to contribute? Or do you think that all your teammates are pretty much tuned in to what you have described?

Jon: I think that they're somewhat tuned in. I definitely am more so, just because I work in a field where you're looking at a lot of things. You see statistically significant things all the time, that you think there's a good chance that they're false. Because you're often betting large amounts of money on them, you need to be really careful with these things.

So I think that's just from experience—I probably have a better nose for that. But there's a number of people on our team who are very talented in these areas, so I don't want to make it sound like I'm imparting wisdom to the uneducated masses. That's far from the case.

James: Maybe another way to ask you is—how do you think others have benefitted from your experience, and your role on the team?

Jon: I think that there's a few ways. I've been through all the winning and losing tons of times before. I definitely don't get too emotionally attached to my results or to specific decks. I have, over the years, played a pretty substantive role in organizing and decision-making for the group. It's been mostly me and Billy [William Jensen]. It's a great group of guys and we generally get along.

But it's like anything else. When you're trying to take a dozen people and make decisions together, people have slightly different preferences and ways to look at things. You still need to put in effort so that you can do the best to keep everybody as happy as possible.

And I think that I'm pretty good at deck selection and tuning decks. I'm probably less likely than a lot of other people to come up with and build a new deck. But I think that I generally end up making pretty good choices. I have a good understanding for when I should trust the opinions of other people, rather than my own.

Generally, it's the case that if one person thinks something is the best and the other thinks something else is the best, one of them is wrong. And in Magic, there's a lot of ways that people try to find ways to say, "Maybe they're both right. Neither is really wrong, and either one is ok." Of course, some things are really close that it's almost impossible to know.

But if you're in a room with five other people that you think are really talented and really good at this—and whose overall skill and decision-making is as good as yours, if not better—it's scary to say, "I disagree, so I'm just going to do what I think is best, rather than having a model that tries to weigh your opinion equivalently with the opinions of these other people."

And so you end up applying what you think is wrong because your model of how much to weigh everybody's opinion suggests that you should actually *not* do what you want to do. You do what someone else wants to do.

I don't know if that made any sense or not—I got a little bit into the weeds there.

James: It makes sense. I used to work for Amazon, and they have this leadership principle called "Disagree and commit." It's not about building consensus, because consensus can be dangerous if you try to cater to everybody. At the end of the day, as a team, you have to weigh the different viewpoints and options and go with *something*. You have to ultimately be willing to own a decision as a team.

Jon: And just to be clear, we don't always play the same deck as a team. But it's important to understand where you may feel that Deck A is the best deck. But other people, whose opinions you trust a lot, think Deck B is the best. And the right thing is almost always going to be going with Deck B. Either you are making a mistake or all four of them are making a mistake. And it's most likely that you're making a mistake than all four of them, collectively.

James: Right. If each of you went to another team, you'd definitely be the star of that team. I imagine that it takes absence of ego and humility to stick together.

Jon: That's certainly a nice way to think about it, and I guess that's true, to some extent. But also, if you want to win—look at basketball, right? People used to talk about Kobe Bryant wanting to win. Kobe Bryant didn't want to win. Tim Duncan wanted to win. Kobe Bryant wanted to be a superstar, and that's very different. He wanted the winning shot. Tim Duncan wanted to win because he was ok to take on a lesser role, or to not be the guy all the time, if that maximized the chances of victory.

James: Kobe was gunning to the very end. Even in his last game, right?

Jon: Kobe has the record for the most game-winning shots in NBA history, and he also has one of the largest downgrades in inefficiency in clutch moments, out of anybody in NBA history. And it's because he always wants to take that shot.

They call that the difference between being correct and being right. And it's more important to be correct than to be right.

James: Absolutely. On that note, what are your goals for continuing to be involved in these teams? What keeps you in it, mentally?

Jon: Yeah, it's hard, and it gets a little bit harder every year. At the end of last year, I was struggling and considering not going to all of the Pro Tours this season. That's not really vacation time for me—it's stressful and feels like work, even if it's something I enjoy. And I do really enjoy gathering with my teammates. They are some of my best friends, and I love spending time with them.

But my teammates, they didn't really have somebody else that they were really excited about playing with this season. And so they said to me, "Hey Jon, are you fine with doing some preparation work on your own, and then maybe coming in for the event, a day or two beforehand?" And that's what happened—I've been doing a little bit more prep on my own, and playing some more Magic Online than I usually do.

I'm not really sure how much longer I'll be going to all the tournaments. It is hard to try to compete when you are getting a little bit older, and also when you're not spending as much time as a bunch of other people who are also very bright and very talented, and fifteen years younger than you are. It's difficult, and I suspect that my career of being competitive probably isn't going to last too much longer.

James: So for you, it's not strictly about winning the next Pro Tour. It's about being *in the game* and being part of the team, it sounds like.

Jon: When I go to a tournament, I want to win. I want to do well and I want to top eight. These things are important to me. This is the tension, because I don't put in the same amount of preparation as some people do. I don't play as much, overall. And this is part of what I'm talking about. I don't want to go to a lot of tournaments and show up and not be prepared.

And not be any good. I certainly can't do that when I'm on a six-man team that's very likely the best team. I mean, we probably have the top three players in the world and we are in first place this year. It's a hard thing for me to half-ass it.

James: I am curious though—because of what you said about the game today, and having limited time to participate. I know that you still play in some Grand Prix and events like that. How do you feel about the Eternal formats?

Jon: I actually haven't gone to any Grand Prix in a while. There was a period when I did—a couple of seasons ago—where I made two top eights, and I hadn't gone to that many Grand Prix. I went to a couple just to pick up enough points to possibly qualify for Worlds. I played maybe only two or three, going back to Kyoto, which was last July.

It's hard for me to jump on a plane on a Friday, fly to some place, win a big tournament on Saturday and Sunday, and then fly back. And these tournaments are huge and there's relatively little prize support. And generally I'm playing formats that I'm not very excited about.

Going to Pro Tours is one thing. I'm willing to put in the effort and the time to try to be competitive there, to go play in those. But generally, for Grand Prix, not so much. I think I only played one Legacy Grand Prix, where I borrowed a deck from Reid. But I effectively don't play Legacy or Vintage at all.

James: Do you have any thoughts about Legacy at all?

Jon: Not really. Again, I don't pay that much attention to formats. I guess the one thing I will say about the Eternal formats—about Modern and Legacy—is

24

that it's nice, and there is a lot more diversity of decks than there is in the Standard formats. But the downside is that they tend to change very slowly, and often because of bannings.

Also, the combination of very powerful sideboard cards and a lot of possible match-ups can create a sort of unfortunate situation where if people draw their huge sideboard hosers, then they're just going to win. And I think that's a bit problematic.

If you're playing a deck that loses to Rest in Peace—and many people are playing at least two of those cards in their sideboards, if not Nihil Spellbombs—it comes down to, *do they draw a Rest in Peace, or do they not?* That makes a huge difference. You're playing Affinity, and they draw their Ancient Grudges or their Shatterstorms. Whatever, their Stony Silences. If they draw it, they win. If they don't draw it, you win.

And I think that is somewhat problematic. So these formats do tend to get a bit stale and the sideboarding aspects—I think it's just pretty bad. But on the other hand, they have a diversity that Standard hasn't had in a really long time.

James: Sounds like it's a double-edged sword. It's diversity at the cost of—you need to have haymaker cards that can instantly answer things. Because the flip side of not jamming that Stony Silence or Rest in Peace is that you just lose on the spot.

Jon: Right. So it makes it kind of random where someone's sideboard has to be ready for ten different decks. But then you're playing your Affinity deck. And at the end of it, you're like, *out of the people I played against, X people drew their Stony Silences.* It's not a ton of fun, or even that interesting, when an entire match comes down to one or two side-board cards. So I think that's a problem, but I don't know enough to solve that problem.

James: I want to ask you about Gamers Helping Gamers. I know that it's a Magic-related charity that you've co-founded to help Magic players with their college tuition. Can you tell me a bit more about this organization, and how it can potentially help Magic players?

Jon: We gave out our first scholarships six or seven years ago. And it was an idea of a friend of mine, Tim McKenna, who used to play a lot of Magic. He's a pretty good tournament player, but never a dominant one. He's worked for years as an economist in New York, and there are a number of us involved who are in New York. We've played a lot of Magic and have been reasonably successful.

Now, when it comes to scholarships, there are scholarships out there for almost everything. But there wasn't that much going on for Magic players. Generally, Magic players tend to be bright and interesting people, and have good, useful ways to view and understand the world. So we wanted to step in and do something to help out a little bit there.

And so, we had the idea to start Gamers Helping Gamers. It's me, Chris Pikula, Bob Maher, Matt Wang, Daniel O'Mahoney-Schwartz, and a few other people. There's Eric Berger, who is probably not as well-known in Magic.

And the idea has been to use it as a way to help and raise some money for the Magic community— to help some Magic players. It's been a pretty big success. We've had a number of winners whom we stayed in touch with, who have gone on to be pretty impressive people.

In our first year, the winner was Dylan Fay, and he ended up going to Yale law school. I know that one of our winners from four years ago, Nathan Calvin, just graduated from college. And he's going to Stanford law school, with a year off to do a program at Oxford in-between. He's another very impressive young man.

There's also Oliver Tiu—probably the most well-known Magic player that we've helped so far.

James: Oh, interesting. Oliver's been through this?

Jon: Yeah. And one of the decisions we made was that we care a bit about Magic results—we wanted somebody who was a real Magic player and reward them if they've done well. But at the same time, we're also not just going to make decisions purely on that. It's not a foregone conclusion that if you're a seventeen year-old Magic player who just won a Pro Tour, then you're definitely going to get the scholarship. But we picked Oliver because he was pretty impressive outside of Magic, in addition to his Magic results.

James: How can folks apply for this program?

Jon: We have a website—gamershelpinggamers.org. At the beginning of every year we start to take applications. Applications usually close at some point in May.

For anyone who is interested in applying, definitely stop by our website.

James: Any interesting surprises since you've been running the program?

Jon: I've been really impressed with some of our winners. I've gotten to know them as people and they've stayed in touch with us. The ones I mentioned earlier—Oliver, Dylan, and Nathan. Really bright, interesting, and motivated people. Good people. And that's really great.

It's one of those things that makes you think that it's all worthwhile. Maybe I made it a little bit easier for this person to get through college, and it looks like they are going to be on their way to doing great things with their life.

James: Are there things that you're looking to evolve in terms of the program?

Jon: Obviously, it would be great if we could get a lot more donations. Then we could expand the number of scholarships we're giving. But generally, I've been pretty happy with how it's been running. Every year, we get a lot of great candidates. We can probably go even deeper and find even more people who deserve the scholarships. I don't think about branching out or reinventing the wheel here, because I think it's been working pretty well so far.

"In Magic, it feels like we have this fantastic community that will gather together and do amazing things. However, there's a bunch of other times where it feels a bit more toxic or self-centered, or silly. And I realize that by being a more positive person in the community, it helps facilitate the game going in the right direction."

—Jonathan Sukenik

CHAPTER 2

JONATHAN SUKENIK

Jonathan, or Watchwolf92 as he's better known in the Magic Online community, found early success as a tournament grinder and streamer. He wrote some incredible articles on Star City Games that revealed to the world what a brilliant young mind he was.

The problem here? I missed all of that.

I certainly wasn't a hardcore tournament grinder. I had my own interests, particularly around a niche format within Magic called Legacy. Legacy was a format where you played all the old school cards from back in the nineties and pretended that newer cards didn't exist.

But the legend of Watchwolf92 found its way to me. I interviewed AJ Kerrigan, a well-known Legacy player, for the podcast.

AJ and Jonathan were really good friends. They belonged to some weird cult-like group named *The Sukenik School of Crushing*. And AJ vouched for Jonathan so hard as a Genuinely Good Dude that I had to follow up.

As I found out, Jonathan happened to be really good at Legacy, too. He absolutely *crushed* games of Legacy in spectacularly unorthodox ways. I saw him play a match with my favorite Legacy deck, Grixis Delver, that completely blew my mind.

My first real interaction with Jonathan was a Skype session where I asked him to teach me the ways of my favorite deck. And Jonathan, bless his heart, did not disappoint.

Jonathan shared his deck philosophy with me in an in-depth one-on-one discussion. I was absolutely blown away. I expected fifteen minutes...and received two hours. My head was spinning from the insight overload.

I instantly became a member of the Jonathan Sukenik fan club. I knew that we had to record a show together.

As I went deeper into the rabbit hole of guest research, I learned that Jonathan went *way* out of his way to be a good sport. In recent years, Jonathan's gone to incredible depths to be good to his opponents and serve as a positive force for the game.

This was interesting to me, because I was nothing like that. I played Magic to win. How does this guy play to win *and* maintain the highest standards of sportsmanship? I wanted to deconstruct Jonathan. I needed to get inside his mind and learn more.

How did Jonathan get here? What makes him so gracious to his opponents? And what's this *School of Crushing* all about, anyway?

Interview recorded in December 2018.

James: We met for the first time in GP Richmond, which was a few months ago, and you were gracious enough to teach me an alternate form of Magic.

Jonathan: Yeah. It's the basic lands game.[3] AJ [Kerrigan] brought this into our friend group.

James: I thought it was really cool because I had never heard about the game before. It teaches you a lot of basic concepts about Magic without having to overcomplicate things.

---

[3] https://www.reddit.com/r/magicTCG/comments/1iacj1/the_basic_land_game/

Jonathan: Definitely. I taught it to a bunch of my co-workers who expressed that they want[ed] to play Magic, and now all they want to do is play the basic land game with me. It's cool.

James: And we were actually playing it between rounds of actual tournament Magic. I thought it was cool that you reached out to teach me.

Jonathan: I think a lot of Magic tournaments should be more about the people than the Magic. Kind of like how this podcast is more about the people than the Magic, right?

James: For sure. Let me start by asking you about something that happened on social media.

There was this meme, kind of a viral thing. I think it was: "If you're reading this, even if we barely talk, tell me your favorite memory of me."

Jonathan: Yeah. So some of [my friends], I would guess what they would say, and then they would say something that I totally didn't expect.

For instance, one of my best friends, Abe Stein. He was the first to comment, and he pretty much enjoyed when I used to stream and we used to play jack-box games, which are like multiplayer games where the computer screen kind of serves as the way a lot of people are able to see what's going on in the game, and you play with your phone at home. So you're playing remotely. And normally, people play in front of a TV, but we would just play through my screen share on the stream, and he said that was one of his best memories of me—just hanging out.

And a lot of people put down times where they first interacted with me, or they first met me, or things about my personality, smile, or attitude, or something like that. But the ones that stuck out were these times that I don't remember at all. Or I remember pieces of it.

So cherry-picking through them, one of them was alluding to this person that's part of a larger friend group, that I would talk to all of the main players of the friend group, but one of the people didn't go to as many tournaments, was a lot more quiet, and I don't even know if I really interacted with him.

But we ended up being paired for the last round of a Grand Prix. He wasn't even sure if I remembered him, but I did when I saw the pairings. And when I went to walk to my table at the Grand Prix, he was sitting in the chair that I would be passing through. I wasn't across the aisle from him, I was on the same side. He went to go take out his deck, and I quickly said, "Stop, I'm your opponent, please don't take out your deck, I don't want to see any cards."

Then I go around the table, sit on the correct side, and I'm like, "Hey, I'm Jonathan." And we get introduced. We played a really awesome match. I did end up losing, but he said that this left a really big impression on him. How you can make a big impact on someone just by making sure that the game is fair and that I didn't accidentally see his cards before the match. He was also happy that I recognized him.

Similarly, there was one person that I met at a Grand Prix, and this was when they came up with the Scry rule after mulligans. We're both X-0 in this Grand Prix, and he's on the play. In his head, he wants to play an Overgrown Tomb tapped, and then pass the turn. But he played a lot more Standard than he played Modern, and they just introduced the Scry rule. So he was used to Scrying on turn one and then passing. So he Scryed on turn one and passed without playing his Overgrown Tomb tapped.

And I don't really remember this that well, but he said I pretty much refused to let him pass the turn without playing a land. A lot of people might have said, "Sure, I'll take my turn now." But I must have insisted that he play a land.

And then there was one time where—this was at Pro Tour Dominaria, which was a very important event for me. When I'm playing this event, I had to go 7-1, including this particular match, to stay on the train. I was not qualified for the next Pro Tour, and it was pretty high stakes.

But despite the stakes, I played against this guy in Dominaria Limited and his deck was definitely better than mine. And he pretty much got mana flooded and I ended up winning the games. And I even admitted to him, after the match, "Your deck is pretty sweet, I'm really sorry about the mana flood," offering my condolences.

And he said to me through Facebook that he was very happy to hear that at the end of the day I ended up being able to stay on the train, going 7-1 that day. And he said that the fact that this is a positive memory and not a bad beat story about how he got mana screwed—it speaks volumes about how good of an impression I made on him.

The last Magic-related story was Theros Block Sealed. I was pretty decent at identifying how I would need to win matches, and one of my Sealed pools had zero combat tricks, despite being Green-White. But I would play a lot of the Heroic creatures, that when you target them, they would get some sort of boost.

And the way I wanted to try to win my matches was by aggressively bluff attacking every single player that I respected, because I knew that they wouldn't block if I did it with enough confidence.

And I had two Glimpse of the Sun Gods in my deck, which was X and a White, instant, tap X creatures, and then Scry 1. So on the very last turn, where hopefully I snuck in enough damage in my Green-White deck by bluff attacking, I would attack with my team, and before blockers, I could tap their creatures and trigger my Heroic ability by targeting my guys.

I ended up crushing the competition and top-eighting when most of my opponents had much better decks. And a player that I looked up to for a very long time, he told me that my performance in this tournament really stood out to him. He thinks about it all the time, like, "How could this happen? How did your opponents not block more? How could they not see that after the game, that you went through x amount of cards in your deck and you did not have any tricks?"

At the end of the day, if anyone called, I would have lost. I would have binned my creatures and then got on with my life. But that pool was not good enough to top-eight, but I took the only route that would allow me to top-eight, and it was cool that I did.

And the fact that this moment just sticks out so much to this guy that—there's so much to be said about Magic as a player playing the cards, instead of the cards just playing themselves.

James: Absolutely. And I want to go back to something you said, which is that people's memories of you are often not significant in your own mind. How these things that didn't even register in your memory were meaningful to somebody else.

Jonathan: There was a time after high school— long after I graduated, I was just visiting my high school. A long time ago, I was a senior in high school, and this guy was a freshman.

When I visited my high school after getting into college, this guy was still in high school. He was like, "I still remember the first time we met." I was like, "Great, I don't." And he said, well, we were in gym class together, and it was raining outside so we were playing a card game indoors. We were playing "BS."

It's a game where you try to lie about how many cards you're putting down and you're trying to get rid of all your cards. And we agreed that as long as someone puts a card on top of someone else's cards on the stack, then you can no longer BS it.

And I'm playing very lazy and very badly the whole game. Eventually, the bell goes off. We have a five-minute warning bell before the period would be over for gym class. That bell goes off, and it's my turn. So I just slam down my whole hand of forty cards on top of the pile, get up, and scream, "Hadouken!" You know, the Street Fighter Ryu pose.

James: [Laughs] Sure.

Jonathan: And everyone is like, "Why did you do that?" I'm like, "I don't know, just keep on going, keep on going." And the next guy puts a card on top of it, and I'm like, "Great, I won!" And they're like, how did you win? I'm like, I put down my forty cards when I "Hadoukened!"

And then this moment stuck out in that kid's mind as something awesome. I was just like, yeah, I do believe that's something that I *would* do, and I just don't remember it. [Laughs]

James: I thought he was going to say something about how you taught him math or calculus and helped him get into a college with an application or something. [Laughs] But that is cool as well.

Of the stories you told me, two stood out for—for lack of a better word—I'll call it sportsmanship. Because you've always struck me as someone who cares about winning and losing the right way.

How did you develop your sense of sportsmanship or "justice" when you play Magic? Is that something from before you played Magic, or is that something you developed as you were playing the game?

Jonathan: That's a very good question. My evolution with Magic starts from when I started playing FNM and I was this kid that was hanging out with high schoolers when I was in elementary and middle school.

I was relatively smart, and I was a little bit cocky, and I would just care about winning, and I would make fun of my opponents, and do these little punky kid things. And I did not regard people's emotions as much. Because from their point of view, I'm this punk kid, and they would almost be amused.

I was a little bit shorter when I was younger, and had a higher voice, and I used to have hair down to my shoulders. People used to confuse me for being a girl just based on looks.

But yeah, I was not particularly someone that I liked at this point in time when I was younger. I would trade a lot to make sure that I had the current decks for Standard. And I would rip off people with no remorse. I would always try to make sure I'm getting a deal that's in my favor.

When I was around 16 [years old] I had my first big finish. I lost the finals of a Star City 5K event with Faeries. And at that point, I was featured on *The Magic Show*. A lot of people reached out to me, and a lot of people gave me pretty big praise for this type of finish.

And at that point, I realized that all this trading and ripping people off monetarily did not sit well with me. And I enjoyed making money through being good at the game. A lot more.

That was the first time I realized, at least from a Magic point of view, that I should probably...just by being me, and being a relatively good person, that I should let my Magic career be *that* instead of focusing on the monetary value. Changing the focus from *me* to *we*. And so, from then on out, I focused on trying to improve myself in the game, and to make sure that my opponent is having a good time.

James: When you were trading—you described it as ripping people off—what was going through your mind? Was it just youthful indiscretion, or something else?

Jonathan: When I was younger, it was much more like... yeah, I only have $200 to my name and I want to play Standard. And Standard costs *this amount* of money. And if I can change my $5 card into a pair of $10 cards because this other person doesn't know the value of their stuff and they've consented, it's fine.

I also justified it from a "youth" point of view. I'm a 10 year old kid, and this 20 year old is willing to trade with me—he knows what he signed up for. It's not my fault he didn't research it. So I would be opportunistically taking advantage of people that were either being nice, or people that did not value their things correctly.

I quickly determined that that was not why I wanted to play Magic, and that was not a world that perpetuates people wanting to interact with me. If anyone ever discovered that they lost tons of money to me in trading...*I* wouldn't want to be friends with me.

James: You were thinking about how you wanted to be treated. That maybe the way you behaved was not the way you wanted others to behave towards you.

Jonathan: Yeah, that's a good way of putting it. It was aligned with hitting puberty and changes in general. That period of time where…I feel like a lot of kids when they're younger, they're a little more self-centered. They feel like they're immortal, or the center of the universe.

And during puberty, it became a time when I realized that a lot of my actions led me to feel more lonely. That, or I didn't have people that I could trust. I wasn't building trust with people through my actions. And then that carried over to how I felt I wanted to treat people in general.

Throughout my childhood, I felt that there were points in time, both inside and outside of Magic, that I might not have been the most considerate to people. And that's not the world I want to live in. I want to live in a world where a lot of people are considerate for me, and I'm considerate for a lot of people.

Pretty much from then on out, whenever I play a match of Magic, I try to live those values. I definitely value these things way more in the, say, past five years, instead of when I first started thinking this way. But I do not want to leave the match until I know that my opponent is OK. Win or lose.

I don't care that my opponent top-decked me but that they still feel terrible about a judge call or something. I will be there for my opponent because we are a community. If there is no one else on the other side of the table, then we can't play Magic.

James: That's so fascinating to me. Because I know a lot of Magic players, myself included, have played the game for a long time. And we have developed totally different views about the game.

I still want to get into the *why* because—it's one thing to have a decent Star City Games finish, or feel that you need to treat people better when you interact with them—but it's quite another to actually think, I'm going to do everything I can to make sure that you have an enjoyable game of Magic.

So I'm really trying to understand that part.

Jonathan: I'm trying to understand that, too. [Laughs] Can you repeat what you said, but slightly differently?

James: For sure. There are lots of people who realize that they have to be better with their opponents, or better with their relationships with Magic players. But you seem to go the extra mile. If you look back, are there specific things in your life that caused you to develop that view, or to form that set of behaviors that you now have?

Jonathan: In general, I don't try to just objectively do nice things. I try to do the things that I think are right for a given person or community. People perceive me as the kind of person that has never told off a person in my life. But I *have* told off people, and I have said things that I felt needed to be said to people. And I have daggered people in order to motivate them to get them to take the extra step.

In Magic, it feels like we have this fantastic community that will gather together and do amazing things. However, there's a bunch of other times where it feels a bit more toxic or self-centered, or silly. And I realize that by being a more positive person in the community, it helps facilitate the game going in the right direction.

So I guess what you could say is—it started off as me trying to be what I think I should be, so much that I ended up just *becoming* that. I might have lost the reason why I do it, and I just do it. It might not be fully justified why I care so much about my opponent.

But at the end of the day, when a tournament is over, or a match is over, I know I can take my losses. I know even if I lose every round of the tournament, I'm going to go home knowing that I hung out with my friends. That I had a great time.

But that's not true for everyone. Some people go through a really tough work week, and then they go to this Magic tournament that they've also been practicing for. And they've gotten very little sleep, and they lose to me. They might have missed day two of the tournament, and that meant a lot more to them than it did to me. And I can understand that person feeling frustrated. I want to do everything I can to make sure that person is willing to do it the next week.

It's tough. Magic puts you in a spot where there's a decent amount of variance, and if you can't take the losses in stride, then it's going to be really difficult for you. And the wins also feel very short-lived.

There was this one time when I did very well at a Pro Tour, and the next weekend, I did not do so well at the Grand Prix. And throughout the whole rest of the week, all I could think about were the mistakes I made at the Grand Prix. The Pro Tour success was so short-lived.

And there's some people that aren't even fortunate enough to have that win at the higher levels.

Yet they're still willing to come out to these events with a dream. And anything that I can do to assist those people with their dreams, at the emotional level, I want to do.

I don't think it's that hard to care for your opponents. Since I feel it's not that hard to care for your opponents, I should do my best to do so, because not everyone is going to ask for help. Not everyone is going to be willing to be vulnerable.

James: Right. Your opponents are not going to come out and say, "Hey Jonathan, I'm having a really bad day here. And I came here just to have a good time." I think it's good that you're trying to give them a good experience. And like you said, there's very little cost to do so, because all you have to do is not be a dick. [Laughs]

Jonathan: Exactly. I do go more extreme than I know a lot of people are willing to. To the point that even if they're someone that I don't like, for whatever reason, I'm still going to shake their hand after the match. I'm still going to make sure that they're relatively fine before I leave.

James: I think it's incredible because at GP Richmond, I saw you lose a couple of matches. I think the litmus test is—when I look at your body language from afar, you look like essentially the same person, whether you happened to win or lose that round of Magic.

Jonathan: At the end of the day, most people are not playing Magic for a living. Most people are doing this in their spare time, and they're doing it for fun.

As people that are highly competitive, or pros, or even people who are doing this full-time—if we don't have the people that are playing this game, as a hobby, enjoying themselves—then our game is not going to be able to succeed in the long run.

However, that's not the motivation as to why I do it. One thing I think is really cool is playing games with kids. You play games with kids, all they want to do is have fun. Sometimes they want to win, but even if they lose, they're like, "Great, let's play again."

I remember going to a Grand Prix and meeting a father and his daughter and son, who were both fairly young. I taught them the basic land game. And I won every single game, but they would just alternate playing with me like, "Ok, great, now it's my turn! Now it's my turn!" And all they wanted to do was play because they enjoyed playing games so much.

And I feel like at some point, when we grow up, we're told that that's childish or foolish. But I think that's pure—pure happiness. And I think the way I present myself at the table, or the way I treat my opponents, is still with that happiness in mind. We are human. We can't just lock away the ability to feel happy after playing a game in general, win or lose.

James: I think we often forget that. Another way to say it is, we often behave as if someone put a gun to our heads and forced us to play in this Magic tournament. And that's far from the case, right?

Jonathan: Yeah.

James: You have people complaining—myself included—about how they didn't have a good round, or got unlucky. But we wouldn't even be playing this game if there wasn't luck involved. We'd all be playing chess or some other game instead.

Jonathan: What's really cool is that I can play against Jon Finkel or Kai Budde, and be 40-60 [40% to win] in the match. To be 40-60 to win against the Michael Jordan of Magic? Or LeBron James? I don't really stay up to date on the basketball analogies. But that's really cool, to have the honor of being able to play with some of the game's greats and have a realistic shot at winning. If I played Bobby Fischer in chess, I'm literally never going to win. There isn't an element of luck there.

James: For sure. I recently heard about this "School of Magic" that you and your friends belong to. I initially heard the name and it sounded so ridiculous that I thought it was some sort of elaborate in-joke. Then I realized that this was a real thing. So tell me about that school that you named yourself after, what that's about, and who's in it.

Jonathan: So, great question. [Laughs]

We call ourselves the *Sukenik School of Crushing*. Trademarked by Evan Buchholz, founding member of the team. In college, I was constantly surrounded by people that play[ed] Magic, and it was a lot easier to work on ideas and be immersed in the game. But when I graduated and started working, I would just play Magic Online. And I lived at home so I wouldn't visit my friends as often. And I had problems communicating with them because I wouldn't make the time after work, and it was probably my fault in the end.

Two books I started reading on my train ride to and from work [were] the Patrick Chapin *Next Level Magic* and *Next Level Deck Building* books. And in *Next Level Magic*, he talks about forming a team of people. He would talk about how he would center it around him and another person that complemented each other as being the core of the group. Then he would identify the weaknesses or the other aspects he was trying to fill and scout out people—that would be his testing group.

My idea was to try that, but in a different way. I went to find three pairs of people and form a group of six, such that people would still have the ability to pair off, or they'd feel particularly comfortable with another person in the group.

So we did this for about a year or so, and we had some pretty decent finishes. There is a four-color control deck that I dubbed Travis control, named after one of the people in the group. That was a Jeskai deck with Lingering Souls that I became more well-known for because I personally put up a decent finish with it. That deck was the first brain child of us just working together.

And when I started the group, I made it clear that the ceiling is that we do amazing things, go on to multiple Pro Tours and crush it as the next Luis Scott-Vargas and Paul Cheon team for Channel Fireball—something like that. But really, the average case, or the floor, is that we interact with each other more and become six pretty good friends.

After a year or two, two of the team members went off to focus on more non-Magic things. The situation happened where we were just friends that would talk whenever we had the opportunity to do.

After that, I randomly won a Modo PTQ, which qualified me for my first Pro Tour in seven years. And I made a Facebook group that I dubbed, "Pro Tour Honolulu 2—Electric Bugaloo." Because as you know, whenever something is part two it has to be Electric Bugaloo. My first Pro Tour was in Honolulu, so it was fitting that my second one was also going to be in Honolulu.

James: There you go. [Laughs]

Jonathan: Exactly. And I invited to this group three other players from the original group that I founded. Soon after that, we brought in two other people.

Originally, we just used this group for testing, coordination, and chat. And after the Pro Tour, we kept on using the group to work together on different things. And before I knew it, we were all talking to each other and planning for events all the time. People would pair off sometimes. Trios would form. We became very close friends.

At one point, Evan said something along the lines of, "Yeah, I mean, at the end of the day, we're all just students of the Sukenik School of Crushing." And I was like, *woah*. And Evan kept on using the phrase "Sukenik School of Crushing," and we stuck with it.

From my point of view, we're all equals. We're all just members of this group. And from a school point of view it's not so much a school of learning, it's probably closer to Xavier's school for—I forgot what he calls it. A school for gifted students?

James: In the X-Men, right?

Jonathan: Yeah, exactly. So it's Xavier's school for the X-Men. Unfortunately—and I've been asked this multiple times—we do not accept applications. [Laughs] It's not really that kind of school, and no one really graduates from it. We're just all trying to help each other improve through—what's it called in the X-Men? The Danger Room. Just through helping each other understand and learn. Being a really tight-knit group.

So that's me. Next is AJ Kerrigan, who was previously on the *Humans of Magic* podcast. Storm expert, GeneralSmallChild on Magic Online. We all refer to AJ in a bunch of different ways. We usually call him AJ. But whenever I want to be more formal or just alluding to something that I feel he has expertise in, I always call him *The General*, because of his Magic Online name.

James: It's a pun, because he has a small stature, which I guess is the reason why he calls himself GeneralSmallChild.

Jonathan: Exactly. He said he made it, and then realized it can have either meaning, and just leaves it up to interpretation. But for me, he's the General of the Small Children.

We actually knew each other way before we [became] close friends. We went to the same gaming store growing up. In all honesty, we didn't mesh that well when we were younger. But when Dragons of Tarkir came out, we realized that we both liked Taylor Swift and we started traveling to Magic tournaments together more.

And at some point, it was just him and I in a car together, and we started talking about more personal things. I [felt] like he was me from five years ago. Everything he was going through at the time paralleled what I used to go through. We would talk about a lot of personal things, some of which I felt like I could relate to. And I would also talk about things that I was going through.

Just the willingness to be vulnerable with each other allowed us to get really close, and we spent a whole summer where he was judging a lot of tournaments, and I was playing in a lot of tour-naments. And we became close after that. Within maybe three or four trips, I already considered him one of my closest friends.

AJ is probably the fastest person in the group at digesting information and growing very quickly. I've always felt like if he could devote a period of time to just playing Magic, he would be going to these Pro Tours with me. But he has a job now, and he was in school before. So I understand his priorities.

He's also pretty good at understanding the way I think. For instance, when a lot of people watch me play Magic, after a match, they will say something to the extent of, "Hey, did you con-sider this?" or "Why did you make this play?" Or something like that. When AJ has a situation like that, he usually says, "Oh, I'm assuming you thought *this*."

For instance, there was this one time when my opponent had a Tarmogoyf and I had a Lightning Bolt and Dig Through Time in my hand. And it just didn't occur to me that I could kill the Tarmogoyf by bolting it and then using the Delve effect in Dig Through Time to shrink it to a 2/3 creature, such that it would happen before Dig resolved. This way, the Tarmogoyf would be in the graveyard already. And other people would say things in a more accusatory way, or ways that might potentially make me feel bad.

But AJ, right after he watched the match, said to me, "Did you forget that you could use Delve to kill the Tarmogoyf?" And I was like, "Yeah." And then that was it. There was nothing else that needed to be said. [Laughs] Everyone in the School is willing to put up with a lot of my junk, but AJ's willing to point out how silly some of the things I do are.

There's a pretty good story where we went to a sandwich shop where you would get sandwich and fries. And each order of fries came with a specific sauce. And I really wanted a certain burger with a different sauce.

So everyone ordered. I ordered last, and I said to the cashier, "Hey, can I get this burger with this other sauce?" And they're like, "No, if you want that sauce, it will be 25 cents extra." I was like, "Okay, that's fine. I'll just get the normal burger with the sauce that it comes with." The sauce that I didn't really want.

AJ suddenly slams his hand on the table and says, "Get this kid the sauce, put the 25 cents on my tab." Since then, I've been trying to be a little bit less silly with incidents like that.

AJ is incredibly funny and great to talk to. He's just very spontaneous.

James: What about some of the other guys in the team?

Jonathan: So Abe Stein is a Star City Games regular writer now.

James: Awesome!

Jonathan: Yeah, it is really awesome. Long time coming. Abe is from the Maryland area, whereas most of the other people in the School are from the New Jersey area.

James: And you're from the New Jersey area, too?

Jonathan: Yeah. AJ and I grew up in Central Jersey. When I first met Abe, we were both playing in a Sealed tournament. Abe's last name is Stein, mine is Sukenik, so it's relatively close. My older sister's boyfriend at the time also had a last name that was close to ours in alphabetical order.

We just realized very quickly that we knew references that we would make, that would play very well off of each other and my sister's boyfriend. We kept running into each other the whole time, and we didn't even know each other. We'd never seen each other before.

We also traded with each other. We both felt like we ripped off each other, so that was very appropriate. [Laughs]

James: [Laughs] That's good. You canceled each other out, right?

Jonathan: Yeah. And I actually still have the cards he traded me, so that's funny. And honestly, I don't exactly remember when we became close. I became good friends with his general group, and then I started talking to him more.

My favorite thing about Abe is that he can compare anything that's going on in life with something in Magic. Any problem I'm going through—he makes the best Magic analogy every time. Any scenario where there's nothing to lose, he would say, "Oh well, sometimes you just attack with all your creatures and you see what they do. Maybe they just put themselves dead on board. How can you just say that? You don't even know what card is in their hand. Maybe they *do* end up blocking!" [Laughs]

He's a really good storyteller. He can re-tell his matches almost verbatim, whereas mine are more flow-oriented. I remember how decisions felt, or how decisions transpired, and I fill it in with things that make sense.

He's also very good at recommending things people would like. Abe has pretty much never recommended a song or anime show that wasn't good. He understands people's preferences very well.

This trio of Abe, AJ, and myself started to become more well-known. We team together for a lot of events. The three of us try to do a lot of things together.

Abe, AJ, and I went to dinner with three of Abe's friends, and it was at a slightly fancier restaurant...The highlight of the whole night is—at the very end—the only dessert left is this dessert that

Abe liked the most. He has maybe two spoonfuls left of the dessert. So first he's like, "Hey Jonathan, do you want some?"

And I was like, "No." I knew he enjoyed it a lot and I didn't want any more of it if it was going to be at the cost of his enjoyment.

"Ok, I'm done," Abe says. "AJ, you can have the rest."

So AJ scoops up this whole cake-like thing on his spoon. He pretty much took the spoon and was moving it towards his mouth. And he legit had his tongue out. His tongue is out at this point and about to make contact with the spoon.

And suddenly, I'm like, "Wait-wait-wait-wait."

Both Abe and AJ look at me, and I'm like, "I would like half of that."

And the other three friends were just, "Tongue out and everything, *and you just cut him off? How can you do that?*"

Well, I didn't want to deny Abe part of the dessert that I know he likes, but if it's just AJ? I'll take half of it. And then AJ gives me a face, puts it down, cuts in half, and then we both eat it.

James: I think that says something good about AJ that he's willing to put it down. If it was me, I would just be, "Whatever." It goes in my mouth, you know? That's very considerate of him. [Laughs]

Jonathan: Yeah. [Laughs] The nicest thing about this group— and I'll get into the other three members later—is that you take any two of us and we're pretty good friends. And in the School of Crushing, we all care about each other a lot. I really do care so much about these guys, I would do so much for them.

I went to a Pro Tour with one of them and I consciously changed what deck I was going to play, and what groups I was in, to make him more satisfied. I had him choose which group he wanted to test with for that Pro Tour. Whatever made him the most comfortable for this Pro Tour.

That way he could succeed. Not so that I could succeed, even though we were both going to a Pro Tour that meant something for the both of us. But I just wanted anything for him to play in another Pro Tour. There's so much selflessness and we care so much about how each other feel, and it's so awesome. I feel like I could take on the world with these people. I want to do everything with these people. I want to go on trips with them. I wish I could be roommates with them. They're just so awesome.

James: How do you think this attitude towards each other developed?

Jonathan: I think it comes down to vulnerability and trust. Really just caring about each other. I guess you can almost view it as how AJ and I approach our opponents. Everyone in the school cares a lot about people in general. A lot of people consider us nice people, and we really are selfless with each other. It builds this unit of trust and mutual caring.

There's this one time we came back from a Magic tournament and the trains weren't running. I lived in North Jersey at that point and AJ was going to school in Drexel. AJ literally passed by his school to drive me home, which took him an extra four hours in total. And it's so nice for him to do that.

Sometimes I have really rough days at work, or in Magic, or in life. I just remember that there's these five people that mean the world to me. It's really awesome.

James: This is beyond a Magic team. This is a way of life.

Jonathan: Every Magic tournament—if no one else in the School is going to that tournament, the incentive for anyone individually to go dives down a lot. But if one of us wants to go, then everyone else is looking through their schedules to see if they can go, too.

As I said, any pair of us is—you're going to have a great time. One thing we used to do a lot is when we used to go to Magic tournaments is—in between rounds, it would be my favorite time because we would play tons of board games. We would play One Night, Ultimate Werewolf, Love Letter. We played Liars, Dice, Skulls, all these different games. And we would invite other people to join, too. It would be a good time.

Then what I started doing, because I was one of the first people to get their own place—is I would host something called Camp Sukenik. I would invite people to participate.

I viewed Magic tournaments as—it is true that we are going to the Magic tournament because there's a Grand Prix and we can qualify for the Pro Tour. But we also get to hang out with each other.

Camp Sukenik is the exact opposite. We're getting together to hang out, and there will also be some Magic on the side. And usually, we line it up with Modo PTQs so that we can help each other out. Some sort of Magic Online tournament is in the background, but we focus on just hanging out. Sometimes the Camp Sukenik events are more fun than the Grand Prix, as a result.

James: There is a sense of—not only friendship, but also play. And I mean that in the best way possible. Because you were talking about how we lose the sense of wonder and playing games for the sake of having fun. I do feel like you guys are trying to actively foster that in the group.

Jonathan: I laugh so hard with these guys, and I feel like I can truly be myself. I don't have to worry about how I'm being perceived, and I get to be very natural in how I want to express myself and do things. And everyone is doing that. It's fostering a very healthy environment of being able to be yourself, and that's what everyone loves about you in the first place. It's really awesome.

James: Who are the other members of the School?

Jonathan: Next up is Travis Perlee. He's the creator of Travis Control, which was an in-joke in the first set of six members we had.

What happened was that Matt Brown, an original member of the School, likes playing Lingering Souls in any deck he could. He put Lingering Souls in Jeskai. And then Matt had to take a break from the School, because he had to worry about work and other things.

And then Travis took the deck and ran with it. Kind of as a stab to Matt and also as a boost to Travis, I call it Travis Control. But Travis calls it four-color. When Abe plays it, he calls it Sukenik Control because he wants to dagger Travis for it.

Travis is extremely good at logical thinking. He went to Princeton and is an extremely smart guy. He's currently working at Google. He's extremely athletic whereas the rest of us could probably do a better job in terms of exercise. [Laughs] He loves soccer.

Travis is really interesting. He's fueled by passion. He's very passionate about coding. He currently has this project called GK MTG. He's developing this website so that people can do things better in organizing and playing Magic.

What he eventually wants to do is run a tournament series. He wants GK MTG to have its own thing, and he has his own ideas for how it works. For instance, double elimination. And he's writing automations that will text you your next round, and tell you what table to go, and use the phone app to report your results. He has very big ideas for what he wants to do with Magic.

Travis' website is called gkmtg.pro, and he's looking to grow this thing. This is a project that he's very passionate about and we're all very supportive of him.

The way I met Travis is really funny. It was at an old-school PTQ, and we're playing a win-and-in for top eight. The format is Extended. I was playing Faeries and he was playing Elf-ball. Travis was trying to summon a bunch of elves and kill me, and I was playing some faeries that people are familiar with.

We both remember the story slightly differently, so I'll tell you how I remember it. We pretty much end up in this board state where I have five lands in play, and he has a bunch of elves. He has either one or zero cards in his hand. And he draws his card for the turn.

I lift up my pen, start counting his board, and just say, "Oh my God, if you have another Lord, I'm dead." And he's like, "Oh, really?" He then plays Imperious Perfect and attacks with his team.

I play Consume the Meek, which destroys all his creatures with converted mana cost 3 or less. So I nailed his Imperious Perfect. Turns out the attack would not have been lethal. It didn't change the clock.

James: Right. Some pretty good mind-game action.

Jonathan: Right. A year or two later, there's a PTQ that I attend, mostly to watch. He walks up to me and is like, "Hey, do you remember me?" And I'm like, "No."

And he's like, "We played in a PTQ. I was playing Elves and you were playing Faeries." I'm like, "Oh, you're the guy that I got with Consume the Meek?" And he's like, "Yeah." And I'm like, "Oh man! What's up?"

And he ends up losing the finals of that PTQ with a pretty innovative deck. It was a green-red beatdown deck with Green Sun's Zenith. It was similar to a deck that Jackie Lee top-eighted a Grand Prix with.

I end up convincing him—either during or after the tournament, I don't remember—that he should try Volt Charge in his deck. That card deals three damage and has the proliferate ability. That way you can add a counter to a bunch of things.

I don't see this guy again for another couple of months, but it turns out that we actually have overlapping friends. I see him later with all these guys I didn't even know that he knew. And he's like, "Hey, I tried Volt Charge in that deck and it was terrible."

And I was like, "Oh my God, you believed me? I got you twice! [Laughs] Once with the Consume the Meek and once with Volt Charge!" At that point, I don't even know why he wants to be friends with me.

James: It was a test. If he passed the test, he could enter the School.

Jonathan: If you can put up with me, you can enter the School. [Laughs]

I think a large reason why Travis and I became friends—moving on from being a guy that I'm trolling, to him actively becoming one of my best friends—I'd say it was his fault. He's the one that made the move that really changed how I viewed him as a friend.

At this point, we've known each other for maybe a year, through interacting at Magic tournaments. We have similar friend groups. At Star City Games Edison, I was catching up with him. We both majored in computer science, so we had some overlap in interest besides Magic.

But at Edison, he asked me to go to his graduation from Princeton. He's like, "There's going to be these cool speakers there, and you get to see the Princeton campus, would you like to come to my graduation?"

From my point of view, it was like, "Okay, this guy that I don't really know that well just asked me to go to his graduation." So me being me, I responded with, "Yes, but I would like to know something." He was like, "Okay, what do you want to know?"

And I said, "How many people rejected your request so far?" I was skeptical that I would be the first person Travis would ask. From my point of view, he was a lot closer with other people in his friend group. And he answers with, "Zero, you're the first person and the only person I'm going to ask." I was like, "Okay, sure."

So then I ended up going to Travis' graduation. It was really nice. Princeton has a nice campus, and it was a fairly nice thing. So he showed me around the dorm he lived in, we went to one of his favorite lunch spots, and we walked around Princeton for maybe four or five hours, and we had tons of heart-to-heart moments.

We both talked about all the relationships we'd been through in the past. We talked about various emotional things and confidence-related things. We really opened up to each other. And maybe that's the theme with a lot of people in the School—or at least, their connection with me.

I mentioned before that the way AJ and I became good friends was that we started driving together more. And we opened up to each other and realized that we can relate a lot to what the other person was saying, and we can help each other out.

And that's what happened with Travis, too. If you spend five hours with someone, you're bound to start opening up about stuff as long as both of you guys are reasonable people. If you're receptive and want to learn more about the other person.

James: If you can have a really good one-on-one conversation with someone for a couple of hours—it usually ensures that you will end up staying friends, or staying in touch. I feel that way with people that I do the podcast with.

Jonathan: I think about the times that I spent with Travis in Bilbao, or the time I spent with Abe in Japan for the Pro Tour. Every one of these one-on-one conversations. Or with Evan every Wednesday. Every so often, I would meet with Evan and we'd catch up on things. The most recent encounter I had with Evan, I reminded him for the millionth time that I think the Sonic X theme song is the perfect theme song. And I'm repeating that in my head over and over again. We enjoy it.

James: Tell me a little bit more about Evan—how you guys met, and how the friendship developed.

Jonathan: Evan Buchholz is from Pennsylvania, whereas Abe is from Maryland, and the rest of us are Jersey-based. Evan and I met through Travis. They're really tight and complimentary to each other. They really understand each other.

James: It sounds like Travis and Evan knew each other super well, and then Evan was brought into the School at the same time as Travis?

Jonathan: Pretty much. I wanted to build a foundation of a bunch of pairs, so they were a pair. Clay and I were a pair—Clay is the sixth member that I haven't talked about yet. When we formed a Facebook group, AJ and Abe came along, so that's the evolution of the school.

So Travis and Evan are part of—I guess you can call it the Crash Course School of Crushing, or whatever. The baby form of it. I pretty much met Evan through Travis. It was through an Extended or Modern—I don't remember what the formats were called back then—but it was at a local PTQ.

I don't think I ever told Evan my first impressions of him. But Evan has this laugh, and I really hope that you, or anyone that's interacting with him, gets to hear his laugh. It's very unique and contagious laugh, and it makes you feel awesome when he's laughing.

James: Can you do an impression of it?

Jonathan: …No. [Laughs]

James: How would you describe it? Is it a hearty laugh, or—

Jonathan: It feels like the air is going into the back of his throat very quickly, and it's just a very loud and… it's just great.

And the two people I know in Magic that have the best laughs are Evan Buchholz and Ralph Betesh. Apparently, when Evan and Ralph went to Spain together for a Pro Tour—and Abe was a part of the testing team, too—there were times where…I forgot what Abe called it. He called it the "laugh train" or something like that. If Evan started laughing—Ralph also laughs very easily, and also has a unique laugh—they would start building off of each other—

James: Like a chain reaction.

Jonathan: —Just this obnoxious laugh, but you can't help but laugh too because their laughs are so funny. But Evan's laugh and his overall way of conducting himself—he's so interesting.

Each of us excels in different things. Travis is very logical, and AJ is very good at coming to conclusions very quickly, through logical reasoning. And Abe is very good at storytelling, recollection, and dissecting things. And I'm okay at a bunch of things.

Evan's style is [that] he's very good at talking to people, and he's very much a people person. He works in hospitality, and I'm willing to believe that he's very good at how he interacts with the customers. He's very good at listening and understanding. And he always wants to help.

I've expressed things to Evan that I've literally never expressed to anyone else. One of those deep, dark secrets, and stuff like that. Evan is the only person I've told certain things to, because he's so warm and understanding.

It's funny, because when he's playing Magic, he can look serious at times. "Warm" is not necessarily the word I want to use. Perhaps "inviting."

James: Very approachable, perhaps?

Jonathan: Yeah, he's very approachable. It feels like he's never judging you. He's trying to understand you.

And I hope I can come across that way to people. That's something I can learn a lot from him about.

The fact that I feel like I can tell Evan things I never told anyone else speaks volumes to how he holds himself, and who he is as a person. And that's something I admire about him.

Evan is the only person in our group that has what I call a real meaningful accomplishment—he lost in the finals of GP "Eldrazi" in Detroit, and then he went to Spain for his first Pro Tour with Abe. It was Evan's first Pro Tour. And afterwards, they're both trying to chase Silver status. Unfortunately, neither of them were able to reach their goal.

And then he realized he could take off a week of work, as did I, to test with Team Cardhoarder for the week leading up to Pro Tour Amonkhet. That was in Nashville. And we ended up having a really good time. We were able to understand how Cardhoarder operates while we were also able to supply some of our Sukenik School of Crushing ideologies. It was a good experience overall.

I know a large part of why Evan wanted to go to Nashville was to experience being part of a Pro Tour testing team. To understand the process and see how he can apply it going forward. But another part was also experiencing the Pro Tour with me.

I end up being in the spot where if I'm 9-7 or better, I reach Silver. And I never had Pro status before, and it was a very stressful...it was an interesting time. I ended up in a spot where I had to win one of my last three matches in Constructed to go Silver, to get 9-7. So then I play a match, I lose. I play my second match, and I lose. It's now the third match—

James: It's down to the wire now.

Jonathan: Yes, down to the wire. I forgot how many times I interacted with Evan during this time period. But I'm definitely walking around, listening to my iPod, trying to chill.

James: What was your mindset going into that third match?

Jonathan: *Man.* The first thing I did was—I ran around everywhere asking people for gum. People make fun of this all the time, but I strongly feel like gum is—not in an illegal way, but I believe that gum is a performance enhancing tool. I don't know the science behind it, but it's either some sort of oral fixation or how the sympathetic versus parasympathetic nervous system works.

I'll explain the one that I believe to be the case, but I don't know if it's backed by science. But when you're in a stressful situation, your body is operating a certain way that is very fight-or-flight oriented, and you're acting more on instinct, or subconscious, which isn't as good for Magic.

Meanwhile, when you're at rest and everything is fine, you're able to do more cognitive thinking, and your body is calmer overall. Your heartbeat is a little bit slower than it would be otherwise. When you're chewing, your brain is like, "Wait, I'm eating? I can't be in danger." And then it triggers the nervous system response that would then calm down your body. I feel like gum could be a good way to calm down your nerves.

I run around looking for gum. I finally bump into Brennan DeCandio, who gives me two pieces of gum—the two most important pieces of gum in my life. So I go and play my match, and I'm chewing one of the pieces of gum. I win game one and lose game two.

The reason why Brennan gave me two pieces—he asked why I needed gum in the first place—I told him the same story I told you. Originally, he was going to give me one piece, but after hearing the story, he's like, "Here, take a second one, just in case you really need it."

And it's game three now. I spit out the old piece of gum, and I'm like, "Ok, I really need the boost here." I pop in the backup gum, and then I end up winning.

And it's weird because I feel like I'm a person that, despite being very animated in my talking, or a lot of people perceive me as very smiley or very outgoing person, I don't display a lot of emotion that often. I don't often feel that feeling of jumping up and down with joy. I don't feel—I don't know. When this match finished, and I end up winning, my opponent was like, "Hey, congrats on Silver."

I thought that when I got Silver, or any kind of accomplishment that meant something to me, that I would go Super Saiyan. To feel like I was on cloud nine, as people would say. And it just didn't matter. It felt like another match of Magic—it was all the same. I thought to myself, *I've done this before. I've won a match before.* This didn't have the magnitude that I thought I would feel.

After my win, I'm de-sleeving my cards and sitting in my chair. I look up and see Evan, and he's peering out from the crowd. And he cocks his head a little and then gives me a thumbs-up in a questioning way to see whether I won. It was one of those wavering thumbs-up gestures that asked, "Did we get there?"

I look at him, and I know that my face was very solemn. When I play Magic, or after a match, when I'm by myself, I'm usually stoic-looking. I look up at him with that same face and slowly raise my hand with my thumb up.

And I'll never forget the look on Evan's face when he saw that I won my match for Silver. He literally jumps up in the air, claps, pushes the people in front of him aside, doesn't care that you're not supposed to enter the tournament area, and runs up to me.

He hugs me, and he's like, "Why do you have to make people so afraid you're not going to get Silver? You waited until the last match to win. Why do you have to do that to us? I'm so happy for you!" And he's hugging me, and still shouting all these things at me.

And at that point, I felt something. I did this thing that doesn't matter to me. But look at this response that one of my best friends had. I'm so happy that he's so happy for me, and now I'm happy.

James: It's like the saying goes—you're doing it for the team.

Jonathan: Exactly. That moment meant so much to me. The fact that he was there, and he had that response, and we shared this moment together. It means so much to me.

James: That made it all worth it.

Jonathan: Yeah. So the Pro Tour that Evan and Abe went to together was Shadows Over Innistrad. And they came back with all of these stories. They had a great time. And something I said to myself was, I never want there to be an opportunity where one of my best friends is going to a Pro Tour and I'm not also there with them.

Since then, Abe went to Pro Tour Hour of Devastation, and AJ went to Pro Tour Ixalan, and I was there with them both times. I've held true to what I told myself. I just wanted to experience my life with these people. I also love how so many different people perceive our group as a whole. It's awesome.

But I guess I should start talking about Clay, the sixth member.

James: Yeah, so Clay. Tell me his full name, how you guys met, and how he became a member of the School.

Jonathan: So, Clay Gereffi. He's one of my best friends from college. When we started the first School of Crushing with Matt and Will, Clay and I were paired together. And the way this formed was— we both went to Rutgers in New Brunswick for college. And we're in the same year.

It was my sophomore year that I first noticed him, and the way he would take his game actions was something that appealed to me. He had a very good presence or aura about him. A very competitive aura. Which is funny, because it's different than how I describe him now that he's one of my best friends, because he's also very kind and understanding.

But when I first met him, I was like, "Man, I think this guy can be great at Magic. I don't know, watching him play, he seems to be pretty decent. And he takes his time, and I like his demeanor."

He's the first person I would say that I've ever tried to train. What happened was that he would come over to my place, and we have an L couch situation. And he would sit in the L couch in a way that, where the two couches meet, we'd be back to back—except we're leaning against cushions.

I was used to playing multiple queues at the same time on Magic Online, by the nature of being a Modo grinder. I would play one match, and then I would also indirectly be playing his match because I could see his screen by turning to my right.

Almost every turn, I would be like, "Hey, what are you trying to accomplish here? What are you thinking?" I would ask very thought-provoking questions.

We did this for a couple of months, of me dual-queueing both of our matches, and he learned very quickly. He's a very smart person. I can't necessarily quantify it in the same way that I can with AJ and Travis, but he's definitely very smart in a game-like way. He's smart maneuvering games.

At his first Star City, I think it was—maybe it was the second event for him, I don't really remember – but he actually top-eighted the event, which was, "Great, he went from FNM to topping a Star City," which at the time felt like a really huge accomplishment.

A lot of my Magic philosophies were trial-and-error based, and I learned by failing so many times. And he was the first person that internalized and understood my philosophies as I presented them. It got to the point where new sets would come out and he would say to me, "Oh, you probably like these types of cards." I'm like, yes, that's right.

And some people think I'm really into Mono-Red because I like playing Hellrider a lot. Or I like Faeries, so I loved blue-based tempo decks. Or I played a lot of Sphinx's Revelation, so I must love control decks. No, I actually like doing these specific macro-things in Magic, and Clay understood that.

And I would say Clay is the first person that I felt would really understand me. I ended up going to a diner with Clay, me, and some people from the Rutgers Magic club. We're sitting down and the waitress comes back and says, "Do you need more time?" And I answer yes, and Clay just, even louder, says, "No, we're ready to order." And everyone else is like, "Jonathan said he needs more time, shouldn't we wait for him?"

And Clay just—Clay has this great laugh-while-talking type of thing, kind of like a chuckle while talking. And he's like, "Oh...no...you don't know...Jonathan. This is what he's doing. See, upon entering the diner, or maybe even reading the menu very quickly, Jonathan already knows what he wants to get. And then he's cost-evaluating all this other stuff, but if we put him under the gun, he will order the thing that he actually wants."

"And by waiting this amount of time, he's trying to psych himself out and see if he can cut a few dollars off, or get something that's slightly more efficient. But it usually doesn't happen. He's just going to take all the time you give him and he's just going to get the same thing, so we should just order."

And everyone looks very perplexed, turns to me, and I look up from my menu, I'm like, "He's right." And then I go back to the menu, and I'm trying to figure it out.

James: He knows you so well. And he's willing to verbalize that, which is really key.

Jonathan: Everyone in the School of Crushing is good at this now, but he was the first person that ever taught me things about myself. I would never be able to put that into words. But because he did, that means I can do it now.

James: Do you think that Clay is super-observational in general? Or is it that you and he have some kind of chemistry, which lets him really understand you?

Jonathan: I think it's both. I think he's really good at understanding people, but I like to think I'm a complicated person and he definitely understands me very well. But maybe everyone is a complicated person.

Clay is probably the person I have the worst record against. He's beaten me more than anyone else at almost any game I've ever played. I think we're both very similar in terms of intelligence levels, but he "gets" me so much better than how I "get" him.

He would constantly say things like, "Jonathan would never do that." And he just knows. It's fantastic.

James: Sounds like he brings out the best in you. And likewise.

Jonathan: Yeah. He means a lot to me. Unfortunately, after we graduate from college, Clay ended up being in the hospital for a little while, and he's currently in a spot where I haven't seen him for—I forget if it's a year or two at this point—but he is actively playing Magic. I do get these reminders that he still exists when he's one of the top draft trophy leaders.

And we have a Facebook group, and the joke we have is that he's in his own version of the hyperbolic time chamber, where he comes back when he's healthy enough. And then he's going to dominate the game.

But really, it kind of sucks. I feel like I wasn't able to share a lot of moments with him that I wish I could have. And he doesn't know this, but I'm not a person that's good at giving gifts. I'm trying to be better about it. I just give gifts to people as it's convenient.

But Will—from the original School of Crushing—and Clay are two people in particular that I like to go out of my way to get presents for. Even before Clay had to stay home more. And since he hasn't been around, I've bought a present for him for every birthday and Christmas that he's missed. And right now, I just have a stack of—it's fairly high now, of just stuff that I bought for him at various events that I've gone to, that I wish he could have come to. Or Christmas celebrations I wish he could have been at.

And all of us talk about how the first tournament that Clay says he's coming back for, we're literally going to drop everything and go to that event, and make it a really big thing.

Abe and I fantasize about me giving him all the presents. What we'll do is like, "Okay, you were on your own for all of these big events. Here's what we're going to do for you." And then it's like, "Christmas 2016. Merry Christmas, Clay! Here is your present!" And then it's like, "March 2017? Happy birthday, Clay! Here is your present!" And we'll celebrate all the things together.

James: Just playback the entire timeline, all in one go.

Jonathan: I don't really know what to say. I really miss him. And he's one of my best friends from college, and it kind of sucks. I don't want to go into too much detail.

James: Let's say that you're looking forward to meeting up with him again—

Jonathan: He's not deathly ill. I don't want to come off like he's dying.

James: You just need to meet up with him at some point.

Jonathan: Yeah. You know how the Beatles used to joke about how Paul was dead?

James: Yes.

Jonathan: It might have been a different person, we don't know. But on the *Abbey Road* album cover, there were clues that Paul had passed away. So people used to ask us, "Where's Clay, by the way?" And we would reply with, "Clay is dead."

James: That's morbid, but it kind of fits.

Jonathan: Or, "Clay is dying," and stuff like that. But at the end of the day, I don't want him to be dead, I very much care about this individual, and we kind of joke about it in a way to forget that it's been so long that we've seen him.

One thing that is very compatible between us—in a similar way that Travis and Abe are compatible—is our sense of humor and how things line up. Clay finds a lot of things I say funny, and he loves listening to my stories.

I would talk to Clay every so often, or in different group settings where he's also present. Maybe others wouldn't have heard my stories yet, but I end up telling the same story in his presence multiple times. Halfway through the story, he usually ends up laughing and says, "Oh, I remember how this one ends, it's great." Or he'll be like, "Oh man, I remember the lead up to this, and I know the punchline is worth it, but I don't remember the punchline. I can't wait to hear it."

He loves hearing my stories over and over again, and I love telling stories. He's just great. I can't wait to see him again.

James: I hope you get a chance to see him soon.

Jonathan: Yeah, we'll celebrate all the Christmases and birthdays.

"If we are here for a very short amount of time, you can look at it one of two ways. One way is, it's the big stuff that matters. It is curing cancer. It is securing a better life for future generations. Another way is, if we are here for such a short amount of time, what is the thing that impacts people's lives the most? It's basically your interactions with other people on a day-to-day basis."

—Gerry Thompson

Chapter 3

Gerry Thompson

Ask any Magic player to name their favorite professional player, and nine times out of ten, you'll hear the name Gerry Thompson.

Gerry T sits on the throne of "the people's favorite" for good reason. He's one of the most respected professional Magic players on the planet, a creative deckbuilding genius, and not afraid to speak his mind.

Gerry has, over the years, consistently put his money where his mouth is. He's taken stances on issues in the Magic community that have hurt him financially but have ultimately advanced the state of the game for the better.

What's more, Gerry has shared his own internal experiences and "growth moments" that have helped many Magic players improve their mental well-being. He's a man of principle, and the community is so much better for it.

Gerry also understands, highlights, and nurtures other players. He is quick to recognize good players and equally good behaviors. A true gentleman, he holds the door open for others – *this* I actually witnessed when I met him in Seattle.

I'd known about Gerry's stellar reputation for as long as I've played competitive Magic. But in 2016, Gerry published some surprising revelations about himself.

In a post he made on Reddit, Gerry wrote about the trials and tribulations of being a pro Magic player. All the things that people glamorized about the Magic lifestyle, Gerry attempted to clarify. It was a bold and honest perspective.

What stood out in that piece was unprecedented, in terms of a top-tier pro openly describing his life-long battles with depression. It's hard to think of any other recent players who have done as much for the game.

Gerry's writing was candid, brave and surprising. How does he deal with inner darkness on a daily basis? How does he dig deeply within himself to muster the strength to deal with the public spotlight, despite not even wanting to get out of bed on some days?

I needed to talk to Gerry. Not only to satisfy my curiosity, but with the hope that his message and learnings could reach as many people as possible.

Three years later, I still think about this conversation a lot. It takes courage and responsibility to reveal something that personal to the outside world and risk being judged. Gerry did all of that and certainly wasn't afraid to do so.

That's Gerry, true to form – an overwhelmingly positive force for the game. I'm constantly wowed and humbled by his energy and grace. He makes the world a better place.

Recorded in October 2016.

James: You recently wrote a very interesting piece on Reddit.[4] It's a unique piece of Magic writing. For full context, could you set that up for us? Take me through what was going through your mind as you were writing your article.

---

[4] https://www.reddit.com/r/magicTCG/comments/58slc5/a_rebuttal_the_lifestyle_of_the_professional/

Gerry: It was a rebuttal to an article that Matt Sperling posted on his blog.[5] It wasn't written by him, but it was written by another professional Magic player.

I had read it a week before I posted my rebuttal and just kind of let it go. But I definitely saw myself in various parts of what they wrote. Basically, about the grind and how everything blurs together—and it's like, "What are we doing here?" It definitely takes a toll on you—all the traveling.

At times being a professional Magic player is not all that rewarding because you're grinding Grand Prix and stuff. One of the things that I always felt kind of strange was just how quickly you're forgotten. You can win a tournament one week, and the next weekend there's already another tournament that somebody else won. They just forget you.

You see someone a month later and they're like, "Yeah dude, I don't remember anything that you've accomplished this year." People forget very quickly, so in that sense it's just not very rewarding, and that adds to it all.

I've definitely felt like that at various points in my career. For me personally, it was—well, depression kind of leads to a lot of that, where everything is dulled. All of your victories are dulled, then the negative stuff just hits you a little bit harder. You dwell on that negativity.

However, [that was] me six [to] eight years ago. Since then, I've learned to be happy with what I do have and figure out the good parts, why I keep doing it.

---

[5] http://sperlinggrove.blogspot.com/2016/10/the-lifestyle-of-professional-magic.html

For me, once my focus shifted a little bit, it wasn't so much, "Oh, I want to win all these tournaments and be revered as a professional Magic player." It was, "No, I really like my writing gig," which I started doing to help pay my bills. But it got to a point where people actually wanted to read my stuff—because it helped them [get better at Magic.]

I would get messages from people: "Dude, you wrote about this deck with this thing, with the sideboarding guide. But you explained this thing that I hadn't really thought about, and that helped me win this tournament." It's just like, *man!* I am kind of making a difference. Then the more I went to tournaments—especially when the Open Series blew up from 2010 to 2011—I found myself signing cards and playmats. I was more of a real celebrity.

It was weird because when I started playing Magic in the early 2000s, there wasn't social media, and these people were not very approachable. I remember players like Antonino De Rosa, for example. I'm just going to throw him under the bus—he was kind of a jerk. If you were a random dude and you tried to go up and talk to them, it'd be like, "Dude, leave us alone. You're not part of the cool kids. You can't talk to us."

Now, you go up to pro players and they're happy to talk. You have a better insight on who they are because you get to follow them on social media. The pros and the random people are far more connected than they used to be a decade and a half ago. That's definitely better for Magic.

But yeah, it just got to the point where I'm signing stuff and I'm hanging out with people, they're taking selfies with me, and it blew my mind. That is part of my job now. I don't want to say that I only do it because it's part of my job—I genuinely like the people.

Between me shifting into this teacher role, and this *person*—I could be this person where part of my job on the weekend, or part of my goal—not even necessarily part of my job—was to brighten people's days. I *want* people to go to Magic tournaments, go home, and be like, "Man that was a great weekend! I want to do this again." I want Magic to be a thing that is all inclusive and super fun for everyone. If part of what they want to get out of going to tournaments is seeing their favorite pros and talking to them—maybe becoming friends with them and stuff like that—it's like, "Hell yeah, I want to be a part of that."

My focus shifted to that stuff instead of the tournaments themselves. I still want to join these tournaments, crush a bunch of people and win. But it's not everything. If you're trying to get that out of Magic—just that part—you might be disappointed.

Reading that article on Sperling's blog, it was like, "I kind of get where this person is coming from. That was me a few years ago. I definitely get that."

Then I watched this Super Smash Brothers documentary, which is on YouTube.[6] I don't know why, but it *connected* with me... I got super hyped up. It's this thing that's about the people of the game. The people who, during their era, were the best. It had a big impact on me, and I loved it. I wish that stuff existed for Magic.

---

[6] https://youtu.be/jX9hbbA-WP4

So, I booked a flight to Providence last minute. [Laughs] Thankfully got everything worked out and I got some cheap flights. Landed, drove to Greensborough, which was two hours away in the middle of the night, to catch my 6:00 am flight.

I got there and my flight was delayed...but I had a couple of hours to kill in the airport. For whatever reason, this article popped up in my mind. "I'm going to write a reply to that." I'm already sleep deprived and making weird decisions, but it's not like I just came up with all that stuff off the top of my head or anything.

I spent an hour and a half writing 1,500 words, which for me is pretty good. I definitely don't write my articles at that kind of clip. This was all stuff that I thought about.

I still am where I am, mostly because of hard work and perseverance and all that happy uplifting stuff—but it was the natural counterpoint to the article that this person wrote. I posted my writing, hands shaking, as I'm hovering over the "send" button. Do I really want to do this? Do I really want to let all these people into my actual life, my feelings, all that stuff? Because I've been burned before.

James: We all have.

Gerry: Yeah, my natural instinct is like, "Nah, don't do it man! Don't do it! Just be surface level." But no, I hit "send" and it made my weekend. It was great—the response that I got was truly phenomenal.

James: I looked at some of the comments there. People coming in saying they had met you somewhere and recounting their stories, it was great.

You said at the end, "Don't do this." It's very hard to make it as a professional player. But then you're also very frank and realistic about how if you *do* decide to pursue this path, this is what it's like. Here is the good and the bad. That really touched a lot of people, including myself.

Gerry: I'm glad to hear that. That was the point. I love Magic. I want it to succeed. I want people to be happy doing this, and I want someone out there to say, "I think I'm good enough. I think I can do this." I want them to do it. You only get so many chances in life to do the things you actively want and just go for it.

James: Do you find that Magic players are unrealistic about this kind of thing?

Gerry: If people were more well informed, I'm sure I would have not felt any sort of urgency to write this piece. If they know this stuff already, there's no point in me writing it. What value does it bring to the table?

Certainly, people are a bit uninformed. They either assume that it's great and we all are rich, or it's awful and we all just live in our moms' basements. Again, it's somewhere in the middle.

James: Yeah.

Gerry: Different people do different things. Luis [Scott-Vargas] is killing it. He basically has four jobs. I'm sure he's fine financially—he's basically the best at what he does. He might be the most successful professional Magic player. But he's got his hands in a bunch of different pots, too. He's got the Channel Fireball thing, working at Dire Wolf Games, doing commentary, and he just top-eights every Pro Tour—he's got a lot of stuff going on.

Then there are the people that only play the Grand Prix and Pro Tours, they don't write articles but have a full-time job. There are the people that live in Roanoke and just make three pieces of content every week, and go to the Opens. For the Roanoke people, the EV [Expected Value] for Open Weekend is probably $500 because they are hella good at Magic and there's no Luis in these tournaments.

So yeah, there are a lot of different ways that you can do this Magic stuff. You can just buy and sell cards. I know that's what a lot of the European pros do when they come to American Grand Prix and the like. Some of the Brazilians buy iPhones and resell them or whatever. There are a lot of things that you can do to make money and it all depends on how much money you think you need to live.

I can live a pretty bland lifestyle. I don't have to go out to eat every night. I don't have to go see movies, or go to the bar and run $100 tabs or anything like that. I'm pretty minimalist, so I don't have to do much. But there are other people that maybe need those things.

James: Let's touch on one of the biggest things in the writing—because it quite honestly surprised me to read it. I don't know if you wrote about this before—it sounds like maybe not—that you had been dealing with depression for most of your life.

Gerry: I can't remember a time where I might have mentioned this out in the open. My close friends are aware—most of them.

But yeah, there's this stigma attached to it. People are not well informed. They don't know that it's a literal illness and not some sort of weakness.

Instead of necessarily trying to change how people view things—instead of [saying], "Look, this is an illness," and trying to speak out about it—it was like, "Well, if they're going to think that this is a weakness, I should probably not say anything, right?"

So, it is a cop out. It is definitely not for the greater good. But it's a big part of my story. It's a big part of who I am and the stuff that I've been through. So it made sense to go into the Reddit post because I wanted to be frank and upfront with everything. Then people were like, "Yeah, I'm going through this too." A lot of people.

James: In the article you mentioned that you've been depressed for as long as you can remember. When did you first realize this? How did you find out about it?

Gerry: I can't pinpoint a specific time or anything. It's weird. Maybe the depression is coloring my idea of things and my memories. I really have no idea. But I know that, at 13-14-15 [years old], I'm sure I felt the exact same way as I do now. Somewhere in high school I realized that this was a thing, but I don't even think that I realized the gravity of it. I was like, "Yeah I guess this is a thing."

Maybe I thought like a lot of other people do, who are like, "Maybe I should just stop being depressed." As it turns out, it doesn't work that way. There is no cure. There are treatments, medication, and going to therapy helps, stuff like that. But medications are different for everyone and there are a lot of side effects, pros and cons, certainly, to taking them. It takes a while for you to actually figure out what works for you because depression affects everyone differently.

So, I honestly don't know. I know that I've felt this way for a long time. I don't remember a time where the switch just flipped, and I was like, "Oh, this is like a real thing and I should try and get help for this." Even up until recently I haven't really done anything about it. Maybe it was pride. Or I'm like, "I'm strong. I can deal with this." I don't know. There wasn't an "a-ha!" moment.

I went back and looked up this article [written by a] friend of mine, Noah Weil, who also now lives in the Seattle area. He was from Minnesota also, which is where I was born and grew up. We knew each other and we'd interacted a little bit. He wrote this article on depression for Star City in 2005.[7] I remember reading that article. I was like, "Oh, this is a real thing and it is very powerful."

James: What's it like? You mentioned things like, "there's some days where you just don't want to get out of bed." What is it like to actually be in that sort of mindset?

Gerry: I'm no expert, but I can tell you how this affects me. It affects everyone differently. So I don't want to speak for anyone else.

James: Sure.

Gerry: But for me, personally, it is—instead of *you have this good experience, this positive experience*—you do this fun thing, or you get rewarded somehow— instead of it being a positive, I feel like it brings me up to even. Does that make sense?

[7] http://www.starcitygames.com/article/11045_Gamers-and-Depression.html

James: So, you should be feeling—I don't know, not *should be*—but you would expect to feel elated or great that you went to the theme park, or you won a tournament. But instead, you just feel *not unhappy*. Is that the way to put it?

Gerry: Pretty much. And then given enough time, my brain could find a way to make me feel unhappy about it. It is not about happy/unhappy, necessarily. It's certainly not about that all the time. But it just kind of dulls everything. It dulls just the amount of positivity you get out of certain things—at least for me. There are some days—and this has not happened a lot or anything—but there are some days where it's just like nothing really feels like it's worth it. Why should I bother getting out of bed, you know?

It is very difficult to get motivated and actually want to do things because you don't necessarily remember the positive reinforcement of the good feelings you had after doing those things. So there are times where I'll sit at home and it's like—I have whatever I want in my house. I have the Internet, Magic Online, and Hearthstone. I have video games and books. I've got all these things that stimulate me. Then there are just times where I just sit here because none of that stuff seems worth doing.

James: I see.

Gerry: One of the reasons I continued playing Magic...I never went to college or anything. I played Magic because I enjoyed doing it and I was good at it, you know? And I don't necessarily like starting over. I'd like to learn how to play guitar for example, but I'm not going to devote 10,000 hours to it. So I just don't do it, right?

But playing Magic for a living gave me the free time to do whatever I want, and enjoy these things that I could enjoy because I love doing them. And now I have so many video games that have been un-played, books that have been un-read, and it's very strange to me.

James: Does depression prevent you from taking certain actions as well? Because I can tell you that while I don't have depression, I have those days too, where I don't want to do anything. Sometimes I wonder what's the meaning of it all. I'm starting to realize with age—you're in your 30s as well, right?

Gerry: I'm 32.

James: We're around the same age. There are some days where you wonder, "What's the point of it all?" Then there are other days where you feel like, "Everything is good. I'm going to do three or four things today, and carpe diem. I'm going to make the most out of the day."

I can't speak for everybody, but for me it fluctuates. I'm wondering if there's any—I'm not trying to be prescriptive—are there any sort of techniques or methods you've adopted over the years that help you deal with that?

I know this question may sound condescending, but I'm wondering if you've tried it? I'm genuinely curious if there are things that you've done, as you're getting older and more experienced, to try to navigate this.

Gerry: I know what you mean and I appreciate you trying to be very careful with your verbiage. I think a lot of people are not [careful with their wording]. But you get it.

So, Pokémon Go was a pretty big thing, but it wasn't for the reason that you might think. It got me out of the house and forced me to interact with people, which is a good thing and brightens my mood. I do love people, and you get out of the house, you walk around, get some exercise and stuff.

Exercise is one of the things that is proven to help with this. It mitigates things a little bit. I would get up in the morning and instead of being like, "Oh, nothing feels worth doing," I was like, "Oh, man, I'm three candies away from a Venusaur or whatever. Let's go find some Bulbasaurs!" Right?

It gets me out of the house, I come back and I feel good because I was out there. I was accomplishing some stuff and having fun. Then from that point, it's easier to do the other stuff, you know? Now that I've been out in the world and I've interacted with some people, and maybe had a run-in with a police officer that was wondering why I was on these train tracks, or whatever, right?

It's like, "Okay, I've interacted with these people. Everything feels a little bit easier. It's not as difficult as it seems. Now I can go to the grocery store." Right? But there are days...now I don't play that game very often, probably because I got hooked into Hearthstone. But yeah, now I'll get up and I'm certainly not going to leave for Pokémon Go because I literally got them all. What's the point? But it's like, "Oh, man! Should I go to the grocery store? I really don't have a lot of stuff to eat." Then it's like, "Well, I don't really want to interact with people, so maybe I'll just order a pizza."

Then I stay in and overall not feel great about my situation. And then there's the self-loathing:

"God! I can't even go outside. This is pathetic!" which makes it worse—this downwards spiral. So yeah, find some ways to get out, interact with people. Exercise in general is a good thing, but if you're playing Pokémon Go and you're walking five miles while also interacting with people—double positive—that's good.

Those are things that help. For all the stuff with my brain telling me, "You don't want to go outside. You don't want to interact with people. You don't want to do anything," doing the opposite of that helps a lot. It's a lot about getting over that hump, and that makes me feel a little bit better.

James: There are things that work, but I think the tricky thing is that your brain also tells you, "Is it worth it?" Sometimes it's hard to reconcile the rational with the irrational.

Gerry: Absolutely.

James: And you're very self-aware. Do you try to keep the way you feel under control? Is control the goal when it comes to this kind of thing?

Gerry: I find it weird that you bring up this question because it's a big part of who I am. I *want* to be in control... It is a big deal for me. I felt, as a kid, not a lot of things were in my control. Now, from 21 on, I'm on my own. If I want something, I need to do it because no one else is going to do it for me. But as far as the feelings, I can't keep them under control, you know? That's the thing. I can't just tell my brain to make myself feel good. That doesn't work. There aren't days where I wake up and I *want* to feel like crap. It just happens.

To some degree, that is one of those things that kind of gets to me. It's like—I should be able to control this, and I can control it to some degree if I get out and do these things. That sort of lessens the effects of the depression. I could get on medication, for example, which I'm currently not on, and I wanted to be on for multiple years. But it's difficult because of that feeling of—if I start taking these pills, it might help my depression, but *am I going to be me?* That is terrifying.

James: That's the opposite of being in control.

Gerry: Exactly.

James: It's great that we're talking about this because I think it's brave. Is there any way we might be able to recognize the signs of depression in people around us? With our friends? Is there anything we can do to potentially help them?

Gerry: This is probably one of the saddest things about it—if not the saddest. You generally can't tell. I feel like a lot of the people who are suffering from depression are very, very good at overcompensating for that when they're around people. Robin Williams I think is the most recent case of a person who was genuinely kind. He was really funny, a literal comedian, right?

No one had any idea that he was depressed. You get so good at hiding it. I don't think a lot of people know I was either. Because you see me at a tournament, and I am *turned on.* My entertainer persona comes out, right? I flip that switch and I become this super outgoing person when I'm close on the introvert/extrovert line, but I'm definitely more of an introvert.

When I go to a tournament that is especially stimulating, as far as dealing with people, it takes a lot out of me. But even when I am on a week-long Grand Prix trip or something, I am able to be my best self on day seven. It's just, how much recharge time do I need to get after that?

So I have no problem hiding it. My natural state is to be this seemingly extroverted person. I think a lot of people do that. It's like, *man*, the people that you would probably think are least likely to be depressed, might be the most likely. It is really tough.

There are going to be times where you're going to be like, "Man, that's just some strange behavior for that person because…" They seem like they're happy all the time or whatever, and that might be a warning sign. You never know.

James: I certainly think you're shattering that stereotype—for lack of a better word—because we're not even talking about introverted or extroverted. You are just a nice dude. When we've interacted—when I see your writing, or how you interact with other people—you strike me as a very generous dude.

Gerry: I think I was raised right. I think my mother did an excellent job. A lot of who I am is me trying to emulate her, right? So, thankfully I had a good role model.

But a lot of it might be overcompensating, too, where I know how shitty I feel on a day-to-day basis, and I don't want that for anyone else. It is kind of selfish, where I want to do good things for other people, just to make myself feel better. But it is coming from a good place for sure, and I definitely try.

James: You're a well-known, recognizable Magic player and you work for Star City Games, so there is a certain image to uphold. Does that ever get tiring—being Gerry Thompson and having to be nice to people?

Gerry: I was not very nice about a decade ago. I think I was a lot more selfish. If someone misplayed against me and beat me anyway, I would lay into them for no real reason. Maybe I thought that sort of stuff would make me happy, right? But yeah, that was not my default setting. I'm very, very good to my friends. For the new people that I meet, I give them the benefit of the doubt. I assume that they're an excellent person and therefore I'm going to treat them very well. And if you're not a nice person, I'm not going to treat you very well. That is constant with me.

My perspective changed and now it's just—no one deserves to get yelled at for making a mistake or whatever. It's stupid, it's childish. Now, I strive to be a good person all the time, I guess.

It does drain me, but that's an after-the-fact thing, and I'm used to it at this point, but during the tournament it's where I want to be. That's one of the reasons why I went to Providence in the last second. It was like, "Why am I home?" If I'm on my death bed, I'm not going to be like, "Man, I should have gone to Providence." But I would be like, "Why did I not do all these things that I knew would make me feel good, or I would have a good time doing?"

So when you look at it that way, it's like, "Hell yeah! I'm going to go to this tournament." If I'm there, I'm going to enjoy myself. Enjoying myself means interacting with people, and hopefully that means making their day a little bit better. I kind of pay for it afterwards, where I'm dead to the world for twelve hours and have to sleep, get up, and take a nap.

But I think even if I played the tournaments in a mask and no one had any idea who I was, I would still be exhausted after the fact. So it doesn't drain on me. I don't see it as a price I have to pay for being a "face of Magic" or anything like that. I genuinely enjoy it, and if I didn't I would be someone else, you know? I wouldn't be writing articles and doing all that sort of stuff.

James: Does your love for Magic help you deal with depression? Going out and interacting with the community?

Gerry: It does in such a way that if I'm at a tournament and interacting with my friends, it is very difficult for me to have depression on the forefront of my mind. I kind of forget about it and I get to enjoy myself as much as I can. So it definitely does help.

But obviously there are tournaments where you go and the travel is exhausting. In round six of Providence I realized I strongly disliked my deck and it was misbuilt, but I knew that going in. It was a throwaway tournament for me. A lot of the time when that happens, where it's like, "Oh, man. I messed up and now I have to play the rest of the tournament with this crappy deck," and you have a middling finish and maybe your friend loses playing for top eight and they are pretty bummed.

It's like, "Man, this weekend sucks!" But in reality you're hanging out with your friends, you're joking around, you create more in-jokes or things you're going to bring up a week from now that are awesome. You keep on telling people the same stories and everything.

All that stuff is great, and you might say, "Oh, man. This was not our best weekend." Then it's like,

"Man, why did I even come here?" But then I get home and book another flight because I know deep down that this is it. This is the thing that I want to do.

James: This is your passion, right? This is what you're into.

Gerry: Absolutely. I tried other games, other jobs, and whatever. None of it hits me like this does.

James: Have there been cases in the past where having depression prevented you from doing that? Not to keep dwelling on that, but you seem remarkably consistent in your output.

Gerry: Writing is easy for me. It is something that I enjoy. Even if I wasn't getting paid for it, I would still do it. It's never been like, "Oh man, I'm feeling bad. I can't write today." Writing is therapeutic for me. It's organizing my thoughts, putting them on paper, and sharing what I've learned with the world. That makes me feel good.

I've definitely skipped tournaments because I'm like, "Oh, I'm tired. I need a break." And I don't think I'm tired. I'm definitely getting old and it's taking more of a toll on me, but I'm never too tired to drive six hours to a tournament, you know? That's not a good excuse. If I'm being realistic, I would say that depression has definitely stopped me from attending events. Providence was a close call, but thankfully I rectified that.

Now that I made the post and I'm having this interview with you, I'm forced to think about it more. I actually go back and analyze my actions. What was causing me to do these things? It's crazy that depression is one of those things that tells you not to do the things that would help your depression.

James: That's it, right? It's something that is a constant battle.

Gerry: Right. Like I said—go outside, get some exercise, interact with people. Anyone who is listening to this—if they can't relate—they're like, "Dude, that's just easy. Why don't you just do that?" It's like, "Well, that's the problem! Because it's very difficult."

James: Well, it's hard for anybody. I mean, I tell myself I want to go to the gym every day and I don't do it, right?

Gerry: Sure.

James: It's not that easy. The human will is not that easily harnessed. On a similar track...I know you mentioned that you matured. You've changed from who you were 10 years ago. But one of the sentences that stuck out when I read your recent writing was, quote, "I resented Magic because it became my life and I thought I could and should be doing so much more." That sentence really hit me and it begs the question—what *are* you looking for in life, and is there a way that you can measure that?

Gerry: I think I figured it out now, but back then I didn't know. I had no idea. I didn't go to college. I had no one that was a positive influence. My mom passed away when I was 18, and she was my role model. She was the good person that I looked up to. With her gone, there was no one pushing me or setting a good example.

Fast-forward four or five years later, I'm playing Magic—and I had done other stuff in-between—but I'm doing that, and then I'm very disappointed in myself. I was supposed to be this smart kid. I pick things up pretty quickly, so what's stopping me from actually doing something that matters?

Obviously, what matters is—I don't know, it's a debate, right? Things that matter, matter to different people....Cure cancer, for example. Could I be a doctor? Could I actually make a difference? It's like, "Yeah, maybe I could. I don't know."

I don't want to be a waste...I would like to do something that does matter to people—and here I am just playing some card game, right? That lingered with me for a while, and there was a lot of the self-loathing. It was like, "Oh man. Maybe it's just Magic's fault because Magic is too good." But it has nothing to do with that. The fact that Magic is good is a great thing. But once I grew up a little bit, I took a harder look and it was, "Now, what do I actually want? What do I think matters?"

Maybe because of my mom dying, the mortality thing really hits me. We are here for so short of a time. She was just forty-two when she died, which is incredibly young. I'm coming up on forty-two, you know? It kind of stops you in your tracks. Makes you think things.

If we are here for a very short amount of time, you can look at it one of two ways. One way is, it's the big stuff that matters. It is curing cancer. It is securing a better life for future generations. Another way is, if we are here for such a short amount of time, what is the thing that impacts people's lives the most? It's basically your interactions with other people on a day-to-day basis.

I'm sure everyone has this—where you have a negative interaction and it ruins your day. If someone cuts you off in traffic, or they don't hold the door for you. Something happens, you're like, "Man, that guy was such a jerk." Then it eats away at you for the rest of the day. I never want to do that to anybody. I never want to inadvertently be responsible for ruining someone's day.

They shouldn't have to go through that. They don't have very many days. So, instead, I do the opposite approach. I want to brighten someone's day. I don't necessarily want them to look back on their day and be like, "Man, that was a good day! That was because of Gerry." I don't care if I'm invisible, right? But if at the end of the day they are happy, that makes me happy. I don't know that for sure, but I try and put as much good stuff out there as I can and hopefully that happens.

James: Quite honestly, you're doing that. That's the beautiful thing about this game called *Magic: The Gathering* is that you are making someone's life better in some way. That's tangible impact, right?

Gerry: It was still difficult for me to grasp what kind of impact I've had, because it's not like I'm speaking publicly in front of 10,000 people. But that is how many people read my stuff. You know, ballpark, something like that. That is a lot of people. When I did commentary and there were 14,000 people watching, it was such a big number I couldn't even fathom it.

It gets so big that it might as well as be empty because the number is so big it doesn't even matter. And that's kind of what I feel about what I write, too. This is a thing that I'm writing for me. I'm writing this to organize my thoughts and show how smart I am, I guess. Yeah, there are a lot of people that read it. I don't necessarily get updates from every single person where they're like, "Oh I won a tournament and it felt great because of your article." Or whatever, you know?

That stuff happens very infrequently, so it's hard for me to take that leap and recognize that maybe what I do actually does make a difference and enrich people's lives. Maybe they do enjoy the fact that I exist, right? It's really tough to make that leap because I'm mostly doing this silently, at least from my perspective. I don't get it a lot.

So, when I did this Reddit post and all these people were coming out, I would say acquaintances, people that I am friends with and would like to be closer to, but our paths haven't really aligned, you know? All these people were coming out and sharing these stories of things that I said to them, that have stuck to them for five or ten years. That's insane because if you didn't tell me, I would have never known. The responses to the Reddit thing was enormous.

It is crazy and puts things into perspective, and it makes me proud of what I'm doing. This is what I want to be doing. I want to be helping people. I want to be enriching their lives. This is an affirmation of that, which is something that I need. So I appreciate it.

James: The thing you posted, which really touched everybody, was on Reddit. On Star City, you're doing strictly Magic strategy. Do you think Star City would allow you to do more "life writing"? Does that ever work, or is that something that does not meet their business model?

Gerry: I mean, Todd Anderson has written diary entries on Premium, right?[8] [Laughs]

---

[8] http://www.starcitygames.com/magic/misc/22690_Constructed_Criticism_Living_The_Dream_Of_Pro_Magic.html

James: [Laughs] Yeah, that's right.

Gerry: So, I give Todd a hard time, but I think it is good to some degree. It is certainly better if the reader feels more connected to the author. You develop that kind of relationship where every week, "I want to see what Gerry's doing. I'm going to tune in to whatever tournament he's at, and I'm going to make sure to read his articles, and maybe I'll play his decks." Stuff like that.

Getting those types of relationships might not be something that is tangible, that you can see, but I do think it helps and that it's important. It's not like I want to trick people into liking me so that they buy cards that go with my decks or whatever. But it is nice because you meet those people at tournaments eventually, and you already have this connection, which I think is awesome.

I definitely have a lot of stuff in my phone as far as notes for things that I want to talk about, and this will be something that I do at some point. But I'm also very bad with deadlines, or very bad without deadlines, I should say. I get my articles and videos in on time almost every week because there's a thing saying that I have to.

But if it's something like writing a book, or making a website, or doing this blog where I write about life stuff, it's just like, "Yeah what's the rush?"

James: It's less structured. So it's a little bit harder to do that, especially when you already have this full-time content creation job.

Gerry: The deadline is me being accountable to myself, but I know that I can't punish myself. I can't do anything that would make me regret not doing this on time, so I just wait. I'm content with the way things are.

I have enough money. I'm doing fine. So do I *really* need to try and make this leap and get this book out and sell that or whatever? Nah, not really. I'm good.

James: Well, it's not always about the money, right? It's whether you feel like this is helping people, or you have a message that you want to put out.

Gerry: Right. But money is the thing that you can point to where it's a reward. It is a reason to do something. But as far as people reading it and maybe getting something out of it, that is less tangible. Like I said, it's mostly been invisible, so it's hard for me to quantify that and use it as a justification for getting off my ass and doing something.

It's not logical. It doesn't necessarily make a lot of sense, but that is how my mind works.

James: That's okay, man. [Laughs] Life is not logical.

Gerry: Agree.

James: The other thing I wanted to talk about is the community aspect. I know we touched on it here and there as well. One of the things in your Reddit piece was that you had this interesting mention: "I could keep in touch better with this person and this person."

Gerry: Yeah.

James: I'm curious here. That sentence, what prevents you from...what's going on there? I'm trying to understand that. That was one part of the article I didn't fully get. Is it because you're travelling around the world? Or is it that you know too many people, and they make demands of you?

Gerry: There is definitely a thing. I don't remember the exact numbers, but it was something along the lines of—your brain can only keep up with X amount of close relationships. Which I firmly believe in. I don't know, Google it. [Laughs] ... I think the number was something like X equals seven.

That kind of falls in line with my experiences and how I felt with this. There's a couple of ways to look at it. The first one is I message them. Say it's Calosso [Fuentes] and it's like, "Man, I miss this dude. I haven't talked to him for three years. I wonder what's going on with his life." I message him like, "Hey man! How are things going? How are you doing?" He's like, "I'm good," and then it ends. Right?

Well, that wasn't really helpful, you know? That's been my experience some of the time. That kind of sucks because we're Magic players and it's socially awkward. All right, I'm going to go off on a tangent here. So, there were a couple of people that I would see only occasionally at Pro Tours and Grand Prix and I'd be like, "Oh man, how's it going? I haven't seen you in a long time."

I'd give them a hug and they'd be like, "Oh, I'm three-and-one in the tournament," or whatever. I started yelling at them, "Dude, I don't care about your tournament. It doesn't matter to me. Just tell me how your life is." I want to talk about that stuff. Yeah, your tournament, you're going to win, you're going to lose. Who knows? Whatever! But that's not what I care about. I care about you as a person, so let's talk about that.

[Laughs] And so the two people—I think I'm fine with just naming them—Josh Utter-Leyton and David Ochoa—they were conditioned to be like, "I'm three-and-one." I think the reason they like me—we don't have a ton in common, they're not two of the most talkative people or whatever—but I honestly think one of the reasons they like me is because I was like, "Stop telling me about your tournament. I don't care." I try to get to know them as people because I genuinely like them and I don't think that they had that experience with many other people.

That is the stuff I want, but it is like pulling teeth sometimes because what do you share to someone that you haven't seen in three years? How close is your relationship? Maybe you went through something traumatic and you need someone to talk to, but maybe I'm not the person you feel comfortable talking about it to. That's certainly fine. I mean, you do you. You do whatever you need to make you feel better.

What do you say to someone you haven't spoken to in three years? And part of it is, if I message them, then suddenly they're aware of the fact that they haven't spoken to me in three years. For me, I feel guilty about that. Yeah, it's a two-way street, but what if it brings up the thing that, "Oh, man. This guy hasn't talked to me in three years. What a dick!" Then they don't want to talk to me. [Laughs]

Obviously, that's not going to happen. Again, not logical. But there is this sort of fear, I'd rather hide and not remind them that I haven't talked to them in three years or whatever.

James: It's interesting that you said that. Let me give you my honest-to-God view of Magic professionals. My view is that they all hang around each other because they like each other's achievements in tournaments. So you go to a tournament, you always see the same guys, there's this kind of bond.

But sometimes, as someone who is more a casual competitive player, it feels like, "Oh, maybe we're on a different level." It's harder for us to relate to you guys, and vice versa. I don't know, it feels stupid to say, but in the past, I also felt intimidated approaching you. What I'm trying to say is that I always thought that pro players hang out with pro players because they're pro players.

However, it's interesting that you said that it's *because* you want to talk about things other than Magic that people value that, as opposed to just—I thought you guys only wanted to talk about Magic because you guys are in it. You spend your waking hours thinking about the game, you know?

Gerry: Don't get me wrong. I love Magic. I will talk about it ad nauseam with anyone as long as I feel like they can stimulate me and add to the conversation. But to your point, yeah, we might not be on the same level Magic-wise or whatever. But who cares?

First of all, if you come up [to me] and start talking about Magic, I'm not going to be like, "Oh, this guy is so stupid." I'm going to try and find that common ground. We'll talk about your deck and your sideboard choices. Do you have any idea how many times I have made my decks go from good to great because of something I saw someone else doing? That is all I do. I just steal from other people.

I'm looking at all the decklists and it's like, "Oh, man! That guy is playing that card. I didn't think about that. That's awesome!" I make sure to look at everyone's deck, and if the deck is even remotely interesting—because they might have thought of something I hadn't—you know?

So, we can try and connect on a Magic level, or we can try and connect on a different level, too. That is completely fine with me. We are people. There is no pedestal or anything that I'm going to stand on when I'm talking to someone else, because that's just ludicrous.

James: The thing that makes it tough—and I am going to make a gross assumption here and say that you're in the minority—is that, for us Magic players, we always use Magic as validation for who we are. I mean, let's face it. We're not doing something else. We're not curing cancer, we're spending our waking hours playing Magic or in a competitive tournament. Reading articles, preparing decks.

In a way, when you ask somebody how they're doing in a tournament setting, *their record is who they are at that point in time.* I have friends who are extremely salty because they are one-and-three in that tournament or whatever. And, I don't know, it's really hard. I wish we could get to a world where people don't feel like their record, or their Magic results, validates who they are. But I feel like we haven't really gone past that. Do you know what I mean?

Gerry: That makes a lot of sense to me. For example, at the Pro Tour I was 0-4, and day two was 4-4. I could have continued playing, but I dropped and went back to my room. Now, part of that was me not feeling well and it was hard to justify staying at the tournament because I wasn't enjoying myself. I thought that I would only make things worse.

But at the same point, I was kind of embarrassed, you know? I didn't want to be at the dead-last table at the Pro Tour, trying to grind it out and—I don't want to say that I'm above that, but my brain is trying to tell me that I should be above that. It's stupid.

Like I said, the results from last week are fleeting. You could win the tournament last week and go 0-2 this week, and people are going to remember you for the 0-2. That's very sad.

James: Right. You're only as good as your last game, right?

Gerry: Yeah. So say I messaged Calosso, "Okay man! How is it going?" It goes fine. I have currently 1,000 people that I'm friends with on Facebook, and I've curated it down to the people that I genuinely like. You know, that sort of thing, whereas before I would just add anyone. Any sort of acquaintance or whatever.

So I have 1,000 people in my life. If I sent one person that message, I would feel guilty about not messaging the other 900. There is a hierarchy to it, you know? I don't necessarily want to figure out what that hierarchy is, because it will make me feel bad, and I don't want to message the one person because then I'll feel like I have to message the other 900 people.

Again, not logical. Very similar to you only being as good as your current record, or whatever. That's not logical either.

James: [Laughs] Speaking of getting in touch with friends, is it difficult for you to get close to people? Because I can imagine that in the Magic community, there's a lot of people you'll say hi to on the street—but do you have a couple of friends who you really feel like you connected with?

Gerry: Yeah. I mean, it's tough for me to get close to people in general because of who I am. Not necessarily because of Magic and how everything is all surface level and stuff like that. I think, judging from my experience of dealing with Magic players, it is difficult for most people to get close to others, especially right off the bat.

If I run into David Ochoa, I'm like, "Dude, what's going on with your life?" He's not going to immediately open up to me, you know? I don't expect that. It can be very, very difficult. I have a lot of stuff that I'm not proud of. I don't think I'm perfect and it's tough for me to share that sort of weakness with people and let them in.

The depression is certainly part of it. It is tough. But it's one of those things, too, where effort happens. When someone sees you for what you truly are, and they're still there, there is no better feeling. So, it is definitely something that I wish I could do more. Logically it makes sense, and sometimes my brain won't let me do it. Just defense mechanism, I guess.

James: Who's the person that you're closest to right now?

Gerry: His name is Josh Cho and I think he would be disappointed if I didn't mention him. Josh and I talk about this all the time. We might be driving to some tournament or whatever, and there's a lull in the conversation and we're having a good time, and he brings this up more than me. But it's like, "Man, how are we friends?"

It's a question for the ages because I was a terrible child. He was a terrible child. We met at a point where if it was one year apart in difference we probably would have hated each other. It's something that we feel is wild because, I don't know, it's one of those things where it's when I met him, I was good at Magic, I was winning a bunch of tournaments and stuff. He was just a dude that played.

Now I think he is at the top of his game and he is killing it, which is great for me to see. But for a long time there was a gap in our ability that was pretty noticeable by most people, and we're still best friends, you know?

That doesn't stop us. It's cool that we play Magic and we have a reason to go hang out, and he was one of the motivating factors behind me going to Providence. If I knew he wasn't going, I definitely wouldn't have gone. But then again, maybe I would have just driven up to DC and hung out with him.

James: How long have you guys known each other?

Gerry: We met at the first Star City Games Invitational, and this is a chronic Magic problem where I don't remember dates or anything, but I remember tournaments. [Laughs] I remember what was going on. So, this was Valakut [era]—like Primeval Titans, Vampires, Blue-White Control. I played Valakut at that tournament, and it was a really weird structured tournament—different than anything else as far as the number of people and the amount of Swiss rounds. No one had any idea what record you needed to make the top eight.

He was this random dude who I had never seen before, being very helpful with tiebreaker math and stuff. Obviously that's a stereotype, but he's not even that good at math, as far as I know. I don't even think the advice he was giving was good, but I was like, "Oh, man. That was really nice and helpful."

We would see each other at tournaments. And I don't even know at what point it was like, "Okay,

next tournament we should get a hotel together."
I don't know—it was like I met him at that tournament. Now we're best friends and there is no in-between.

James: It's hard to describe these good friendships, right? It's really hard to go back and be like, "Yeah X, Y, and Z happened, so that's why we're good friends." Sometimes you just have this chemistry with somebody.

Gerry: Yeah, absolutely.

James: Does he know most of what you're going through? Some of the things that came out recently in the writing? Your situation and your challenges?

Gerry: Yeah. He does not suffer from depression, so it's kind of tough for him to relate. It's tough for him to pick up how I'm feeling, which is fine. But I would say that for the most part he "gets" me. He understands my motivation and what we're going through.

Part of why we're friends is that we can have some sort of ethical discussion and we're basically on the same page at every point, which makes it really easy.

We just "get" each other and our lives are pretty different. He was working full time, married, and going back to school now. He is trying to find time to play Magic. Last year he hit Silver, deferred his Australia Pro Tour Sydney invite, so then he had two Silver invites because that's just how it works.

Then he won a RPTQ, so now he has three invites for this year. So, he's got to juggle family, school, Magic, all this other stuff. He's like, "Can I make a run at Gold?" So we're talking about that stuff and now he's a little bit more involved in Magic than in previous years.

But yeah, our lives are very, very different. We have incredibly different backgrounds. But our ethical compass is on point, which I think is pretty important for both of us.

James: That's key. It sounds like Josh is juggling a lot of things in his life. That's pretty admirable.

Gerry: He's busy. For me it's like, "Yeah, I have to get up and record a video." That's really tough for me, but Josh slept for five hours. He had a hip problem for a little bit, and he had a lot of back pain. Despite that, he was just go-go-go—getting all this stuff done. He was even finding time to go catch Pokémon, too. He's a pretty big inspiration. It helps me motivate myself when I have people like that— that have a lot of stuff going on, and he still manages to get it all done.

James: I know it's really challenging to go through everything. I hope you had the chance to get everything off your chest, in terms of this interview.

Gerry: I did, absolutely. Like I said, I was nervous about posting the Reddit thing—scared of people getting a glimpse at who I am, maybe shattering the illusion a little bit. Where it's like, "Oh man, this guy has it so good," or whatever. Kind of scared about doing this podcast also. But it feels good, you know?

James: I do have something I want to ask you. You're talking about something that a lot of folks don't directly experience. It's Magic celebrity. Mark Rosewater wrote a really good article about it.[9]

---

[9] https://magic.wizards.com/en/articles/archive/making-magic/celebrity-2012-07-30

Do you feel that other people treat you differently because you are such a well-known pro? It's impossible to know, but have you ever had incidents where you feel, "Yeah, this person only likes me—or doesn't like me—because I'm Gerry Thompson, the Magic player? Not because I'm Gerry Thompson, the human being"?

Gerry: No, this is a great question. I love this question. I have a few people on a list, where I'm like, "This person is a scumbag." They do a lot of things for selfish reasons. My radar is not often wrong. It is not uncommon for me to be like, "I don't have many interactions with this person, but I don't like them." A lot of my close friends [might say], "Oh that's weird," because normally you have some story—something that backs this up. And then six months later [that person] get[s] banned for cheating.

Then there are people that are just bad people... There are a lot of people that I'm like, "Man, I really like that person." Then someone is like, "Nope! Story, story, story, story." And I'm like, "Wow!" I would never have guessed that.

A lot of it is because people are on their best behavior around me, trying to curry favor. Maybe if they get in with me, I can hook them up with the tech or whatever. That's one of the things that I mentioned in the Reddit post—some people are just so fake. It's tough to figure that out.

I would say that most people are on their best behavior around me, and I don't get to see the real side of people. It makes me cautious a lot of the time, where it's like, "Alright, this guy has been really nice. *What does he want?*" Or, "This guy just seems like a genuinely nice person, but a lot of people hate him. *What am I missing?"*

People are very complicated. I'm also a person who had a very bad reputation—a well-deserved bad reputation—about a decade ago. Where [someone might say about me], "No, this guy is an asshole. He blew up at me for no good reason and I hate him." That hurts, but it doesn't hurt because they're lying. It hurts because it's true.

I'm fully aware that people can turn it around. Perspective is a very powerful thing, and once you get some of that, it's harder to justify doing a lot of the stuff that impacts people negatively. I'm willing to give people the benefit of the doubt a lot of the time.

But I'm also not necessarily going to believe that you are as good of a person as you present yourself. I'm cautiously optimistic a lot of the time. We can have a lot of good interaction, but if there's something telling me that I shouldn't be best friends with you, then I'm probably going to listen to that. Because my gut has been right—a lot.

James: One of the things I realized as I started getting in touch with people to do this podcast is that there's a lot of drama in the Magic community. It's sometimes ridiculous how much of it there is.

Gerry: I love drama. I love it at arm's length. A lot of my good stories do not involve me, for example, because I'm a wallflower a lot of the time. But I love the drama. I love hearing about it and, to some degree, I intervene at times and try to fix it. Especially when it is about stupid stuff.

I want to know who's dating who and all that stuff. It's my reality TV, except it's with people that I know. I'm pretty good at getting people to tell me stuff, but I'm also very good at not betraying their confidence. I don't go around spreading rumors. But I love the fact that people are willing to tell me stuff because then I get to know the drama.

James: That's part of any community, right? People have stories and experiences, and people want to share them.

Gerry: Yeah, absolutely. Maybe it's because I like the people and the psychological aspect of it, where—what drives people to do certain things? Why did they make these actions? Stuff like that.

James: That's absolutely why I love having this chance to talk to you—because I want to get inside the minds of people and figure out how they work. I think this is a marvelous time where we can do this through technology. To wrap things up, did you have any particular shout-outs to anybody?

Gerry: I like everyone. If I haven't talked to you in a long time and you think that we should be friends— maybe you thought we were better friends—I am truly sorry for that. My mind is very weird and I'm sorry I haven't messaged you. That's a thing that constantly bothers me.

Josh, you're the best. Star City Games helps me pay my bills, which is great. Wizards of the Coast makes the best game ever. I love the community. Thank you everyone that responded to my Reddit thing. I'm very touched and I'm glad that it affects so many people—just the things that I say, the things that I do. Maybe even me talking about depression, opening up about it. Raising awareness. I'm very happy that I'm in the position that I'm able to do those things.

"I can become obsessive with some of the things—like wanting to win. Not necessarily wanting to beat the other person, but there might be some perfectionist aspect to it, which isn't always a good trait to have."

—Wilson Hunter

CHAPTER 4

WILSON HUNTER

Wilson is, without a doubt, the most competitive person I know. This says a lot given all of the Magic players I've met over the years. His competitiveness permeates everything about him, whether it's exceling at Magic, playing ping-pong, or dominating his fantasy baseball league.

Wilson exemplifies the blue-collar Magic player – someone who became really good at the game through sheer obsession, excellent practice habits, and force of will. He burst on to the scene in 2011 and has gone on to top eight a few Grand Prix events and finish solidly in a couple of Pro Tours.

Most notably, Wilson and his good friend Phillip Braverman took Pro Tour Ixalan in 2017 by storm. They unleashed a brand-new deck for the event – Mono-White Vampires – that surprised a lot of the best players in the world. In that tournament, Wilson and Phillip demonstrated their ability to think outside of the box and brew innovative decks at the highest levels of competition.

Wilson's full of strong opinions and honest takes. I respect his willingness to lay it on the line and speak his mind about what works, and what doesn't, in the realm of competitive Magic. When Wilson talks, you listen.

I had known about Wilson by being a listener of his Magic podcast, *The Brainstorm Show*. Later, when I looked for ways to promote my first book, I reached out to him and asked if I could be on his show. It was an honor to join his show and speak to his audience, who shared many of the same interests I did.

Afterwards, we kept in touch. A friendship, on the basis of mutual respect, was formed. Later, when I looked to get the *Humans of Magic* podcast off the ground, his name immediately came to mind.

Today, we are partners in a Magic startup called CardBoard Live. The venture is a culmination of the trust and rapport we've built, as well as our shared values and outlooks on life.

My involvement in CardBoard Live couldn't have happened without this interview. I was fortunate to get an inside look into who Wilson is. It revealed more about him than meets the eye, and that unlocked the possibility for us working together in a professional capacity.

Life can surprise you in wonderful ways. I am truly grateful for being part of this community, which allowed me to meet folks like Wilson from the other side of the world.

Recorded in November 2016.

James: You're someone who I've admired because of *The Brainstorm Show* podcast, as well as some of your results on the Magic circuit. I understand that you're primarily a Legacy player, correct?

Wilson: Absolutely. Legacy has been my favorite format since 2010. I'll play everything for the most part, but Legacy is a timeless format for me. If work gets heavy for a while, family stuff, or anything—Legacy is always there for me. I really enjoy the complexity of the format and personally feel that it has a very high ceiling.

James: It's pretty early over there for you, but it sounds like you're used to this routine-wise.

Wilson: Well, last night was a little more extreme with only four hours of sleep. Every Wednesday night I play some soccer, and that's my physical outlet. Sometimes it's just...I don't know. I just lay there. I was completely dead, but I couldn't fall asleep for a while.

In general, because of the amount of work I've had lately combined with family stuff, I haven't been getting a ton of sleep. But that's alright. It's a kind of thing where your body gets used to it and you get into marathon mode for a while.

James: It sounds like four hours of sleep is something that you're getting used to.

Wilson: Yeah. That sounds sort of depressing, but I'm a little more used to it. I have a two and a half year old daughter. When she was an infant, that completely changed my sleep schedule in a way that—even if it's not the same as it was before—it hasn't come back since that point.

James: So it's been two and a half years of not getting eight hours of sleep.

Wilson: Well, yeah. I don't even know if that's because of my daughter, though. That phase sort of ended six months to a year into it—having to wake up during the night for her and everything. For me at least, it did something to my internal clock where it trained my body to not need as much sleep as before. It's actually good because I operate at weird hours of the night and day. I'm really a morning and night person. I struggle the most from 3 to 5 PM, but because of that I get a ton of work done late at night and in the morning.

James: It sounds like you've got the best, or the worst, of both worlds. Depending on how you look at it. [Laughs]

Wilson: [Laughs] Something like that.

James: Wilson, there's so much I want to talk about. Let's just start from the beginning.

I know you online, and you have a hit Legacy podcast, but I want to know more about Wilson Hunter, the person. Can you tell me a bit about yourself?

Wilson: I spent most of my childhood in Central Virginia, in Charlottesville. I have one younger sister. My dad is, and was, a traveling sales rep, so he worked very hard and always on the road. The house I grew up in for most of my life was on a farm—pretty rural setting, maybe 20-25 minutes outside the city of Charlottesville.

I went to a really small rural school, before going to a more "normal" high school that a lot of people experience. I do think that growing up, I had a... well, there are a lot of people out there that grew up in rural America somewhere, or whatever country they live in. It's a different experience, and a lot of my friends have had this experience.

There's just some things that go with that [rural upbringing], that change your life a little bit. I went to Appalachian State University in North Carolina, and now I live in Johnson City, Tennessee. I moved here for the job when I got married, and have been here for about five years.

James: What about your mom? What did she do?

Wilson: Right now my mom designs gardens for people. When I was growing up, she was a stay-at-home mom, and she was an awesome mom. A lot of my desire to solve puzzles and do some of these things came from her fostering a lot of that. There [are] a lot of really cool stories of things that she would do for me.

I remember that one time—this is a very specific memory, and there's a lot of stuff like this—she gave me this huge blank book. It was two hundred blank pages. She knew that I really liked the Amazon and all these Amazon creatures and stuff. She started filling it out with me as a field guide for the Amazon. I was a really young guy, maybe six years old. But it was cool because I ended up making this very simple book of all these creatures I liked. Looking back on it, I took that kind of thing for granted, but that was such a cool way of getting me creatively involved in learning.

James: Right.

Wilson: I credit my mom for fostering a strong desire to learn that carried over to my hobbies now, and what I enjoy doing now. It was great for our entire family that my mom stayed home and did a lot of that stuff with me. I credit both her and my dad for being great parents, growing up.

James: And you said that your dad was in a traveling salesman type of role?

Wilson: He sold yearbooks to schools. That is actually one of the things that I do now. But he was driving all over the place. He worked long hours, and it's somewhat seasonal, so we had a decent amount of time in the summer. He's a hardworking guy.

That's sort of his personality. So there's some elements, too, where he needs to be thinking in steps. He's the opposite of me in a lot of ways. He'd never do something like play Magic, so if he's not working, he has to be...it's almost like mowing the grass is therapeutic for him. That's the opposite of anything I would ever enjoy doing.

James: I have the sense that you're a hardworking guy. Even when it comes to working around the clock—you mentioned that just now. I imagine there's some part of your dad's personality that rubbed off on you.

Wilson: That's a good point. That might be the elements of the parenting culture. I just don't feel like we think the same way. But the way that my life is now, I definitely credit a lot of these values to him, for sure. Personality profile-wise, the Myers-Briggs thing, I'm an INTJ [Introversion, Intuition, Thinking, Judgment]. My mom is the same. My dad is completely opposite hers. I don't know what he is. You're right though, I was definitely affected by both my parents in different ways.

James: You mentioned that you grew up on a farm, so you must be pretty good with your hands, right?

Wilson: We did a lot of stuff that somebody who didn't grew up on a farm wouldn't have done. But we didn't have tons of cattle or anything like that. We lived on a horse farm, and some people kept their horses at our house. I have some memories of working on a chicken coop with my dad, or doing some gardening activities. We had chickens and stuff. But the farm aspect wasn't a business-type of farm.

I had some friends that did work and live on a legitimate working farm with tons of cattle and things like that. It was definitely a different experience than that. When I say farm, to some people that sounds like a farm. To people who grew up on a farm with cows and all of these things—it wasn't that type of experience.

However, I did a lot of outdoor type of things when I was a kid because of that. There's lots of acres and lots of areas to play. We had a decent amount of woods and all that, sort of behind our farm where the pastures were. My sister and I would play outside a ton, so that that was a great area to foster creativity, for sure.

James: What kind of stuff did you like to do when you were a kid, and throughout high school?

Wilson: Going back to the story of the book that my mom gave me—there's a ton of stuff like that—both indoors and outdoors activities. As a young kid, when your mom is still very involved in some of the things that you do, that started some of the things I did on my own.

I remember building this huge fort that was poorly built, tons of boards nailed to the tree and stuff like that. That kind of thing was fun. I also absolutely loved board games. I remember at a very young age I loved Axis and Allies...that was one of my first introductions to gaming.

Before that, there were games like Risk, but Axis and Allies was my first game that was a little more complicated. It made me think, "Wow! Some of these games are so deep and are so cool." It was hard to nail down my dad to get him to play that game with me, but I had some friends who played, and an uncle who was a very cerebral dude and loved playing.

I mean, I had some other interests across the board, too. I got into sports. My dad was more of a sports guy, so I got exposed to a lot of those things from him. I loved soccer, and like I said, I'm still playing today. For me, that's the best way to exercise. It's hard for me to lift weights or do stuff that's super repetitive. I like having a competitive goal when I'm playing, so I did all kinds of sports. Baseball, soccer, basketball, all that stuff.

James: At what point did you find *Magic: The Gathering*?

Wilson: It was in middle school, which was tough for me. Part of the way that I grew up—with some of the things that I was doing—a lot of these things were introverted in nature. I didn't grow up in a neighborhood setting where I could just run down the road and be part of a gang of five kids, or something like that. So, going to middle school was pretty rough. I felt like I was a little bit of a weird kid, and I'm still a weird big kid now. [Laughs]

James: We all are, right? [Laughs]

Wilson: Yeah, that's right. But Magic, I found out about it in middle school. No one really taught me how to play the game for a while. I had some cards and I tried to see if I could use them in some way—with another kid in middle school who didn't have a lot of friends. We were basically playing some game that wasn't Magic, we were mostly just playing with Magic cards. That was fun.

I also enjoyed the art and all that kind of stuff. I remember getting the Deckmasters set—the [Jon] Finkel versus [Richard] Garfield box set—for Christmas one year. That was a turning point when I got those cards, then maybe I got some more cards here and there, and I started to get more involved. At some point—I don't remember exactly when that was—but at some point I did start to figure out the rules.

But I didn't understand the game well until high school. In middle school I was probably playing an entirely different game—not even Magic—but it was cool because it provided an outlet for me. Magic was, even at the very early phases, a big part of my life, during that difficult phase in middle school. It was a way to get out and do stuff. I remember the guy that I was playing with, he probably had a rough middle school experience, too. We didn't really talk to anybody else other than each other.

James: You mentioned earlier that you went to college. How did Magic evolve as a game for you as you got older?

Wilson: I'll bridge the gap a little bit with the high school stuff first.

When I was in high school, I got to know Paul Michel, who also played a lot of Magic. He's the co-host on our podcast now. He became one of my best buddies in high school.

My high school was great. It had good academic opportunities, which was another important outlet for me. Generally people start to grow up in high school and embrace different groups of people. I know that's not true everywhere, but that was my experience.

Paul Michel was one of my best buddies in high school and he had played Magic at a very young age. He knew how to play the game very well. I think he was on the—what is it called? Junior Super Series?

James: I think it's the Junior Super League, or Super Series. Something like that.

Wilson: Yeah. He was competitive at the age of nine.

James: Oh, wow. [Laughs]

Wilson: Paul knew all the rules. He had these old decks that were all tier one Standard decks. He had the Parallax Wave deck, the Psychatog Upheaval stuff. This green Stompy deck from Urza's Saga with Masticores and Gaea's Cradles and stuff.

James: This was a new world for you, right? This guy is essentially a master—relatively speaking. He sounds like a sharp dude.

Wilson: Yeah, absolutely. I remember just whipping out our cards because we found out that we both played Magic. He had these decks that were all tuned and meant to accomplish a very specific goal. I remember taking out my Deckmasters tin with my motley crew of half Deckmasters cards, half cards that I just jammed in there. I didn't really know how they worked.

James: Right.

Wilson: Paul helped me learn and understand the game. We started going to FNM in high school. Neither of us had any disposable income as high school students, so we got really scrappy to get a Standard deck that we shared and would take turns playing it at the FNM.

Let me flash forward to college. I ended up at Appalachian State and I started playing FNMs there. It was a great way for me to meet a lot of people which was something I started looking forward to every week.

I quickly started getting to a point where I wanted to be competitive and build the right decks, I wanted to win when I was at the App State FNM. I dove into that pretty quickly. I think I went to FNM the first week I was there. I liked the crowd and started making some good friends through that. Some of my first friends Upstate were Magic players.

Then, something sort of changed in my head. I started to enjoy building competitive decks. They weren't net decked competitive decks, it wasn't about trying to play the tier one deck that a pro was playing, I was trying to build my own decks that could beat those decks. Sometimes I was successful, sometimes I wasn't. I was often not successful in the beginning. But it quickly became one of my favorite things to do.

James: It sounds like it became your number one thing.

Wilson: Absolutely. I'm not sure why I went into it so heavily. I guess it's because that was my first experience living on my own, so I didn't have the introverted outlet anymore. I didn't go back home to a lot of space, where I could go do something by myself and be creative.

I gravitated towards something that I was comfortable in, which was playing games. I wasn't into the heavy socializing scene, even though I did do some of that. I went out with friends and I did meet some people outside of Magic. But in general, that wasn't me.

I was looking for something else to do with my time in college that I enjoyed. So I went heavy into Magic. I remember—and a lot of people can probably relate to this—but on the non-FNM days I would be on the Internet forums, and putting my cards together. Magic became more of an everyday part of my life, and that was new.

In high school, we didn't think about it every day. There were some weeks where we would play-test at school during independent study, or lunch, or whatever, but it wasn't every single day. In college it became...it's on my mind every day and I'm doing something with it. That's a big reason why I kept getting more competitive to the point where I wanted to start to travel to some of these events with friends.

James: I know from our past conversations that you mentioned that you're hyper-competitive. Did you start honing this hyper-competitiveness at this point in time, or did it come later?

Wilson: That's a personality trait I've always had, and there are some positives and negatives about that. I think people are competitive for different reasons. I've never been somebody who's focused on beating the human that is in front of me—I spend very little time focusing on my opponents.

I'm extremely competitive about winning or beating a puzzle. It's got to be something...it's a mix between the games and activities that I was exposed to as a kid, and also my personality.

James: So you're saying that even when you were playing board games—way back, before Magic—you were competitive?

Wilson: Yeah. There's a joke in my family about this kind of thing about how even as a little kid, I would never let the people playing games with me say, "Let's go take a break." That made me really unhappy.

James: Yeah?

Wilson: We really had to sit down and play the full Axis and Allies game, or I would not be happy with the situation. With Magic, my friends will be able to tell you that I'm a strangely extreme person. Part of that is whenever I get into something—an activity—I take it to the extreme. I inevitably get really competitive in whatever it is that I'm doing.

The key distinction is that people compete against different things. For example, I played soccer last night. I'm really not focused on the people that I'm playing against. We had some guys on the other team trash talk us last night. Those guys seemed so focused on not only beating you, but being better than you.

James: They want to get you off your game. It's a personal thing to them.

Wilson: It's personal to them, and that just couldn't be more different from the way that I feel about it. In any competitive activity, I am trying to beat the game. In Magic, there happens to be a human pilot for the other deck. The way that I approach it is simply to just beat the deck in front of me.

James: Have you ever been competitive in a non-human scenario? For example, playing a single-player video game and trying to beat the computer? Or does there have to be a human, or actual opponent behind the game?

Wilson: I liked playing some video games in the past, as I was growing up. I didn't get as into that as some people. The best comparison I can make is to school and academics. I was extremely competitive with myself, just trying to make good grades and take it to the next level. That never had to do with anybody else.

It really came down to, "I got 80% on this test. How can I do a ton better next time?" So in that way, I really liked school for a long time because of the competitive aspect of it. I liked the feeling that I could get better. If I wasn't doing well, I asked myself what I could do to conquer that class. Does that make sense?

James: It does make sense, and it's a wonderful quality to have. It sounds like you're motivating yourself in the right way.

Wilson: Well, I appreciate that. I mean, I think there are a lot of positives to that. But just like anything else, there are some negatives, too. I can become obsessive with some of the things—like wanting to win. Not necessarily wanting to beat the other person, but there might be some perfectionist aspect to it, which isn't always a good trait to have. It's the desire to think that a B-grade is definitely not enough. Even receiving an A-minus grade in a class, I feel like I'm missing something, and that may have taken away from my enjoyment of some things.

James: Has there ever been a time that you thought you took things a bit too far in this realm?

Wilson: James, I always take it too far. That's a pretty common element in the things that I do. I know that's subjective, but a lot of people would see what I do and say, "Man, that's pretty extreme!" When it comes to Magic, I don't get to play it a ton right now. So, if I don't have good results—if I don't have a good result at the one tournament I go to, because there's not a large sample size—it becomes really frustrating.

There's no immediate way for me to fix this feeling. There's usually no tournament the next weekend that I can try to do better at. I have to sit around for a couple of months to get another chance because of my schedule. There's a lot of frustration that can cause, and you miss out on a lot of other things.

If I get super honed in on one thing, I'm definitely missing out on some other elements. There's always been a social aspect that I've missed by doing some of these things. I'm not in these huge friend groups of people that are going out to eat all the time, socializing, and hanging out. I'm usually focused on beating some game somewhere, and in school, I was always trying to make good grades. There are definitely some downsides to all of these things, for sure.

James: How do you handle losing?

Wilson: I'm a not a super emotional person, so I tend to look at losses on a logical level. If anything, I'm frustrated that I can't fix something immediately. I don't know if this makes any sense, but when I lose a game, I'm not frustrated at variance. Instead, I feel a general frustration that I didn't possess a large enough sample size to do variance justice. Especially if I have conviction that what I'm doing is a good approach.

My number one frustration is—if I feel at the end of a tournament that I didn't do well at, that I made some decent deck building decisions—that I didn't have more tries to prove I was right. I don't have an opportunity to get out and prove it using a larger sample size. There's also an element of stubbornness to it—I think that I'm right, and I'm still losing.

I'm sure that sometimes I'm wrong and just being stubborn, but that's the biggest thing for me. I never get emotional or mad at my opponent. It's more of a frustration that I wasn't proven right. It feels incomplete. It's hard. I don't believe I'm better than anybody else. It is just my personality of internalizing things, and being introverted. I don't know what it is, but I've never really cared a ton about the people aspect of things. I can tell you where some of this came from.

James: Sure.

Wilson: I think that having some difficult childhood social situations shaped who I am. Growing up, I spent a significant amount of time not having good friends and struggling with the middle school experience. It was even the same with elementary school, to some degree.

My parents were always telling me not to care about what people thought—all that stuff. Things that other parents will tell their kids in those situations. But it was extreme for me. I internalized all of it every day, and I had to convince myself of that to survive at a young age. It became part of my core being in a way that I didn't even think about. It's not like I'm actively doing it, but it became instilled in me.

To this day, if I wanted to change that, I probably couldn't. There's a lot of negatives that go with that. You don't think about this all the time, but if you do care what people think about you, you'll do some things that are net positive, or nice things for others. I'm not saying that I don't have empathy, however I do think that, for whatever reason, the thought of "don't worry about what people think" drives me in a lot of aspects of life. Especially when I sit down to play Magic.

James: You created a protection mechanism for yourself. That also affects how you view others, and how you treat others.

Wilson: I'm trying to go back and point out to myself where all that came from. Some of it is also just personality that was inherent in the general traits that I have. It's a mix of both of those things. I'm not shut off from the world or anything like that. Friends who know me can attest to that. I really do care a lot about people, it's just a smaller group.

Sometimes I have a hard time with large groups of people, and having lots of empathy towards them. I'm extremely loyal to the people that I like. Loyalty is an extremely important trait for me as far as the relationships that I have.

James: It is about quality over quantity. You top-eighted two Legacy GPs. You also had some other things going on, with solid finishes at SCG events. Whatever it is, it seems to be working for you.

Wilson: Well, I appreciate that. I don't think my results sound remotely impressive compared to some of these other guests on your show—people like PV [Paulo Vitor Damo Da Rosa] or Gerry Thompson. Compared to them, this is almost a joke. But for me, the few tournament results I do have in Legacy have been the pinnacle of my competitive drive. It felt good to reach some of those high points even though I haven't taken down any of these events.

That's my goal—to win a Legacy GP. Also, I talk to some of these other Legacy guys, like Jarvis Yu, and we have a friendly competition. Jarvis has top-eighted a couple of Legacy GPs. We have one coming up. He doesn't even know if he can go to the next one, but we're challenging each other. We say things like, "No one's ever top-eighted three Legacy GPs. Who's going to be the first to do that?" It's become an ongoing thing between us.

James: Friendly competition.

Wilson: Yeah, exactly. But it's fun because that kind of thing drives both of us.

James: As you said, Legacy has a lot of interesting decisions and possibilities. So I believe you're sticking with the right format. I think you're doing something right.

Wilson: Legacy's a blast. The friends that I've made in Legacy—that's been cool. It's a subculture within Magic—people who are extremely passionate about one specific thing. I think Legacy players are more likely to produce cool content. Maybe that sounds elitist, I don't know.

The Source[10] has all these active people. There are people I talk to that are playing Legacy day in and day out, wherever they are, around the world. And I feel it's a cool community to be involved with—to talk to those people and learn what they're doing.

James: If you could look back at some of those top eights, what's been your preparation process?

Wilson: It was a lot different when I was in college than it is now. But I can talk about both of these things.

I top-eighted Legacy GP Providence in 2011. That was the first event that we decided—me and my small friends' group—we're going to drive to

---

[10] http://www.mtgthesource.com

Providence, Rhode Island. It was an insane slog of the East Coast—it ended up being a 20-hour drive. Before that, I had only ever gone to closer regional Star City events, and this was my first Grand Prix.

I've played in eight total, but that was the first one. It was a big experience. It's a little different from the Star City Opens, but the preparation towards it—even if it was my first Grand Prix—we were very prepared. I don't know how this happened, but I was super fortunate to be at a school with some other good Legacy players, at Appalachian State. You would never think that.

James: It's a hotbed, man. [Laughs]

Wilson: It's crazy. Part of it is that we all came out of the woodwork due to each other. For any one of us, if we were the *only* player around, we probably wouldn't be Legacy players. But we all had similar interests, we came together and everybody became a lot better at Legacy because of each other. The collaboration was huge for me.

Phillip and Mike Braverman, and my friend Dylan Squire, who doesn't play a ton of competitive Magic anymore—they were good. Everybody knows players like that. Dylan—nobody will know who he is, outside of our friend group because he just played in a couple of events—he's so good.

You know, that's the thing about Magic is that there are some really good players out there that you've never heard of. We harp on the big names in the community, and they are still extremely good at the game, but there are lots of unsung heroes like Dylan. I felt lucky to have been able to meet him and the Bravermans.

We would go to somebody's house and jam tons of Legacy. The four of us, we'd build tons of decks, hone our skills more and more, and we were taking it to higher levels of competitiveness. Phil is super competitive too, even in testing. Not in a negative way, but everybody wants to win. That's fun for us to want to win, even when we're testing.

James: There's no off switch. It's competitive all the time.

Wilson: Absolutely. Because of that, we analyzed things really well even in testing. Not just jamming a bunch of games and not analyzing, we kept taking it to the next level. By the time I went to GP Providence—you know, there are a lot of good Magic players out there, but I was surprised that it seemed people didn't do the same things we did. I never really realized that, if that makes any sense.

James: It felt normal for your group to put in the work. But not everyone else did.

Wilson: It was my first Grand Prix and I thought everybody out there was going to be—

James: Everybody was going to be a ringer, or grinder, or something. [Laughs]

Wilson: Yeah. Even people that were grinders—they don't necessarily play a Legacy deck in the same way that we played our Legacy decks. Looking back on it, I felt like we had a big advantage in almost every round in the way we prepared for it. But we didn't go into it knowing that.

Flash forward to now, because of family and other obligations, it's no longer about jamming tons of games with my college buddies. The biggest preparation is thinking about the decks and planning things in my mind as I'm driving on the road. That's been huge for me. Active thought that is actually getting you somewhere in your analysis, or taking you to a new opinion, or next step, is really huge in preparation.

You can think about something all day and never change your opinion on it, and never get to the next level. But if you're spending a lot of time actually making changes—realizing why you want to make those changes, even when you're not playing games—your brain is building it to the next level. You're honing this over and over again in your mind, even without having to test it out and play games.

James: It's great you mentioned Jarvis earlier, because it feels related. When I talked to him, he had the same kind of process, really. He doesn't play Legacy for forty hours a week. But because he had built a wide range of experience within Magic, he could think about situations and work out optimal builds in his head. You guys seem to share similar approaches.

Wilson: I have recently gotten to know Jarvis a little bit. I still don't know him super well, except online. We're in this Legacy chat together, and of all the people in there, we seem to consistently agree on so many things. I think that's interesting. He and I are always like, "Yeah, it seems like we're on the same page again." There's a lot of great players in that chat that are really fun to talk to. You know—Miracles players.

James: That's cool to hear, because I've never talked to him about anything outside of Magic, really. But I can tell he does think similarly, in some ways.

Are you able to prepare and think about things, while you're in the car, because you've played so much Legacy in the past? Or do you think that this skill can exist independently from your past experience?

Wilson: That's a great point, James. There's got to be both. You have to have a foundation of feeling out how things will play. But there is also an element of problem solving where you don't have to play infinite games to get to that point. You absolutely have to have some sort of background in trying a lot of different things in Magic before you can independently start thinking about that stuff. At least, that's the case for me. There are probably some geniuses out there who don't have to do that. But for me, the foundation was absolutely crucial.

James: Are there lessons that you've learned, from playing Magic over so many years, that you could generalize for us? Perhaps even applied to things outside of Magic?

Wilson: I'm working on a few work-related things now, where the Magic type of problem-solving has been really good for me. That's definitely a specific one. The business world, tech, all this stuff—there's a ton of things that revolve around the problem-solving process. You can find a lot of interesting ways to be successful just by solving a problem that somebody else hasn't solved.

For me, a big part of Magic is saying: "I can play this deck of 75 cards, and I can learn how to play it." But I feel I'm missing a bit of the potential there, because I'm not asking the question, "What can I do differently to make this deck the best? Is there something unique out there that's the best approach?" Once you've explored all of those questions in life and business—if you find something that nobody else has found—there are a lot of opportunities to be successful. Honing those skills in Magic, I absolutely go through the exact same thought processes in my work.

James: In terms of your problem-solving process, is there a framework that you always go back to?

Wilson: To get into specifics like deck building—and this can be a long conversation—we conduct an activity called sideboard mapping. We want to optimize all of our cards across a metagame. In my head I'm naturally starting to weigh a lot of these factors, but you can do it on a spreadsheet and come up with equations.

Once you start playing the game enough, your brain creates these equations that are able to problem-solve. If you get a good idea of how popular some decks are, you're able to create a list of decks in your head. Tier one, tier two, all that stuff. You're weighing those factors. If you have your 75 cards, you're assigning values to those cards in every single matchup.

My goal for deck-building is, post-sideboard, to always have high value cards against everything. The emphasis will be on the highly-played decks in the format. The biggest problem in deck building is that people cling to their emotions too much, and they throw together a lot of cards that are there for some emotional reason.

It could be due to something they lost to, or something they *should just have* because someone told them that. Maybe they read it in some article. But then they play an event and they've never even thought about their side-boarding before. They end up leaving in a Terminus against a Show and Tell deck. Then you look at your decklist and think, "Why did I put myself in this position?"

Deck building to optimize something is a formula. It's not a complicated formula. It's something that you can do in your head, but because the format is so complex, and there are so many different decks, it gives you a ton to think about. To sit down from any opponent at any event—even if they're playing an unusual deck—you can still put that deck into a category. You want to say to yourself, "I feel good about my approach to this. Even if I haven't thought about their specific deck, I have thought about decks similar to theirs." That's the specific process I follow.

James: People often underestimate how tuning that last card, or understanding how things go in and out of your deck, gives you those edges. Especially in a complex format like Legacy, that goes a long way.

Wilson: Absolutely.

James: Switching gears now—you're a family man. You're a responsible adult with a wife and kid. How does that change your relationship with Magic?

Wilson: There's a lot to talk about here. But I value Magic a lot more than I used to.

Some of that is because of the limited time I have. But—being a parent is awesome. It's the best thing in my life, for sure. It's also one of the hardest things I've ever done. Lately, with how much I'm working, and trying to be the best dad and husband I can be,

I put a lot of pressure on myself. Because of that, I really appreciate having an outlet like Magic when I get the chance.

Magic has become more meaningful in my life. I look back on college, and Magic was a blast then. But I took it for granted, because I could play the game whenever I wanted. If I'm bored, I could go down to the shop and sleeve up a deck. I could text a friend who's as bored as I am, and we'd jam.

Now it's not like that anymore. We haven't put together an episode of our podcast [*The Brainstorm Show*] in a long time just because it's hard to get everybody together. Everybody's got their lives and jobs and stuff. But we're coming back soon. It's been a while.

James: I'm happy to hear it.

Wilson: Thank you. Magic has been a bit of a battle. I've been tough on myself. I've asked myself, "Am I being selfish by playing this game?" I'm trying to be a good dad. My daughter is two-and-a-half-years-old now, and I don't want to be missing anything in her life to go do something that's just a hobby for me. I don't want to be traveling too much to go play card games when my daughter is growing up.

So it's definitely these deeper feelings I have, and I need to find the balance. I told myself that if I could balance these things, I can be a better dad because I have some outlet for myself. But it's definitely a balancing act, and it's easy for me to do too much of it. A part of that is me being selfish, and I'm not saying that people are being selfish when they play Magic, but it feels like with my parental responsibilities right now, it's my personal struggle. Thinking about where to draw the line, and how much gaming is too much.

James: Yeah.

Wilson: I know that you wrote a book on this. It's part of your book.

James: You're talking to someone who continuously feels guilt about this type of thing. The only thing I would say here is that it's very human to feel that way. It's good to feel guilt or question your actions, because it shows self-awareness.

I also want to know, however, if you've ever talked to other parents who may have felt the same way? Maybe not even with Magic, but in general. How do they spend their free time, away from their kids?

Wilson: Definitely. I don't want to put words in their mouths, but the "Magic dads" I know have similar experiences. I've received some messages from people who listen to *The Brainstorm Show*. They've said things like, "Hey, man—I'm also a dad. Love listening to your show." I get a strangely high number of those.

James: Nice.

Wilson: It tells me that other dads are consuming podcast content. It makes sense to me. If we can't always be playing the game, a podcast becomes perfect to our schedules. Through that, I'm able to connect with those types of people. A podcast is something that a dad or mom is more likely to do. That's what I've gathered over the last year or so—of running into people who listen to the show. It's one of the demographics.

James: That's amazing.

Wilson: Outside of Magic, I think it's something that any parent will struggle with, especially people that enjoy social activities. I know a lot of parents who are purely social people, and they have friends around who will do lots of social things—and their kid is involved in all of these activities.

But for people who are more focused on these cerebral games, or outlets for introverts, it's harder for your two-and-a-half-year-old child to be enjoying these things with you. It's always, I don't use the word "struggle," but it's always a balance of trying to figure out how to do that.

James: That's how it is with life. You always look at what's going on with other people. Sometimes you think that they've got it all figured out, but I'm sure even the social ones have their own struggles, too. We all do.

Wilson: That's absolutely true. They are probably 180 degrees different from you on something else. It's just my perception. Another big one is career choices. That's a balance when you have kids. I've always pondered about these two extremes.

For example, I could have the perfect job to support my family, which I might hate. I could probably find something that makes a decent amount of money, and I could spend more time at home. But I might hate the job. Or I could do something that is totally awesome but makes no money. Travel the world but never see my family. Those are the extremes.

James: Yeah.

Wilson: I obviously don't want either of those extremes. It's about finding the middle ground and then having your outlet. Growing up, I always wanted to be a marine biologist. That's the ultimate dream. I probably can't follow my dreams to an extreme, based on having a family. But what can I do, somewhere in-between? To have the outlet and also be there for my daughter as she grows up? That's the question.

James: Do you think you've found that balance?

Wilson: It's definitely in flux. I'm starting to get a better understanding. When I graduated college, I almost had this idea that I had to do something that I didn't like doing, to overcompensate for this feeling. I felt that, in order to be a good husband and eventual dad, I had to do a job that I hated.

I'm not saying that I hate my job, but I'm saying that the question of "am I going to like my job?" never crossed my mind. I just assumed people worked really hard and didn't get tons of enjoyment out of what they did. A lot of that is absorbing certain cultural values as I grew up, but the process is learning that I can be a good dad. I can be there for my family and also be doing things that energize me.

James: It sounds like you're heading in that direction now.

Wilson: I haven't gotten to the point yet where I can say I've solved it, and I don't know if I ever will. But at least I'm asking the questions now and it's really making me look at things differently. Introspection has changed my life trajectory. We'll see where it takes me. It's been a huge year—all sorts of different changes, and thinking about the future.

James: Has this been one of the most challenging years for you, in your life?

Wilson: Last year was.

James: Can you explain?

Wilson: This year's been challenging, time-wise, but I'm starting to get over the hump of realizing how to get things
to come together in a way that I can enjoy. Last year
was tough because it got to a point where I needed to
look at things differently, I just didn't realize it yet.

So many frustrations were building up, but I
didn't know why. Once I figured it out, I still wasn't
able to solve all of those things. But it felt a lot better
to have a game plan moving forward, and understanding myself more. I know that's completely
ambiguous, but last year I started getting frustrated
without realizing why.

It was something within myself. I also felt
trapped in certain things—daily routines. I felt like
I *had* to do certain things. I took a step back and
asked, "Why am I operating like this?" After realizing that I had more power over my life, it changed
how I looked at things. I realize that's vague, but it
was a journey for me.

James: No, it's good. We all feel those struggles at different
times. The bottom line is that Magic feels more like
a privilege to you now than before.

Wilson: Absolutely. I value every tournament that I can go
to. I try to make it more of a scheduled thing now.
I'll try to attend a tournament every three months or
so. It still feels like a lot, as far as my family and stuff
goes, but it's good for me. It also gives me something
to look forward to when I'm doing things that are
tough, in my work, or just the daily grind of driving
on the road.

I can say things to myself. "Okay. On January 6, I'm going to Grand Prix Louisville." Having that in the back of my mind allows me to relax a little bit more, and gives me a personal goal I can reach. It's big for me to have those things planned.

James: Is that the main thing that keeps you going, as far as the game of Magic is concerned—the goals and the competition?

Wilson: I always love top-eighting an event. I'd love to win an event, which I haven't done yet on a large scale. At some point I hope I can hold a trophy, but as much as those types of things drive me, I enjoy coming up with a new deck and being the person to come up with a new strategy. It's like solving a puzzle that hasn't been solved yet.

Every set that's printed, every shift in the metagame, it's an opportunity to do something different. It's exciting and just as much of a competitive outlet for me as playing in the actual events. Not because I want to be recognized for coming up with a particular deck, but because I love to solve puzzles. If I can look around and realize that nobody else has solved it the way I did, then I've accomplished something really cool. That's a good feeling for me.

There are other elements, too. Phil and Paul are some of my best friends, and I talk to Phil daily about life stuff. I drive on the road all the time, and we'll talk on the phone. We're both strangely introverted guys, so it's cool to have found each other to connect with. My buddies are also all on the same page. We're a group of people who don't waste time talking about meaningless things. We all fall into the

INTJ personality profile, where we just can't handle the small talk.

So we just dive into all of these cool things to talk about. That's been a good experience, building relationships based on similar values. Through the online communities, I also meet a lot of cool people all over the world that play the game.

James: That's awesome.

Wilson: It's been interesting to realize the way that I look at things versus the way my friends look at things are unique. Everybody thinks differently about the game and solving puzzles. Being in my own head, I always assumed that everyone was thinking in the same ways, but once we started podcasting and talking about Magic, I realized that we all thought about things differently.

It goes back and forth. I learned a lot from other people's feedback and what they think as well. It's opened my eyes about a lot of things. The things that people think are cool, I'll sometimes tell myself, "I never thought. I just took that for granted." It's both learning and a process of appreciating things. I realized that I needed to get better with my analysis.

James: Sounds like you guys are having a great time. Just to close things, do you have any shout-outs you want to give?

Wilson: Oh, man. I didn't even think about doing a shout-out. Had I known, I would have prepared something really trollish—

James: [Laughs] I put you on the spot here.

Wilson: It's good that you put me on the spot, because had I prepared, I would have come up with some really strange trolls for a bunch of people. In general, I'd say Paul and Phil have been my reason for enjoying the game as much as I have, especially over the past couple years. It's been a great experience to record the podcast with them.

The biggest shout-out is to my wife for allowing me to do this hobby. Well, not "allow"—that's the wrong word—but being very supportive of it, because she's so different from me, personality-wise. She doesn't have something as extreme as this that she has to be doing. She's got a lot of hobbies, but she's been very selfless and putting herself in my shoes and being extremely supportive of it. She's definitely the biggest shout-out for me.

"Work hard at what you love. Try to be a good person. That's what I think is most important. I have played so many matches against people where they tell me afterwards that they had a good experience playing against me. That makes me feel fantastic."

—Noah Walker

Chapter 5

Noah Walker

Noah is one of the youngest guests I've ever interviewed. At the time of our interview, he was barely 21 years old and already crushing tournament Magic to incredible rates of success.

Noah has been playing Magic since he was 10. He started off as the youngest person in the room, written off by others as "that kid" or "too young to be good." That became the proverbial chip on his shoulder. Noah used those slights as motivation to get better.

It didn't take long for him to start dominating Magic, and he hasn't looked back since. To date, Noah has four Grand Prix top eight finishes and has won two Star City Games Opens – records that most Magic players twice his age would be lucky to have.

I'm sure Noah's accomplishments will only snowball over time, as he is truly a student of the game and always looking to get better.

Noah serves as a source of continuous inspiration for others in ways other than just Magic. His personal story is one of overcoming challenges in life and trying to be the best version of himself.

For those who've not had the chance to talk to Noah, don't let his serious tournament demeanor fool you into thinking that he's an unpleasant character. When the heat is on and you see Noah in a camera feature match, he can be one of the most intense competitors to play against.

But when the match is over, Noah is one of the nicest people around. He possesses a zest for life that becomes immediately obvious within a few minutes of conversation.

Since this interview, I've run into Noah several times at high-level Magic tournaments. Every time, without fail, Noah will stop what he's doing and say hi. He's fun to talk to.

Noah's great, and I'm proud to highlight him here.

Recorded in September 2017.

James: Where is home for you?

Noah: Home for me right now is in Framingham, Mass. But I'd also say it's where I'm at right now—at my mom's house in Florence, Mass. This also feels like home to me.

James: I hear that you're riding up with a whole bunch of friends to Eternal Extravaganza 7 tomorrow, to play some Legacy?

Noah: Only two. Just a couple of my close buddies that I've known for a while.

James: Do you have your deck choice, and what you're going to play, all figured out as well?

Noah: Yeah, of course. It's actually been a while since I've been able to play any paper Legacy. Every chance I get, I jam a MODO League because I love the format. It's so much fun to play.

James: What deck are you on right now?

Noah: Right now I'm playing the 4-color control deck, or Czech Pile, as it's called. I put my own little spin on it, of course, but it's mostly a stock list. Right now, I'm trying out some Wastelands in the main and a [Life from the] Loam in the board for the mirror. It's been pretty good.

James: Do you think it's the best deck in Legacy right now?

Noah: I don't know if it's the best deck, but I think it's up there. I always think the pillars of Legacy, or the best decks, are Lands, Grixis Delver, and Storm. I feel like these decks go back and forth on being the best deck. There's also Sneak and Show, stuff like that. But I think 4-color control has a lot of game in a lot of matchups.

James: It never feels like you're really far behind in any matchup, right?

Noah: Exactly.

James: I recall from our chats you had been working at a camp during most weeks. Is that right?

Noah: Oh, yeah. It's mostly just in the summer. This summer I didn't get to work there as much as I'd like. But I work at a summer camp called Rowe Camp and Conference Center. And I worked there for four weeks this summer. Last summer I worked there for seven weeks. It varies depending on how much time I have with Magic.

James: How many years in a row have you been working at the camp?

Noah: I've been working there for three years now. But I've actually been going there as a camper since I was eight years old. So it's been a big part of my life for a bunch of years.

James: What exactly do you do there?

Noah: Basically my job at this camp is camp counselor,
           but I'm part of the cabin staff. Most of the counse-
           lors that work at the camp, they stay in their own
           quarters. But when you're cabin staff, you sleep in
           the same cabin as the campers and it's cool. You get
           to monitor them a lot. But it's mostly just a camp
           where we try to empower youth as much as possible
           and give them a lot of choices and fun stuff to do.
           Kind of like any other summer camp—games and
           fun stuff.

James: What do you enjoy most about working there?

Noah: You feel like you're changing these kids' lives, to
           some extent. Especially for the age group that I nor-
           mally work with, 12 to 15 year old kids. You get to
           feel like…I don't know. I'm at the age where being
           a camper feels like so long ago, but it really wasn't
           that long ago. So I can still relate to them pretty
           well. And you get positive feelings from spending so
           much time helping kids become good people.

James: For a lot of kids I would imagine that's a critical
           time. They're still trying to figure out who they are,
           and all that stuff. What are their attitudes like?

Noah: Some kids are really against camp. They say, "My
           parents sent me here and I hate this. Why am I
           here?" But other kids, they've been coming here
           for so many years and they look forward to the
           camp every single year. For those kids, they make
           it a special place for the other campers. It's not
           like I get paid much. Some camps, you get more
           than others. For this camp, they don't have much
           budget. It's really about the experience, and the
           campers, for me.

James: You implied that there's a particular type of background that campers have when they come here. Is there some kind of specialization?

Noah: The camp is a Unitarian Universalist camp, but a lot of people aren't exactly UU. It's an all-encompassing camp of really good people. I went there on a scholarship that my mom got me into, because both my older sisters went there. But neither of them followed up and went back as counselors.

James: It sounds like it's a passion for you.

Noah: Of course, yeah. I wouldn't do it if I didn't love doing it, because I'm not getting paid that much for how much we have to work. [Laughs]

James: That's awesome. The way you talk about it makes me feel that you're into it. But what's the toughest part of working there?

Noah: It can definitely be tough, because there isn't any contact to the outside world. It's not like we're directly in the woods or anything. If I need to talk to someone, I could probably do it somehow. But it can feel a little overwhelming—not being able to contact anyone at any time. But at the same time, that's one of my favorite parts about the camp. You get to escape to this place where no one can contact you and you focus on having a good time and impacting people. So much is happening in these kids' lives and you're directly influencing it—so you worry, sometimes. It gets difficult. But it's a great place and I love it.

James: Do you ever worry about how some of them will carry on, after they leave camp for the summer?

Noah: For sure. It's not like all the kids are getting the message of "togetherness." A lot of kids think the stuff that you're doing there is dumb and they want to act however they want. But it's not like the camp has all that many rules. We try to encourage inclusive behavior of kids, and not being mean to each other, basically.

James: Good values, right?

Noah: Exactly. But some people are like…it's ingrained in them in different ways. So it's hard for them.

James: Do you remember what it was like for you, when you went to the camp as a kid?

Noah: Of course. I was actually…I don't know. I don't want to put myself down. But let's say that I wasn't the best kid ever. I was often competitive in a bad way. I played a lot of Magic when I was younger, and I was pretty good. I should say—I wasn't bad. I did well at my local PTQs. Never had all that much success. But my attitude towards Magic and life and everything was so much more toxic. I didn't understand as much as I do now about why playing Magic is important to me. Or why winning and good sportsmanship are important. It was all about being the first, and being the best.

James: You were very competitive at a young age.

Noah: Yeah, for sure. At the ping-pong tournaments at camp, I thought I was the shit.

James: If you could look back—do you know why you were so competitive?

Noah: I think it definitely had a lot to do with self-image and being self-conscious about what other people thought of me—and wanting to be great, as a result.

James: I think, as kids, we all care about our self-image. I mean, I would be lying if I said that I didn't care about that when I was younger. Or even now to some extent, and I'm much older now.

Tell me about a time when you wanted to show someone how awesome you were at something.

Noah: Well, before I even started playing Magic, I played Yu-Gi-Oh competitively, but I was never really good. I wasn't bad, but I was young. I was eight or nine [years old], but I didn't feel like I was ever the best. But I felt like I was pretty good. Of course, young me was always cocky in everything I did, so it didn't matter to me. But I remember one time specifically playing against this dude and playing this OTK deck [a "one-turn kill" deck]. And I kept beating him over and over again. And he felt so demoralized.

Any game that I play, when I would see someone think of me as just a kid...I don't play video games all that much, but I liked playing Soulcalibur II on the Xbox. And a couple of my neighbors, back when I was 11 or 12, they would invite me over to play with them. But they were all high school or college students...And I would beat them every time. I don't think I lost more than two games of Soulcalibur II over at my neighbor's house when I was 12 years old.

James: Do you think you were naturally talented at fighting games?

Noah: Maybe that. Just games in general. I just have a good mind for games. Always have.

James: Let's backtrack a little bit. I would like to know what it was like for you growing up, even before you got into Yu-Gi-Oh or Soulcalibur. Describe what it was like growing up at home.

Noah: I grew up mostly with my mom. From the time I was born and up until I was about six years old, I did live with my mom and my dad. And it's not like I don't feel like my dad is a part of my life that often, but he isn't. He is such a busy, preoccupied guy that he really can't be. For the most part, I grew up with my mom. And I have two older sisters and an older brother on my mom's side. And even though they are all technically my half siblings, I strongly identify with them as my family. And on my dad's side I have a lot more siblings, maybe four or five, but I haven't met all of them. I know some of their names and I've seen some of them. My dad's from Jamaica, so it's different—the culture that he's come from and the culture that he's used to. It's how he's been raised. But he's been a really sweet man to me and always tried so hard for my mom. But he views things differently.

James: I see. What does your dad do?

Noah: At the time, he was a mechanic. Right now, he helps people with special needs, 24/7. I don't see him very often, even though I don't live far from him. Most of the time during the week, he's always working and I'm always busy on the weekends playing Magic.

James: What about your mom? Is she a stay-at-home parent? What does she do?

Noah: All my siblings are older than me, so I'm the youngest. I'm 21. My older sister Alicia is 24. My older brother Jacob is 28. And I think my older sister Crystal is …I want to say 34 or 35. I'm not even positive at this point. My mom doesn't have to take care of any of the kids anymore, but my sister has two sons, so mom has the grandma duties. But also for work, she is a nanny to these two children. And occasionally she cleans houses.

James: You're closest with your mom. But what about your siblings? Which brother or sister are you closest with?

Noah: My family is really weird. I feel like we're all so pre-occupied with things that I don't even get to talk to most of them anymore. Sometimes I'll talk to my brother. I'm close to my brother because we have a lot of similar interests, but he's off doing his own thing a lot of the time—where I feel like I don't get to connect with him. And my older sister even more so, because she is so busy with kids and she was finishing college. If I was younger and you asked me this question, I would immediately say my oldest sister, Crystal. She has always been the one I had no problems with, and has always loved me, because we've been so far apart in age. I guess I'd have to say my oldest sister Crystal. I feel if I needed to talk to any one of my siblings, I feel like she'd have my back and I'd be able to talk to her. They all love me, I'm sure. And I love them all.

James: Growing up in your area, what was it like?

Noah: Most of the time when I was younger, we lived in an apartment complex. Most of my interactions with other people were other kids at the park or with my siblings back at home. My older brother was kind of a dick. Unintentionally, you know. It's not like he meant to be mean to me, but I was such a sensitive kid. He'd be kind of put off-ish. And I remember one time distinctly—I thought that a shaved onion was an apple, and he told me it was an apple. And I took a giant bite out of it and I was crying and yelling. And my mom came in and scolded my brother, "What are you doing?" I was screaming.

But yeah, I'd say for the most part as I was growing up, it was me and my older sister Alicia. Crystal was off for most of it. And my brother was old enough at that time, where he was living with his girlfriend. For a time, he did live with us. But it was pretty tough because at the time, he had a lot of anger issues. He was hard-headed, so our interactions were not good. And I was an annoying child, so it made sense. And now we get along much better.

Now I feel much more connected to my siblings, specifically my brother.

James: Is your brother a lot more calm now, compared to back then?

Noah: I think he's much happier with his life. Things are going much better for him, so he's good.

James: What was it like going to school? Let's start with elementary school.

Noah: It was tough because for some reason or another I ended up moving a lot. I'd say I went to at least four different elementary schools. My mom's on Section 8 and has been since I was younger. I came from a family like that. It was never like we got evicted or anything [from our home], which does happen to people and is really sad. But my mom would have altercations with some random landlord...and we ended up moving a lot. And I was always pretty good at school, but I didn't really care about it. Schools are a weird and different thing for me that I kind of coasted through it. I was good at math, but I didn't care for anything else. So it was hard for me.

James: Did you feel like school is just something you had to do?

Noah: Yeah, for sure.

James: Having said that, did you develop any close friendships with people? I imagine it might be tough because you're always moving. But did you remember someone from back then that you were really close with?

Noah: Yeah. Luckily, I started off in the Amherst area and then ended up back there as well, so I have a couple of close friends. One specifically was my best friend since third grade, and is still one of my best friends—Garrison. I don't get to see Gary all that often, but he's definitely still one of my best buds. Every time I'm in the area with him, we have a gym session and maybe play some ball afterwards. Just hang out.

James: Did you ever play basketball for your school team?

Noah: I never played for my school team because, honestly, I don't even think I was good enough. For so many years I was this super chubby kid. I was relatively coordinated because I was good at DDR [Dance Dance Revolution] when I was younger. But I wasn't that athletic until I turned seventeen and started losing a lot of weight, going to the gym a lot more. Played more basketball to the point where I could keep up with people and feel like I'm not that bad. I definitely don't think I'm that good by any means, but I can hold my own.

James: You mentioned DDR. I lost so much weight from playing DDR.

Noah: Dude, yeah. DDR is the truth.

James: [Laughs] Obviously, I'm a lot older than you, so I was already in high school when DDR came out.

          Let's go back to your school days. You found Yu-Gi-Oh and started playing it. How did you go from that to finding Magic?

Noah: I was playing Yu-Gi-Oh at my local game store and I would do pretty well. Most of the local tournaments that we'd have, I would win first or second place. I'd get some packs as prizes and start opening them. Some people playing Magic came up to me and said, "Hey, you're pretty good at Yu-Gi-Oh. You should learn Magic.... It's even better. You can get packs with your winnings from Yu-Gi-Oh and try to start learning with us." I was like, "Yeah, I'll think about it." I ended up grabbing some packs of Magic. Back then the Ravnica set was out, so I bought packs. I cracked them open, saw the cool cards, tried to start playing. I wasn't very good but I liked it a lot. I started getting into it a lot more. I started traveling for PTQs when I was around 12 and kept going from there.

James: That's a big jump. You just described opening packs to travelling to PTQs. You've got to walk me through that journey.

Noah: I had a good friend, Jody Keith, who helped me get better. Not "Lands master" Jody Keith that you might have seen on Star City Games coverage, but another Jody Keith. Jody would build me different random decks to play at FNMs with, and I would go 2-2. On a good week, I would 3-1. And I started liking it a lot. I don't know exactly when I made the competitive leap. I can't think of a pivotal moment when I went from not playing competitively to playing competitively. It just happened. It was like any other game that I would play. I didn't feel I was that good, but I felt like I had to keep playing. And I invested a bunch of money on packs. Cracked open a bunch of Kamigawa packs and hoped for the best. At that point, it felt so fun and new to me that I didn't picture my future with Magic. It was just a game that I was playing.

James: Did you feel, even back then, that you had a good grasp of the game fundamentals?

Noah: Yeah, it felt okay. I'm trying to think of one of the first drafts when I felt like, "You know, maybe these people aren't much better than me. Maybe I am getting to be okay." Because I analyzed these Magic players—the type of players who I would now happily play against in every round of an event. No hate on them or anything, but they didn't pursue Magic the same way that I have. It's very different for them.

James: Did you feel like you had a deep understanding of the game?

Noah: At first, not so much. It wasn't until I started playing in PTQs, and playing against players that were a lot better than me, that I could reflect on my games. I'd ask myself, "What happened in that game? What can I do to get better?" And I mostly started out playing Limited and Standard. My local gaming store always held drafts, so all my fundamentals started out from Limited. That's why it's no surprise that I love playing Limited now. It's one of my strongest formats for sure. I felt that I had a pretty good grasp on the game, but I always wanted to be better. Of course, I felt strong because I was such a cocky little kid. I felt like, "Oh, I'm the best. I can do anything!" But really I was just not a bad player. I had some pretty good theory behind Magic, but I didn't grasp it all that well. I probably didn't realize my mistakes as I would now, which is what I think is one of the most important parts of the game.

James: Do you think it was Jody or your friends that pushed you to get better, or was it coming from within?

Noah: I think a little of both. The way that I've functioned for a long time is that if I like something, then I'll pursue it and try to get really good at it. A lot of things I gave up on because I'm not good at, which kind of sucks. But if I really show interest in it, then I'll get good at it. I remember playing ping pong at camp one year against people and just losing, losing, losing. I was not very good. Then I practiced with the intent to get better. The intent to learn every time I'm playing, and I started getting better. Eventually I was one of the best players in camp, even beating some of the best counselors. A similar thing happened with me and Magic. I really tried to play against better players, and watched a bunch of videos, and learned as much as I could.

James: Was Magic the first game that you started traveling to tournaments for?

Noah: I started traveling to tournaments with Yu-Gi-Oh. I played a couple of the regionals, some random local events, which were never that big and I never managed to top eight. You needed to top-eight for nationals. I would top-sixteen sometimes and do okay, but I never did all that well. I probably haven't traveled to more than fifteen Yu-Gi-Oh tournaments in my life.

James: You started traveling at quite a young age. Did your mom or your family have any issues with that?

Noah: There were definitely some issues—to some extent. But my mom had always been rebellious in her own childhood, so she tried to not judge what I wanted to do with my life.

James: Was she ever worried about you when you were out there?

Noah: At first, especially. She's given me all this money every week, and I'm not really bringing any money back. It's like, "Where is the money going? I can't do this forever." Because my family never had that much money, so it was always tough.

James: Did that have something to do with you wanting to improve?

Noah: For sure. Just top-eighting or cashing a tournament— or not earning any cash, doing okay in a PTQ—is not going to off-set how much you're spending to buy food and travel to all these places. Back in the day, when I traveled to the regular PTQs—when they would have them almost every weekend in Massachusetts, and they were just one-day events—I wouldn't win. Eventually, I ended up winning some of them as I got older and much better at Magic. I became much more patient with learning and life-related matters.

James: What was the first big Magic victory or tournament success you had?

Noah: I hadn't day-two'd a single Grand Prix or cashed anything until around 2014. My first GP that I ended up day-two'ing was GP Indy, and it was Limited. And I almost finished day one with a 9-0 record. I went 8-0, losing the last round. I had a chance to 3-0 the rest of it to top-eight, but I ended up with a 12-3 record. In the end, I top-sixteened. That was my first GP cash, and it felt so good. For such a long time, that was all I wanted—to be up there and competing.

James: Did you feel like that tournament was something special, as you progressed through it?

Noah: I felt like I knew the format well. I thought that I had built my decks well, and I felt good the whole time. I felt like I had been wanting something like that to happen to me in Magic for so long. At the time, it was bittersweet. Obviously, the 12-3 finish felt good and I was ecstatic for doing well in a Grand Prix. But I still didn't reach my goal of qualifying for the Pro Tour, and that was the next step. I top-eighted probably 16 PTQs before I won any of them.

James: Did you feel like you were on the verge, and that you didn't play well, for whatever reason?

Noah: Exactly. A lot of them felt similar. I would do well in the Swiss rounds. My day one record would be decent. Then I'd get to top eight and lose. And I felt like I was solid, but didn't get there. I'm not sure what happened to get over the hump. I took a break, came back, and won two PTQs in a row. It was the end of Khans block.

James: Why did you take a break? Were you frustrated, or did you have other stuff going on in your life?

Noah: I took a break—I think it was for camp—a lot of times, because I would be gone for several weeks. Back then it was as a camper, so more of a three-week break. At the time, I was traveling every weekend or every other weekend. Maybe it ended up being a month or a little longer of not grinding Magic. Maybe playing occasionally but taking it easy on Magic. I wanted to play as much Magic as possible, but at the same time, it didn't feel feasible. I never really got there. I felt like one of the best players that I knew from my area, but it never got me to the next level.

James: You said you had multiple chances to reach your goals but you didn't quite get there. Was that a dark time for you? Were you frustrated?

Noah: For sure. I felt like the hard work wasn't paying off. And it can feel that way so much of the time. Magic is a frustrating game sometimes. You want to be where you want to be. So when you're not there, it's tough to cope.

James: Did you think about what you needed to do to level up?

Noah: That was one of the tough parts for me at the time. I didn't realize what I needed to take it to the next level. I was really frustrated. "Why can't I do this? I've been trying so hard. I'm getting better...I think." I realized my mistakes, sometimes. I didn't understand why I couldn't get there. And I feel like my attitude towards that changed in that time period. Just taking every match for what it is—one match at a time. Not having giant expectations. Thinking, "If I lose this one, then I'm out." Just trying to think about things differently.

James: But how do you do that? How do you become more relaxed about it? It seems like most people never figure it out.

Noah: I think that's easily one of the toughest parts of Magic—your attitude towards the game. Towards yourself as you play the game. You want to beat yourself up, to some extent, so that you don't blame luck every time. So you can actually grow. Some of the best players that I've ever met are constantly saying how bad they are, and how bad they're doing. It's really funny, every time I'm at an event, I don't know Martin Jůza very well, but I know him by association through some friends. I always ask him how he's doing, and he'll entertain me and say something like, "I'm X-2," or whatever, "I'd be X-0 if I actually played well."

James: Right.

Noah: But it makes sense. You want to be hard on yourself so you can get better.

James: Here's one of the greatest Limited players in the history of the game, and he says he's not doing well. Or that he's doing badly.

Noah: Exactly.

James: This mental growing up and leveling-up process that you went through—did you figure out a different perspective from talking to people? Or did you figure it out by yourself?

Noah: It definitely was a lot of internal stuff. For so long, I thought I was so good. So it didn't make sense to me. It wasn't clicking why I wasn't doing well. It took a lot of energy to look at the situations in different ways. Even looking back on it now, it was difficult. I looked back on every tournament that I played in and it's a struggle to stay positive about the game. Even when you are doing well, Magic is a game of so many swings where it's tough.

James: Did quitting ever cross your mind?

Noah: Of course. Spending all this time and money in the game and not getting anywhere. I could do well at some major tournament at a local level every once in a while. But every Grand Prix I played in, I would go 6-0 then 0-3. 6-0, then 0-3. I was always doing well for the first couple of rounds and then I don't know what it was. I would lose focus, lose track, start playing poorly. Of course quitting would cross my mind. Why would I want to keep playing? But the game was so much fun and the community was so good—my friends. And that's really what keeps bringing me back to the game is the people that I get to be with on a weekly basis.

James: Who are some of your best friends right now in the world of Magic?

Noah: I'm pretty close with everyone on my team, and I love them all. That's Team Cardhoarder. Outside of the team, one of my closest friends is Oliver Tiu. We've been playing together in Massachusetts for a very long time. We've always been the super young guys. And he broke out in the scene last year. Or maybe it was the year before. He went from nothing to Platinum. He's always been someone to look up to, which sounds weird because I'm a couple of years older than him. But it was nice to know that I still had potential, because I never looked at Oliver as someone who was crazy better than me. He's one of my good friends, and gave me a lot of hope towards what I could do.

James: How long have you guys known each other?

Noah: We've been playing together for a long time now. I don't think we've been that close for all of the years that we've known each other. But recently we've both been grinding towards PTs. Every Sunday we would video chat and I'd help him with his Sealed pool for the PTQ or whatever. Sometimes I'd be playing in it, and we would both help each other with our pools. I met him when I was around 13, so it's been about seven years now.

James: What's one thing that people may not know about Oliver?

Noah: Oliver often needs a lot of help keeping his stuff together. I travel with Oliver a lot and—

James: You mean, being organized?

Noah: More like *not losing something*.

James: What's the most valuable thing that he's lost? Or has it not happened yet, because you've been watching out for him?

Noah: Yeah, I usually watch out for him. He's been known to leave his wallet in the Uber. Or leave his phone in the Uber. Or just anywhere. I don't want to bad-mouth Oliver like that. [Laughs] It's not like he always leaves stuff around.

James: Are you guys very different, personality-wise?

Noah: Yeah, I'd say we're both different and similar. We're both chill, laid-back people. We work well together. I'm teaming up with him for the Team Limited GP in Providence at the end of this month.

James: Awesome. He sounds like a good guy. He's very humorous on Twitter.

Noah: Yeah, that's basically what Oliver is best known for—his Twitter account. But he's a good guy. He has a good heart and he loves the game. It gets frustrating for him and for everyone at times, but he has a lot of love for the game or he wouldn't be playing it so much.

James: I'm wondering if you see the same things that he's going through now, that maybe you went through a few years ago?

Noah: Yeah. Especially for him, Magic is even tougher. He came in playing competitively and basically didn't lose for a year and a half—maybe two years. When he loses now, he gets super down on himself. And it's bad because variance didn't hit him as much in those first couple of years. Now, when it does, it's harder on him. At the same time, he does work hard. It's important to keep up your game as you keep playing in a tournament. Not getting discouraged by a loss, misplay, or anything.

James: Are there ways that you try to give him advice, or give him encouragement when he does feel like he's not quite getting there?

Noah: As much as I can. I'll go up to him and try to have some small talk. Pep talk him back into it. "You're obviously great. You can't win every match." It's just hard. Having these high expectations, as he does for himself, and sometimes not meeting up with them. It's tough when you've done so well for so long.

James: Going back to the times when you were close to winning tournaments but you didn't quite get there—did you feel like you had mentor figures, or friends, that helped you through those situations?

Noah: For sure. One of my friends is like an older brother. His name is Roberto. I teamed with him for a Team Grand Prix a long time ago, at one of the first GPs I played in. Roberto taught me a lot about *how to be*. Everyone thought they knew how I should best live my life. Especially growing up with all these older people when you're a young kid playing this game. They tried to steer me in the right direction. Especially Roberto. But yeah, I can think of Roberto and Greg. Greg was always teaching me so much about drafting. That's easily one of the reasons why I love Limited so much, to this day. I'm grateful for everyone back home.

James: You're still close with those guys today?

Noah: Yeah. Roberto lives a little further now. He's out in Connecticut and he's always busy because he has kids. But every once in a while, especially when I'm in the area, I try to hit my local FNM for a draft. We don't have quite the community that we used to have. We would have at least three drafts a week, sometimes four.

James: You've weathered the storm and you're a Gold Level Pro now. You're playing in Pro Tours. What kind of goals are you working towards right now, as a Magic player?

Noah: I want to be as intentional as I can about Magic. I want to play well. I want to prepare well. It's so hard to make it right now as a Magic pro, and I don't view it as something I'll be able to do forever. I want to ride it for as long as I possibly can. Hopefully get some more ties within the Magic community. But I hope to re-up Gold for as many years as I can. Maybe get lucky a year or two and hit Platinum—keep playing and growing as much as I can. That's the most important to me. I don't want to just keep playing at a mediocre level and feel bad about myself. I want to keep growing with the game.

James: That's interesting—what you said about being intentional. It sounds like you're not focused on the results, but on approaching the game the right way.

Noah: I think a lot of the time Magic players are too hung up on results and being results oriented—because what else do you really have to base off of? I understand it to some extent. At the same time, for me, what's important about Magic has always been the process. I've wanted to approach it the right way and feel like I'm learning the most and doing the best that I can be doing. Of course, it's always nice to do well, and it feels good. But if I'm doing well and playing poorly, then I still don't feel great. Even sometimes when I'm doing poorly and I'm playing great, I feel okay. It's not like I would tell myself, "I'm so happy that I 0-3'd this tournament." But I would know that I played well in my rounds and I'm learning more. There's a lot of different ways where you can look at Magic, and I feel like it's easy to look at it in a bad way.

James: Do you feel like you have it mostly figured out—in terms of the mental approach to the game?

Noah: Well...I don't know if you ever really can, but I'm trying as much as I can to keep it under control. There's one thing that bothers me the most while playing—and I hate that it bothers me. If someone makes a misplay and I see it, then I'll get tilted for a bit and I have to tell myself to stop. I try to think of it as every time that it happens, your opponent is giving you more percentage points to win. So, why be frustrated? Be happy!

James: Oh, that's interesting. You're not saying when *you* make a misplay. You're saying when you see your opponent make a misplay.

Noah: Yeah, exactly.

James: Is that because you want to feel like you're both at the top of your games, and that you still won the match without your opponent making any obvious mistakes?

Noah: I don't want my opponent to play poorly and still beat me. Then I won't feel good about their chances with the rest or the tournament. Or feel good that I lost to them. Every time I've lost to a good player, I generally feel fine. "I just lost to Reid [Duke] last round. It's fine." But every time you have to say something like, "I lost to this dude last round, and they played awfully," it feels bad.

James: Do you still feel that way today? Do you feel tilted if that happens?

172

Noah: I try not to—as much as I can. But I'd say that's one of the things that still to this day tilts me the most about Magic. I'm trying to work on it. And sometimes it doesn't bother me—I'm trying to view it more as them giving me an opportunity to do better in the game, as opposed to them throwing away their chances and still beating me.

James: It's variance, right?

Noah: Exactly.

James: I know you're a content creator as well. Is there something about content creation that really excites you?

Noah: This past year I haven't been doing as much content as I'd like to. My deal with Cardhoarder doesn't involve content anymore. Maybe in the future I'll start doing more content again. But I have videos up on YouTube that people can feel free to check out—mostly of me playing Grixis Delver in Legacy. But I have enjoyed making content. It's fun to feel like I can share what I think, or what I'm good at, with other people. It also means a lot to me when I get feedback. Last year, when I was making content more regularly, I'd have people come up to me at events and be like, "Hey, man. I read your content. It's really good. I picked up Grixis Delver in Legacy and your videos have helped me learn." It's little things like that that make everything worth it for me.

James: Being a content creator is also one of the ways that you can make a living in Magic. It's not just about the tournaments.

Noah: Exactly.

James: Are there content creators out there that you especially enjoy?

Noah: Honestly, I haven't been watching or reading as much content as I'd like to. But every once in a while I'll read the set reviews. Sometimes people produce content on a deck that I'm currently playing, and I'll read it. I like Andrea Mengucci's content because he's one of the only Legacy players out there right now that's a big name. He's always playing Legacy. There are Legacy specialists out there that stream, but Andrea makes a lot of great content. Any chance I get, I also check out any Limited articles written by masters of the format. I might read about Standard decks when I'm preparing for a Pro Tour. That's when I'll read most of my articles, the week before a PT. It helps to check out Star City Games and hit up some articles of what they think a good deck could be. But most of the time it will be a few cards different from the optimal list, because who would want to give up the best list right before a PT?

James: Yeah, unless you're Gerry Thompson. He seems super open about sharing whatever is on his mind. He's not worried about getting an edge. I don't know if you know him well, but he's all about being good for the community.

Noah: For sure. I don't know Gerry all that well, but I've had some interactions with him. He's been a nice guy and he's working hard to be good for the community. That's important.

James: Are there any players in particular that you respect and look up to?

Noah: I love watching technical players go to work. That's my thing, you know? When I see someone make a cool play, it's awesome. And it's even better for me when I've met them or talked to them and they happen to be kind people. Of course, Peach Garden Oath is so much fun for me to watch. Reid Duke, William "Huey" Jensen, and Owen Turtenwald. Having played against some of them and having had interactions with them, they've all been genuinely positive. And they're all great players, so I love watching them play. Also, Lukas Blohon. Just a really kind dude. Always been nice in every interaction I've had with him, and a great technical player. Corey Baumeister and Brad Nelson, too. It's crazy watching how much they crush. There are so many pros that I feel like I get to learn so much when I'm watching them play, or playing against them. That's what it's about for me—getting better, and watching these players.

James: Have you thought about working with some of these guys more closely, to try and level up your game?

Noah: That's always the goal—working with the best around so that you can get better. But I love working with people in general. My team is great, a lot of solid players. But it's hard to feel like we're growing as a team all of the time. I don't want to feel like I'm trying to mentor people, or teach them, all the time. I want to be the one that's being taught. My ideal setup would be me on a team with a bunch of people that are way better than me. That way, I can learn as much as possible. As opposed to when I feel like I'm teaching people. But in the same respect, both things have a lot of weight.

James: As a camp counselor, or one of the better players on your team, you might think that you're not getting much in return. But it can also be rewarding to show other people the way.

Noah: Yeah, exactly.

James: You mentioned that Magic is not going to be there forever for you. You have to balance Magic with life obligations. How do you do that now, and how do you see it going forward in the next three to five years?

Noah: Right now, I'm trying to play as much Magic as I can while picking up any job I can find. It sounds pretty bad, because right now all I've been doing is playing Magic, and it's not sustainable—getting a sponsorship from Cardhoarder and earning money from tournament winnings. For the next couple of years, what I see myself doing is looking at ways that I can apply my Magic skills to other things. I've never felt passionate about doing that many things, so it's hard for me to pinpoint what those things are. I often think about this. If Magic just vanished, what would I do? If it's the next day and I've never played Magic before, what would I be doing with my life? I'm not sure. Probably something involving fitness or personal training. Being a personal trainer, perhaps. Maybe I'd go to the gym five days a week and do as much as I could there. I don't know.

James: For you, Magic is about the grind, the community, the fire, and the competition. It might be hard to find a direct replacement for that.

Noah: Exactly.

James: You touched on fitness. How is fitness related to your lifestyle, and to Magic?

Noah: In the past year, I spent maybe every other weekend playing Magic, sometimes two weekends in a row. Just grinding GPs all the time and playing in PTs. I ended up qualifying for all of the Pro Tours. It was hard for me to maintain my fitness level. I was eating out too often. I wasn't going to the gym as much as I'd like. I was gaining weight and feeling bad about myself. It was really poor. In the past few months I've been getting back to the gym a lot more, and making dinner almost every night with my girlfriend. It's felt good. I didn't even realize how big a role fitness played in my life, until I stopped doing a lot of it. I was chubby for so long—from age 11 to 17. Between the ages of 17 to 19 I lost a ton of weight and was working out all the time with Gary, my best friend. We played a lot of basketball. I felt good about myself. After that, when I spent so much time playing Magic and getting out of shape, it was tough. Even though I was happy and having good success in Magic, I had the underlying issues.

James: It's tough because a lot of people never find that balance, but it sounds like you have. You had a wake-up call at some point, in terms of the physical stuff, right?

Noah: I'm getting out there and starting to feel back in shape. I've been going to the gym three or four days a week, and getting back to running. I used to run a lot because my friend Gary lived close to the gym. He's close to Amherst College. Since he worked there, he could get into their private gym, so it was a nice place to be working out. And we jogged there every day and worked out for a couple of hours.

James: If you could go back in time five years, what would you tell the younger, 16-year-old Noah Walker?

Noah: I'd probably tell him to keep working hard at what you want to do. Work hard at what you love. Try to be a good person. That's what I think is most important. I have played so many matches against people where they tell me afterwards that they had a good experience playing against me. That makes me feel fantastic. Whether I win or lose a match, I want to have fun. We're playing a game and I want that great experience for everyone. So, I'd tell myself to value things differently. When I was 16, I still had a toxic mindset when it came to Magic. All I thought about was how to win. Not even *how* to win, just thinking that I *want* to win. That's all I wanted. So yeah, I would tell myself to reconsider what I thought was important and to value growing with people, and being the best me I could possibly be.

James: What would you tell a kid, or someone younger than you, that wanted to get into Magic for the first time? Maybe he or she has started playing casually and is now thinking about playing in tournaments and becoming more competitive. What kind of advice would you give that person?

Noah: I would tell them to play as much as they could, at as high a level as they could. And not to just play, but to think about what was happening in the games. It's so easy to go on autopilot and play a bunch of games of Magic, and not learn anything. And blame everything on, "Oh, I got so unlucky. I got mana screwed every game." But the way you want to look at Magic is—what can I be doing every single turn to optimize everything to be the best, instead of worrying about the whole outlook and just thinking about winning? You never really win a game of Magic. You win a game on every turn that you're playing, so you have to take things slowly and not get discouraged. Just try to learn.

James: Great advice, man. Noah, thank you so much for spending the time with me. I really appreciated you coming on here and sharing some of your Magic background.

Noah: Yeah dude, this was great. Thank you so much for having me. There's so much more to Magic than just the game, and I don't think people realize it all that often.

"And he looks at me and says, 'Well, if my best friend is going to be a girl, I'm going to be the first one to buy her a drink.' And takes a sip at his and winks at me. That was kind of the, 'Things are going to be okay [moment],' I guess."

—*Emma Handy*

CHAPTER 6

EMMA HANDY

Emma Handy is one of the most popular personalities in Magic. Competitor, thinker, marketer, writer, commentator, advocate – Emma wears all of these hats, and is extraordinarily talented in several aspects of the game.

Emma is a fierce champion of the LGBTQIA community and has done plenty to raise the profile of this under-served group within Magic. Her fans look up to her, beyond what happens when a deck of Magic cards is shuffled up and dealt.

Today, she's a writer and commentator for Star City Games. You can watch and listen to her commentary as part of the SCG Open series.

What people may not know about Emma is that she has overcome a lot to get to where she is today. Emma is a transgender person and has struggled with self-harm and depressive tendencies at various points in her life. She has contemplated suicide. To say that she overcame certain hardships in life is understating her journey.

The moment Emma mentioned that she was a fan of *Humans of Magic* in her tweets, two things happened. One, the *Humans* Twitter account following grew by 60% overnight. Two, I knew that I needed to interview her.

Emma has a fascinating story to tell, and it's a story that is inspirational to others dealing with similar difficulties in life. Of all the interviews in this book, I spent the most time preparing for this one. Not because I was concerned about doing poorly as an interviewer, but because I wanted to properly convey her story.

In the end, the interview flowed well and Emma bravely answered everything I threw at her. It's one of the episodes I feel proudest about. Judging by the community's reception, it managed to hit the right notes.

I learned something about Emma, but also about myself, in the process. Leaving one's comfort zone, and pushing boundaries, is an inevitable part of growth. Not only for Emma, but for myself as an interviewer and content creator.

I'm glad to have had the opportunity to interview Emma, and honored to be able to share this conversation.

Recorded in August 2018.

James: Emma, there are a bunch of topics that I wanted to ask you about today, and I thought that we could start off with something simple.

You're a pretty well-known Magic personality. You put yourself out there—whether it's your tweets or your writing—and you have quite the collection of fans. But what's one thing that people may not know about you? That they may not know just from reading your content, or seeing you play on camera?

Emma: I don't know. I guess it depends on how dark we want to get. I think the fun thing to say is that I'm well-versed in music. When I was in high school, I played in a lot of rock bands. I can play drums, guitar, bass, piano, upright bass, and I was a singer for a while.

If we are talking about something darker, then the answer is that I'm a lot sadder in person than I am on the Internet. But that stuff is not something you want to perpetuate. You want to try to put good in, so you get good out, you know what I mean?

James: Oh yeah, totally. We often have—whether consciously or unconsciously—an online persona that is a bit different from the person we are in private life.

Emma: Exactly. I have a private Facebook and a public Facebook. There is a pretty stark contrast between them.

James: Do you see two aspects to your personality? Or is the public Emma just a more exaggerated or highlighted version of the private Emma?

Emma: I think a lot of it is...I think I'm fairly good at marketing. Especially marketing myself.

I always joke that it's not my Magic results that have gotten me to where I am today. It's because I can write well, and I'm also charismatic.

That isn't necessarily who I always want to be, but I think it is important in a lot of ways to be my best self when under the public eye. I think that might be the best way to phrase it.

James: The fact is, the way the world works—at least in my cynical understanding—is that people don't want to associate or follow somebody that makes them feel negative all the time. They want to follow somebody that potentially inspires them and makes them feel good.

Emma: I completely agree with that. Especially with something like Magic, which is a hobby, people don't go to their hobby to feel upset or to feel bad. They go to escape and feel good.

Sometimes it means living vicariously through someone else. Sometimes it's just wanting to say,

"Wow, I could get to that point someday because someone else has gotten there." Or, "This person is going to help me feel better about something, or be better at something." And I think that is more important than just making people feel worse.

James: For sure. I had no idea that you were such a talented person in terms of knowing all these instruments and playing music. How did you start?

Emma: I wasn't that interested in music until later in middle school. I hung out...well, I didn't hang out that much, but the people who were closest to being my friends—I call them "acquaintance-pluses"—were mostly band kids.

And I didn't play anything, but then I got into Guitar Hero and wanted to try to play a couple of the songs because I really liked them. I had pretty good hand-eye coordination—I could type 110, 120 words a minute when I was thirteen or fourteen.

And I decided, let's try out guitar. And then I decided I liked bass more. I just liked fingerpicking, I liked the feel of the strings more, I liked the feel of the bass, and then that made me want to learn upright bass, and that's such a rhythmic instrument. I ended up moving over to drums and learning that as well.

And finally, I just learned piano because at that point I knew enough about music theory to fudge it a little bit. I'm not a great pianist or anything, but I can sit and play first, third, fifth chords on the piano, and I can do some arpeggiating. I don't know if that's the correct verbiage.

Besides that, I played in enough bands where I either had to fill in on vocals because the singer was sick, or I was the singer in a couple of bands. I learned enough about music, and you can at least do punk rock songs even if you aren't very good at holding a pitch. You're just screaming into a mic and teenagers go crazy. [Laughs]

James: Yeah, that says a lot about punk rock in general, but I will reserve my music elitism for another day. [Laughs]

Emma: [Laughs] I don't think it's a bad thing. A lot of it is conveying emotion over music. I don't think that's wrong. It's a different way of doing things.

James: It is interesting that you mentioned going from one instrument to the other. I feel like you might be downplaying it a little bit.

Emma: A lot of it is the fact that I can't do just one thing. I have a very addictive personality, and I think this is pretty common amongst Magic grinders. I imagine you hear this from most people you have on your show.

I can't just play some Magic. If I were to quit, I couldn't come back to the game for a draft, enjoy the draft, and then go back to not playing anymore. I would come back for a draft and then I'd go, "Wow, I like this card. I've got to build a deck around this for FNM." Next thing you know, I've got to go to the IQ. And then I've got to go to the Open. And then I've got to go to the Grand Prix. And then I've got to try and qualify for the Pro Tour.

Music was very similar where it's like—alright, I learned how to play some songs on guitar using the basic chords. Then you look around and that bass that person is playing, it looks like they're enjoying it—I should try to learn bass because that's something that can influence my songwriting. And I already know this other rhythmic thing, and I'm pretty coordinated, so I bet I can mess around on the drums enough until I just know how to play it. That will help with my synchronization as a bass player. And I want to write piano interludes, but I need to be able to play them in order to record them. So I guess I should learn to play the piano, too.

Ironically, I'm not nearly as competitive as most people would assume. I want to be the best person I can be, and if that's not better than other people, then that's fine with me. All I can be is my best, right?

In Magic, for example, I'm never going to be Jon Finkel. I'm never going to invest enough time. I'm never going to reach that peak and be better than Jon Finkel.

And that kind of goes everywhere else in my life, too. In bass playing, I'm never going to be a Billy Sheehan or Victor Wooten. In drumming, I'm never going to be a Mike Portnoy. I'm not going to be a Neil Peart. I can list musicians for a long time.

But I was content—or am content—just being the best person that I can be at the things I do. I do push myself, though, to try and be the best I can be.

James: You just want to be a better person today than you were yesterday, right?

Emma: Exactly. Nail on the head.

James: I always like to start these interviews by going back in time. Can you briefly tell me where you grew up? Tell me a little bit about your parents.

Emma: Sure. I was born in Orlando, Florida. Specifically, Altamonte Springs. I lived in Stanford, for anyone who's been around Central Florida. I moved to western North Carolina, a city called Ashville, when I was five years old.

I don't remember a whole lot about Orlando, but because I was younger at the time, my internal temperature was set to Orlando's weather. It's funny—I'll be comfortable up until 90 degrees Fahrenheit. But if it gets down to 65°, I'm ready to burst out the bubble coats and pumpkin spice, so to speak. I get cold very easily.

Ashville is in the Southeast, and it's a pretty liberal city by American standards. I grew up there and lived there until I was 25. I went to school there and didn't go to college. I started to sign up for classes, realized I didn't like the things I was good at, and didn't want to sink myself into a bunch of debt for the sake of something I would hate.

I started working instead. I worked in construction for a little while. I don't really look it now, but I was bulkier for a while. A little under 200 pounds, I think that was the heaviest I ever was.

After that, I worked in a call center. Specifically, as a manager for Blue Cross Blue Shield in New Jersey. The Medicare sector. I answered a lot of health insurance questions, dealt with a lot with that, and trained a bunch of people on Medicare-related health insurance.

And then I started grinding Magic after I started working at a card store in 2014. I really put my nose to the Magic grind in 2016.

As far as family goes, I have a biological mother and father who were both in the picture for a very long time. They divorced when I was in the fifth grade. I've had two stepmothers and one stepfather.

My relationship with my biological father is not great. For anyone who does not know, I am transgender. And for reasons related to my transition, I am no longer on speaking terms with my father's side of the family.

On my mother's side, my mother and my stepfather are both amazing. They've been nothing but wonderful to me. And in a lot of respects, my stepfather is really my dad, and not just because of the bad situation with my biological father. He taught me a lot about growing up—how to drive, how to handle myself in public, and how to get a job. He is a great man.

I have two biological sisters and one stepsister. They're all younger than me and they're all fantastic. One of them is really into animals. One of them is currently a guard at Guantanamo Bay. Another one is a rising comedian.

James: Trying to unpack that a little bit...which family member are you the closest with right now?

Emma: That's a little bit tough. [Laughs] If I had to rank them—this feels bad because it feels like I'm picking a favorite family member, and that's not the case. I'm probably the closest with my biological mother and my two biological sisters. I'm close with all of them for different reasons.

I was kind of a party animal growing up. And by that, I mean I've done some bad stuff, and it's not great. I started drinking when I was fourteen. As a result, I can relate with one of my sisters, who also likes to party a little bit. I don't think it's at the same level, though.

But the sister I'm the closest in age with is also the sibling that I "grew up with" the most. I don't know if that makes a whole lot of sense, but we shared a lot of similar experiences. We were usually in the same schools and everything.

And my mom and I get really catty and all curled up on the couch and watch stupid movies. While it's playing, we gossip about family and stuff, and that's really nice.

I'm quite close with those three family members, but all in different ways.

James: If I can retrace a little bit, what was your childhood like? Let's say between the ages of 5 and 15.

Emma: That's roughly from kindergarten to eighth grade. I went to two different elementary schools because my family moved after the first grade. All that was fairly uneventful. I didn't really have a whole lot of friends. I excelled in elementary school. I picked up on basic arithmetic very quickly and was labeled as gifted. I also read the Harry Potter books. I swear that was the thing at the time—teachers thought that they were going to have the next Stephen Hawking or genius in line, if they could just read *Harry Potter and the Sorcerer's Stone.*

Then in middle school, I lost most of my friends from elementary school because we had different classes. Instead of regrouping with those friends, I got further into trading card games like Yu-Gi-Oh and Magic. I played Yu-Gi-Oh before Magic.

I have a friend named Randy, and I have been friends with Randy since I was 12 years old. But other than him, I didn't really have any good friends until the very end of middle school. So I got deeper and deeper into trading card games and did that with my free time.

James: What about your interests in music? Did you make friends through that channel as well?

Emma: In a lot of ways, I suspect that was why I got into music. There were a lot of reasons, but one of the big reasons is that it was something to do with other people. The people whom I had classes with in middle school and early high school, they would play instruments.

And we started to get into metal—System of a Down, Disturbed, and stuff like that. If we're being honest, it's pretty easy to pick up a guitar and learn to play those kinds of songs in a couple of weeks. Lots of bar chords, which is placing your finger flat against three strings, as long as the guitar was tuned for it. And music was a way to have people to talk to.

James: When you started playing Yu-Gi-Oh, what was that like?

Emma: This is kind of its own little timeline. I started with Pokémon. My mom got me a starter deck when we were going to the beach when I was six years old. I got ripped off for my holographic first edition Machamp card at the Books-A-Million Saturday Pokémon trade thing. I traded it for a Starmie and got made fun of by my friends so badly that I went home and learned to play the game. And I ended up getting quite good at Pokémon. Have you ever played the game?

James: I have. I remember that back in the day—and this is really dating myself—my brother and I started playing Magic when it first came out in the early 90s. For us, Magic was the first trading card game we played. But I do remember that we got into Pokémon very briefly at some point. And I think we got ripped off, too.

Emma: We've all been there. There was an Alakazam damage-swap deck that I had a hand to help create, in the early days of Pokémon. If you know the rules at all, it didn't play any energy, which was a pretty rare thing. It decked the opponent out the hard way, to win. And from there, I picked up Yu-Gi-Oh because it was kind of like—oh, Pokémon is for kids, and I'm supposed to play the big kid game now.

James: Yeah. Level up to Yu-Gi-Oh, right?

Emma: Exactly. So at a Yu-Gi-Oh trading event, someone advertised that there was a card store opening up locally, and there weren't any of those before. And they said that they were going to have some Yu-Gi-Oh cards and a Yu-Gi-Oh tournament, which was a big deal at the time.

I had never even heard of a card tournament. I go to this place, and I see it's mostly Magic on the walls, and I'm kind of confused. After a few months, I ended up learning to play Magic, and I was *awful*. I was god-awful. I had no idea what I was doing.

At my first FNM, I played an eighty-card mono-blue artifact deck and got crushed by Affinity over and over. And I didn't realize why Affinity was as busted as it was. In Pokémon, the trainers didn't have mana costs. And in Yu-Gi-Oh the spells and troops didn't have mana costs, either. So I didn't realize how busted free spells were.

I would get my ass kicked for three rounds in a row. My opponents would go, "Alright, Disciple of the Vault trigger, you're dead." And I'm like, "Wow, your deck is really good. I sure got a lot to learn!" I just assumed that's how Magic worked.

I wasn't really competitive in any games until I graduated from high school and I made this conscious decision to do so. I said to myself, "Alright, I think that if I'm going to start working instead of going to school, I can't afford to sink money into this stuff like I did in school. I need to either get good at these games, or I need to sell my stuff and stop wasting money on it."

And I got very competitive in Yu-Gi-Oh in a very short amount of time. I was kind of a finance guru in that game and played a little competitive Yu-Gi-Oh towards the end of my run with that game.

And then I got pretty competitive in Magic towards New Phyrexia, and then started grinding hard around Battle for Zendikar.

James: When you say that you're a financial guru in Yu-Gi-Oh, what does that mean?

Emma: There were about six months where my only job was peddling Yu-Gi-Oh cards out of the back of my car. That's all I did. I also wrote for a website. You can probably do some research, if you know my deadname, and find those articles.

James: For people who may not understand, can you define what a deadname is?

Emma: A deadname is the name I went by before I transitioned. I was assigned male at birth. Emma Handy ain't the name my momma gave me. [Laughs]

But I'm not really proud of the articles and don't want to share it as a result, at least here. I'll make people do a little bit of leg work if they want to dig that up. But I wrote articles about price speculation and strategy, and in about six months...let me think. I made about $60,000 peddling Yu-Gi-Oh cards.

James: Wow. That beats working in construction or a call center, right?

Emma: Yeah. This was after construction but before the call center. I liked the construction job a lot, believe it or not. I know that sounds silly. But it feels rewarding to come home after a long day of work and feel tired. It feels like you earned your money, so to speak.

And it was a very...saying "easy job" is not correct, but it was...there weren't office politics or anything, and the money was decent. You got in at nine o'clock, they would tell you what you had to get done, and it would have to be done by five o'clock. If it was not done by five o'clock, you got fired on the spot.

At the end of every Friday, if you were not fired, everyone would line up and they would give you four $100 bills. It was all under the table, and they did not ask you any questions. I don't know. It was pretty nice. But I was also young and strong enough to get everything done in time.

James: It sounds like an honest job. You go in, use your hands, and literally get something done. It's very black-and-white.

Emma: Exactly. There was a contractor—that guy was the boss. And then there was everybody else. And we got told what we had to build that day. We had to put up some walls in a certain building, or build a bunch of furniture for another building.

I ended up not working for them anymore because they were based out of Charlotte, and they completed the job that they were doing in Ashville, and I wasn't willing to relocate to Charlotte. It was a good job, but it wasn't a "relocate a few hours away" kind of job.

James: You chose to deal cards, and you did that for about six months. Had you considered buying and selling cards for longer?

Emma: So, there was kind of a problem where…what's the best way to phrase this? Let me go ahead and lay this out upfront. I used to be a much worse person than I am now.

I think a lot of what I'm about to talk about is incredibly immoral, and by the end of it, I think it will be very obvious why I hold that opinion.

In Yu-Gi-Oh there was an era where there was not a specific website or price guide that people went by for prices. So a lot of times, it came down to reputation. "That person is probably the smartest person in the room with prices. Therefore, their prices are probably correct."

What that means is that it was very easy to take advantage of people, including buying cards from people and then buy-listing [reselling] them for more than that. Buy list prices are already not great, so if you're buying for less than that, that's pretty rough.

I killed a lot of the Yu-Gi-Oh scene in western North Carolina, northern South Carolina, and eastern Tennessee. I would buy someone's $1,000 collection for $100, and sell it online for $500. And people would buy the cards from me because I'm selling them for half of what they're worth.

But then the person I bought the cards from, they're done with Yu-Gi-Oh. They don't have a collection anymore and they have $100. When they go buy back in, they realize they can't get anything close to what they had for that $100, so they stay gone.

It wasn't sustainable because eventually I was buying people out of the game for low amounts of money. Entire local areas would stop playing the game over the course of two, three months.

James: But do you really think that you *single-handedly* had such an impact on the community?

Emma: There were four people who were buying cards for me, so it wasn't just me.

James: So you were scaling it out, you actually had a small group working for you?

Emma: We had a small team, and only three of us were really trading. One of them was just there because he was so good at the game that he would enter whatever tournament we were going to, and usually turn a profit even if it was a slight one.

It's not that we did it single-handedly, necessarily, but there is kind of a...what's the way to phrase this? "A catalyst might not do something by itself, but it's the first domino." Does that make sense?

James: Yeah.

Emma: There's a point where—if a community is 25 players and 60% of them show up to locals each week—if you take out 5 of those 25 players, then only 12 people are playing in tournaments. And if you take out another 5, then next thing you know, there's barely enough players for an eight-person tournament.

At that point, people who do well are barely getting enough prizes to cover their entry fees, which means they're less incentivized to keep coming. That means that they're going to go to the mall instead, or spend money on Magic cards instead of Yu-Gi-Oh cards. People don't get ripped off in Magic like they do in Yu-Gi-Oh.

James: Let me play devil's advocate here, Emma. I would argue that it is not immoral because it is the player's responsibility—or the collector's responsibility—to figure out what they should be paying for cards.

Some kid might need the $100 cash, even though his or her collection is worth $1,000. Maybe they want to liquidate their collection, or they feel like they want the instant gratification of the $100 cash in their hands. It's not like you're stealing the cards from them.

Emma: Not literally, no. A lot of what you're saying is how I justified it to myself at the time. Everyone agreed to everything, and it was all on the table. But I wasn't telling the truth about what a fair price for their cards was. I think there's a point where capitalizing on someone's ignorance to that degree is immoral.

James: You stopped after half a year. Was there some kind of realization?

Emma: Yeah. I was making more dollars in Yu-Gi-Oh than my local store was, each week. I almost got banned for it because I would just sit out in the parking lot and sell cards to people. And I heard an employee complaining about their store sales numbers, and my numbers were higher than theirs.

That was kind of the point where I was like, "I'm doing better than a store from this parking lot, that's kind of cool." And then I thought about it more. I was like, "There's probably something wrong with this because I'm not full of myself to the point where I think this is necessarily a good thing." Does that make sense? It shows that some rule is being broken.

James: Did any of the players that you dealt with confront you in any way? I'm trying to figure out if that was a part of it.

Emma: I've had people chase me out of a convention center because they knew how much money I had with me. When you're a floor trader, you tend to have a bunch of cash on you. And I've had situations where…there was a Six-Samurai deck that I sold to someone before a tournament for $500. At the end of the tournament, they wanted to sell the exact same cards back to me, and I gave them $60.

Of course, there are situations where cards are worth more before the tournament than they are after the tournament. But I think we can agree that's a pretty drastic extreme.

James: And how did that make you feel?

Emma: Honestly, it was a pretty depressing time for me, so I didn't feel much.

I will concede that it is completely self-diagnosed, but I am under the impression that I struggled with depressive tendencies for most of my life. And that was a low point for me, at least in terms of mental health.

It's not the worst that I've ever been, and we might touch on that later. But I didn't feel a whole lot. I think it is immoral to do the things that I was doing, which shows that I had gone to some lengths to numb myself emotionally to certain things. That doesn't usually limit itself to lows—it also tends to dull the highs as well.

James: And since we're on this topic, were the depressive tendencies—is this something you felt like you've always had since you were a kid?

Emma: Okay. This is related to me being trans. I was very confused and upset a lot of the time when I was younger. And I struggled a lot with my identity because I presented as male until I was in my early twenties. And for most of my life, basically, I was under the impression that I was a girl and that the world didn't allow me be one. Does that make sense?

This is about being gender-role normative, so to speak. I would try to play patty cakes and hop-scotch. I would try to do those things and then get made fun of by the girls. And boys would punch me, or whatever. I learned very quickly that was not what I was supposed to do.

And there are worse things that happened with my biological father. I did not come out to him, but he reacted very negatively to people who were assigned male at birth and then tried to be women when they were older. And I think that is when I started to realize that something might not be wrong with me, but things were going to be very hard.

I was not going to feel fulfilled in the ways that I wanted to. I wouldn't be able to do certain things.

I wouldn't be able to dress in certain ways. I would be expected to act in ways that didn't make me feel comfortable. I think that's a lot of it, and that started when I was thirteen. In fact, the first time I ever self-harmed was at that age.

An email went around about a trans beauty pageant in Japan. My biological father sent it around—they were one of those chain emails from back in the early 2000s, with jokes and everything. It talked about the contestants. My father added, "I thought you'd really enjoy this."

And halfway through reading it, I started getting excited and thinking, "Oh my God, he gets it. He gets it. This is so good, and I'm so happy that I have a parent that gets it." And at the end of his forwarded email, he writes, "But here's the twist—these are all actually men!" And it just felt like I was punched in the stomach.

At the time, I thought, "Wow, these are people like me. This is amazing. I can grow up how I want to be. I can be perceived as I want to be perceived."

And I brought it up to him later that night. He looks at me, smiles, and starts laughing and goes, "Oh my God, I know! Weren't they fucking disgusting?" And then I realized that his email had been making fun of them the whole time.

That was sort of the beginning of me dealing with a lot of self-loathing issues. I don't know. Emotional distress, we'll say, as a chronic condition, rather than something that came and went.

James: It sounds like you always knew who you were. But the world, or the people around you, would not make that easy.

Emma: Exactly. I think if I had been born a cis woman, I would have still been a bit of a tomboy. I liked the Power Rangers when I was little, for example, and I think I still would have liked the Power Rangers.

But other things would have been very different. I wouldn't have had rocks thrown at me for trying to do things with the girls. I wouldn't have had talks with my teacher about the inappropriateness of a line of girls holding hands.

I would hold hands with the girls and skip down the hallway, and be told that that it was inappropriate touching for me. But not for them. Those types of situations were confusing and painful to me, as a kid.

James: Yeah. I can't even begin to imagine that. Society expects us to fit into these neat boxes.

Emma: Absolutely. For a lot of people, there's this sort of roadmap where—this is what they did in order to be successful or to be happy, right? Because for so long, I was treated as my parents' son. To use the father-son thing as an example, a father gets to where they did by acting like a man, and making decisions that fall in line with being a man and doing man stuff.

There's this sort of assumption that because there's someone who is born like them, they perceive it as, "Alright, my kids should be doing things similar to what I did because I was able to get to the point I am in life doing that, and to be successful. So if they want to be successful, they also should follow this."

And there's almost this social contract that follows that. Boys grow up to be men, and girls grow up to be women. This is how it works, because that's how it's always worked. That is how people have grown up to lead fulfilling lives, so that's what we should encourage. Which means discouraging things that don't fit that paradigm.

James: Yeah. It's kind of, "Damn it, this is how it's always been done. Don't deviate from the script."

Emma: [Laughs] Exactly. "The plan is good, we're sticking to the plan, don't mess up the plan."

James: So through this process of growing up, how did the other members of your family react?

Emma: I worked hard to cover it up. I was a sneaky kid. My biological father was under the assumption I never had a drink until my 21st birthday. When I had my birthday, he made me drink with him and all that. He was like, "Alright, I'm glad we can have a beer as men," or whatever, despite the fact that I had been drinking for almost a decade at that point.

This is kind of a trans trope. But whenever nobody else was home, or when it was late at night, I would take clothes out of the hamper and do what I thought was cross-dressing. I would make myself feel better that way, but I never talked to any of my family members about it, other than watching shows that might have been more in line with femininity.

James: What about outside of your family? Did you have any people that you confided in?

Emma: It was basically all to myself. The first person I ever came out to was in 2014. It was my best friend, Jake. We've played on teams together on a few Opens, and we've been roommates for a long time. He's probably the best person in my life, and that's a lot of why he was the first person I ever came out to.

But before that, I think the closest I ever came to telling anybody was...I told an old roommate of mine that I was not exclusively a heterosexual man. And he was like, "Oh, so you're bisexual?" And I said, "Yeah, yeah." And then I chickened out and didn't tell him.

James: I can't even begin to imagine what it's like to live twenty-plus years of your life without being able to tell people how you really feel. How inhibiting, or restrictive, or painful that must be. I'm not trying to trivialize things—

Emma: You're not trivializing things at all.

James: —that must have been incredibly difficult. I don't even know how you begin to deal with that.

Emma: You fabricate a personality. I mean, not everyone does. But the way that I handled it was—I did whatever I thought that I was supposed to do. I got beat up when I was a kid and was conditioned to think that I had to learn how to exhibit behavior that I would be rewarded for. Does that make sense? I know that's an oddly specific way to phrase things.

James: Yeah. I mean, you don't want to get physically harmed, right? Or even emotionally abused. So you want to have pain avoidance. That's pretty understandable for any human being.

Emma: Exactly. And a lot of it is, "Alright, so girl stuff is bad, and I should not do that." But I didn't exactly learn what guy stuff was, so a lot of it was me feeling out what I was supposed to be doing. I was almost exclusively into men, sexually, until I was a sophomore in high school. That led to me dating girls because I thought I was supposed to do it.

My first girlfriend, for example, was someone I wanted to be friends with. I felt close with her and felt an emotional connection, but not in a romantic way. But because she was one of the few girls in our friend group...you know how high school is. A lot of times they assume you're going to date someone in the friend group because you are close.

I ended up feeling pressure from a lot of my guy friends to end up trying to be in a relationship with her. That ended up tainting and defining the rest of the time that we were close together.

And then I dated someone else because I found out they liked me. I thought, "Well, I guess that's how things work. If a girl likes you, you're supposed to ask her out because you might get to touch her tit or something."

James: When you were in these relationships early on in your life, did the other person understand what was going on?

Emma: I didn't disclose things with any of these people pertaining to my gender, or anything. The first girl was someone who...we ended up breaking up after a week because I wasn't affectionate. We didn't kiss. I didn't hold her hand. We hugged, but that was about it. And she said, "It doesn't really feel like you're trying to be my boyfriend." And I couldn't tell her that it was true.

And then the second partner, after we made out a bunch for a couple of months, we ended up breaking up on Christmas that year. And she said, "I feel like you're much closer with this girl you used to date than with me." No matter what I did, I couldn't convince her that it wasn't me just trying to be friends with this other girl. Because I wasn't really into the relationships in the first place, it was a pretty tough sell, right?

James: You are now very open and public about being queer and being trans. What was the turning point for you? There must have been some events that helped catalyze it, right?

Emma: Absolutely. I'm trying to think of the best way to describe this. Around 2013, my partner at the time went out of town for a long time. She got an internship with Disney, and I couldn't afford to move to Orlando with her. As a result I ended up having a bunch of alone time, and had time to learn about what trans people were.

It involved surfing the Internet. I saw Caitlyn Jenner in the tabloids and started to think, "Wow, that's very similar to how I feel—that's kind of eerie." Before that, I didn't really have a word for trans people. It was just those confused men who wanted breast implants, or those faggots trying to be women. Or those gay guys who are so desperate for a man, they're willing to be a woman. It wasn't a respected identity—it was something very derogatory. Those weren't "real people," it was "that weirdo." I don't know if that makes a whole lot of sense.

But the Caitlyn Jenner thing started to happen and then I learned about Laverne Cox on *Orange is the New Black*. And she was on the cover of a big magazine. I think it was Vogue. It was a big deal that a trans woman was on the front cover of that magazine. And Feline Longmore was starting to break out on the SCG Tour at the time, the Open Series, playing her High-Tide deck, and she got an article written about her on a gaming website. Trans people were starting to show up and be known by people.

A lot of the things I associated myself with came from gender dysphoria, and I was afraid that people would find out. It was something I'd worked to keep under wraps for a very long time. The southeast is not very kind to trans people. I thought that if people found out, my life as I knew it would be over. All this work I had put in—to making this identity of who I used to be—would all be for nothing.

And I started having a lot of panic attacks in public, at home, or anywhere imaginable. And the attacks got pretty bad. The Khans of Tarkir pre-release came around, and through a confluence of wild events—the only other employee in the store had to go to a different city to take an exam that determined if he could graduate from college, and the owner had to go to the hospital—I ended up having to work the entire Khans pre-release by myself.

That meant opening up the store at 11 a.m. on Friday, and closing it at about 5:30 a.m. Saturday morning. Then I would come back and open on Saturday morning at 11 a.m, close at Sunday morning at 4 a.m. Open once more at noon on the Sunday, and then closing at 2 a.m. Monday morning. It was a pretty absurd amount of hours to be working with no other support.

And I'm having a hard time keeping it together. I'm pretty exhausted at this point and my panic attacks are really bad. After everything wrapped up on Saturday, I ended up taking a gun home. I decided that I was done, and I was going to try and kill myself.

I decided that it was going to be an easier out than trying to be openly trans. I didn't want to deal with things anymore. It didn't feel like I had anybody I could be honest with, or talk about it with. Without any kind of solution, I figured the way I was living wasn't the way to live—but the alternative wasn't the way to live, either.

And I failed at killing myself.

James: Sounds like it was a close call.

Emma: Yeah. We'll say there was a mechanical malfunction. I don't really want to get into the full details of it, any more than I already have. But I ended up being mad at—at the time, I was depressed because I thought, "I can't even kill myself. How can I be this bad?" But I basically cried myself to sleep. My alarm goes off the next day, and I was like, "Well, if I'm not going to be dead, I might as well go back to work." And I went back, I finished my shift, and a couple of weeks later, I still hadn't come out to anybody, but I got very drunk and was genuinely considering killing myself again, or at least trying again. But instead of that, on a limb, I texted Jake, who I mentioned before. I said, "Hey, I'm drunk right now, but tomorrow, I need you to make me tell you something. It's very important, I can't tell you right now, but you'll know what I'm talking about when I tell you the truth." And the next day, when I was sober, I told him.

James: And what was his reaction?

Emma: We had a wedding that we were going to that day, actually. It was our friends Josh and Sharla. We were driving to get clothes for the wedding, and I tell him, and he just goes, "Okay." My heart is in my throat, I'm tearing up, I don't know what okay means. And I say, "Okay?" And he goes, "I need some time to chew on that." And at the time I was like, "All right, that's fair." So I told him he was the only person I'd told, and that was kind of the end of that specific conversation.

But later that night, at the reception, there was an open bar full of beer and he goes, "I'm tired of this beer, it's filling me up and I'm not getting drunk enough." I was like, "All right, cool. Let's get a couple of Jack and Cokes." He agrees. We go to the bar and I order a couple of Jack and Cokes, he moves me out of the way, buys them, and I was just—at the time, we alternated buying drinks and it was my turn, and I go, "What the fuck, man? It was my turn to buy drinks." And he looks at me and says, "Well, if my best friend is going to be a girl, I'm going to be the first one to buy her a drink." And takes a sip at his and winks at me. That was kind of the, "Things are going to be okay [moment]," I guess.

James: Yeah.

Emma: But that was the single happiest moment of my entire life.

James: Right, because you were probably scared of how he might react, right?

Emma: Yeah. We ended up going out to my car when the reception was over, and just sitting in my car and talking about it while sobering up, for two, three hours. I don't think we ended up getting home until almost 6 a.m. But it was—even just telling someone, even when I wasn't sure if I was going to transition or anything, was such an enormous weight off my shoulders.

James: I assume that this diffused you wanting to end your life because you felt like maybe there was some light at the end of the tunnel. But what happens after that? What did you do over the next little while?

Emma: Two things in that statement, one at a time. One, starting to transition has not completely fixed everything as far as the issues I have, combatting suicidal ideation. I have not had a real issue in a couple of years now, but there were a couple of times where I felt like I would never be a real woman, I would just be some scarred-up confused freak, all these things that are self-doubt creeping in, right? But for the most part, things have gotten much better for the reason you said. It's easier to see a light at the end of the tunnel when I can see my progress and see the direction I'm going.

But to go with the second part of what you asked, the actual timeline from there, that was October 12th, 2014, that I started transitioning. It was the first time I shaved my legs, started seriously looking at women's clothing, thinking about names I was going to pick out. Then I started hormones the following March, that was through Planned Parenthood, who is by far the best trans healthcare provider in North Carolina. I cannot say enough good things about them, they are fantastic. Then I went full-time presenting as female, only going by Emma that following July. My trans-niversary was just a few days ago, actually. I think it was the 26th. Yeah, July the 26th of 2015 is the first day I started going by Emma all the time.

James: That's awesome. It's obviously an ongoing process. The last couple of years, did you have a good support network, friends or family, to guide you through this?

Emma: My support network is absolutely fantastic. I only lost, other than my dad's side of the family, I only lost a couple of people, friends-wise, so to speak. Most of the people in my life stayed in my life. Almost every time I would talk to someone I would go, "Hey, I need to talk to you about something in private." And as anxiety-prone this generation is, almost all of them—after I told them—would breathe or sigh of relief. They were like, "Oh my god, I thought you were mad at me or something." They were so relieved that they hadn't fucked up, and they were just, "Oh, but yeah, yeah, that's totally cool. Is there something you'd like to be called?" Something to that effect. They might have some questions, but for the most part, everyone was incredibly receptive. Jake's girlfriend at the time, and one of my better friends, Chloe, she gave me some—what we called "girl lessons." Just teaching me to paint nails, and we would do traditionally early 20s women hanging out, like eating ice cream and watching *Kitchen Nightmares*, and drinking wine or whatever. It's a little thing, but it was so nice at the time, that it was important for me, developmentally.

James: I know there may be people listening to this who may also be dealing with issues of self-identity. Is there anything you would tell yourself if you could talk to the Emma from five, six years ago?

Emma: That's tough. I wish I had been able to convince myself to try to transition earlier in adulthood. But I don't think I could have done it as a child. I don't think there's anything teenage me could have done to get a traditionally female childhood. Obviously, my biological father is not on board with having his eldest kid be a daughter. My mother was a little slow to come around. At first, she was resistant to things, but then she saw me as Emma a few times, and saw that I was happier, I treated people better, I was better in a lot of ways. Seeing is believing, right? And she was like, "Wow, this really improved my kid's life, maybe there's something to all of this." And she went through a lot of work to try to understand things. She read a bunch, and found an online support group, and that really helped her understand things. But I don't think it would have been possible for 14-year-old Emma to exist. But I do think it would have been possible for 19 or 20-year-old Emma to exist. So I wish I could tell myself, "Hey, you're living on your own, you're the only one paying your own bills. If this is what's going to make you happy, you should just do it."

James: Yeah, I think that's the difference between being a child and an adult. To expect someone to figure all of it out at a young age, it seems to me like the odds would be stacked against you. You're making such a fundamental change to who you are.

Emma: Yeah, exactly. And the permanence of that is kind of—even that is a little iffy, right? A lot of things that you see trans teenagers doing is being put on puberty blockers instead of anything that causes their body to change in a permanent way. Instead, it kind of goes, all right, so 14-year-old kid who was assigned male at birth wants to present as female, let's give them these drugs that will make it so they don't necessarily grow as tall and they don't grow a beard. But also, their hips don't expand in the same way and they don't develop breast tissue. So it gives them time to figure themselves out. And the effects of that have been shown to be mostly reversible. It's kind of hard to say everything is completely reversible because you're not going to know what anyone would have looked like if they had started puberty a couple of years earlier.

James: Maybe another way for me to ask the question is— how would you give advice to people who are going through something like that in their teenage years, or in their early 20s?

Emma: The best thing I can offer is to try and become self-sustaining, financially speaking. It basically puts you in a position of power, where you have control over your own life. I've been lucky in my life, right? There are a lot of ways—I think you could make the argument that being trans is kind of a life-long role, where it would be much easier not to be trans. But financially, I've been dealt a reasonable hand. I've never been wealthy in my life, but I have had fortune smile upon me, and I've had jobs that can support me living on my own. And if it is possible for anyone who is thinking about transitioning and isn't sure if it's possible, the best advice I can give is to try to reach a spot where you are relying on yourself for bills. Because then you're in a spot where there's nobody who can hold anything over your head based on the decisions you make. Your parents can't go, "I'm going to kick you out," if you're under your own roof. Your parents can't take your car away if you own your car. And so on.

There's a sort of freedom that comes there, as well as a freedom to experiment, privacy, and all kinds of things that make it easier to figure yourself out, and be your truest self.

James: Emma, are there any drawbacks at all, from your personal experience, with regards to transitioning?

Emma: That one is tough. Yes. The short answer is yes. It's generally a cost-benefit analysis, where there are certain things that become a lot harder. It's pretty frustrating sometimes when-- if you see me in person, I think if you look, you can tell that I was not assigned female at birth. And you'll get people in positions of power that treat you poorly for it. You go to a store, and a cashier is crummy to you because they think you're weird. Or you go to the DMV and the DMV person doesn't really want to go out of their way to help you change your name, so they find a reason for there to be red tape that you have to wade through.

James: People can be vicious.

Emma: Yeah. And I've also hit spots where I've been kicked out of gas stations because they don't take too kindly to ladies with stubble. That was a few years ago. And I've been forced out of bathrooms. I've not been able to go to the bathroom because I was not assigned female at birth, so I can't use the women's room. But I'm not a guy, so I can't use the men's room. So I just kind of had to hold it. There's a lot of crappy situations that can arise, and that's on top of the rejection that can come from transitioning, either from friends or family. A lot of people don't understand it, and a lot of people don't want to put in the work to understand it. It can be really hard in that way.

James: I have a lot of respect for people who are trans because I can relate to the kind of stigma and societal reaction that comes with it. I know it's not easy. I always think to myself—for someone to go through that incredible step, it must mean that they truly believe in it. And who am I to discourage them, or not encourage them to be who they are? It's so easy to be invisible and present yourself as male in your situation. The alternative is far easier, and in life, we always want to do things—again, subconsciously or consciously—that are easy for ourselves.

Emma: Yeah, absolutely, and I appreciate the indirect kind words there. But in a lot of ways, it's worth it. There are things I would not have ever been able to achieve had I not transitioned. Outside of happiness, there's a lot of things where-- we haven't even gotten that far into how dysphoria tends to work, or how feeling wrong about your body can work. Or the flip side of that, how feeling right about your body can work. And then to use myself as an example, pre-transition, I had no desire to have kids. I just did not want them. It sounds awful, but I absolutely did not want kids. But since transitioning, I want nothing more in life than to be a mom, and that sounds great. I had no desire to be a dad, but I want to be a mom more than I want literally anything in the world. And that would not have been possible without transitioning.

James: Sounds like it's brought a lot of good into your life and who you fundamentally are as a person. How do you feel now?

Emma: Some days are harder than others. I feel really gross about myself, or I don't feel great about how I fit into the world every single day. Not just in a, "I don't feel like getting out of bed" kind of way, but in the self-doubt and things I was referencing before. Or feeling like I'm wasting my time, that I'm not going to reach my goals—that's the depression talking. But in a lot of ways, completely being full of myself here, I'm a pretty big Emma Handy fan. I've worked pretty hard to get to where I am today, and a lot of the decisions I've made have been on the back of, all right, where do I want to end up? What is something I would be proud of doing? What is a decision I'm not going to regret later? Because honestly, a lot of my decisions are rooted in regret. There are lots of things in my life that I wish could have gone differently, or I could have done differently. So I would say, overall, I'm pretty fucking proud of where I am today. I don't know if I would say I love myself, but I *think* I love myself.

James: We all have to be our own biggest fans, because who else is going to be our own biggest fan, right?

Emma: Yeah, exactly.

James: I can relate to a lot of what you said because I think it doesn't matter who you are, if you're a human being, you're going to go through periods of self-doubt, and "what am I doing?" Whether it's a career choice or something much more major than that, there is always that questioning of the self, you know?

Emma: Yes, absolutely.

James: If I may switch gears a little bit, can you talk about how you got into the public spotlight with Magic?

214

Because you talked about Feline Longmore and people who identify as trans and make their mark on Magic. How did you start making inroads with Star City and being more and more visible in the community?

Emma: I've been traveling to Magic tournaments since New Phyrexia. The first open I went to was either the first or the second open where Splinter Twin was legal. Or Deceiver Exarch was legal. I've known a lot of people who have worked for Star City Games for a long time. A lot of those people came up from an area close to mine. It was easier for me to go to these Grand Prix because I knew people. Which led to me continuing to go after I transitioned.

There were a couple of positive interactions that came at Opens after I transitioned that made me feel safer at Opens than I did at Grand Prix. Grand Prix, for example, for a while were crappy about only sending checks in the name that appeared on your DCI card, which meant that I had to put my deadname on my DCI card because it was incredibly expensive to legally change my name in North Carolina. I couldn't afford it yet. And that was stressful, whereas Star City Games would let you separate your DCI information and your tax information.

Then there was also an event where my purse that I left on the table got stolen or turned in at the front somehow, I don't know. I don't know how it got from A to B, but it ended up in the hands of Kali Anderson, who I did not know at the time. And over the loudspeaker, she called out, "We have the purse of Emma Handy, please come to the booth." And everything in my purse was under my deadname.

My prescriptions, my ID, my bank card, all of that. But she looked in the software and saw the only person with Handy on their name was Emma, and there was makeup in the purse, and it was a purse. Her putting in that extra effort not to shout my deadname over the loudspeaker or anything made me more comfortable at Opens.

From there, I crushed IQs and PPTQs for a while. There was a season in PPTQs where I scooped-- it was either six or seven finals in the same season, because I wanted the money more than I wanted the RPTQ invite. And also, my boyfriend and I, we were on ecstasy.

James: [Laughs] Okay, it's a thing, yeah.

Emma: [Laughs] Yeah. And we were just cuddling, talking about things, and his eyes get so big and he goes, "I don't know why you don't try to actually make it in Magic." And I was like, "What are you talking about?" And he stops, looks at me and goes, "Are you kidding? You are so good at Magic." And he brought up three instances from PPTQs from the last few weeks where he was like, "There is no one else in 100 miles that would have won the game when you came back from blah, blah, blah. And then you destroyed this combat step with your stupid Butcher of the Horde deck. But you're handicapping your-self because you like this deck. What if you just play the best deck and go to the tournaments that mat-ter?" And he and I had been rivals for a long time, and I perceived him as better than me. So for him to go that far out of his way and— obviously, the drugs made it a little easier to do that.

James: [Laughs] Yeah, for sure.

Emma: [Laughs] For him to go that far out of his way and say all of that... you don't forget about that. And the next season on the SCG Tour, it was season one of 2016, and there were only two Opens that were more than eight hours away. I decided, you know what? *Fuck it.* Fuck it, I can probably afford to go to these as long as I cash every other one or something. And I'm just going to do it. I started writing articles on a blog called cardconfidants.com. They're little 500 to 1,000-word things, a couple of them were pretty good, but for the most part they were just me rambling in a Word document. I started going to these Opens. I did well with the Rally the Ancestors deck, the weekend that Reflector Mage came out, and I was the best finishing Rally player in the tournament. I didn't top eight on tiebreakers. And that was demoralizing, but I was happy to do well. And that got me some attention and a guest article on Star City Games, writing about the Rally the Ancestors deck, which got me a bunch of attention on my Twitter. I got a few hundred followers from that, when I only had probably fifty at the time. Then an article a few weeks later, I did the— are you familiar with Sam Stoddard's "Fearless Magical Inventory" article?[11]

James: Yes. One of the best Magic articles ever written, in my opinion.

Emma: Absolutely. I completely agree. I agree so much that I wrote one for myself and talked about his article, and that got picked up by Erin Campbell, who is also a fairly prominent transwoman in the Magic

---

[11] http://www.starcitygames.com/magic/misc/15107_Feature_Article_
Creating_a_Fearless_Magical_Inventory.html

community. And she passed it over to Evan Erwin, who was the content coordinator at Gathering Magic, which got me a writing gig at Gathering Magic. I started writing for them, I was still going to SCG events and did well enough that I started getting featured in Magic pretty consistently, people knew who I was, I was starting to get in the "crowd." And by the end of the year, I hadn't— I wouldn't say I submitted myself as a known person, but I at least was a blip on the radar, so to speak.

And in 2017, I went to a few Grand Prix and had, at best, an 11-4 record, and never quite broke through. But I did well enough with oddball decks like the Blue-Red Prowess, or Blue-Red Delver deck with Thunderous Wrath, to get that put on the map, which got me some attention. And I ended up getting invited to the LoadingReadyRun pre-release, and started streaming full-time and offering Magic coaching, because I had a few people who would pay me for what were effectively Magic lessons. And I liked doing that more than I liked waiting tables, which I had been doing part-time at the time. And decided to take the full leap into Magic.

James: Wow. There's a lot there.

Emma: Yeah, it was a long saga, but I figured I'd get the whole thing out.

James: First of all, I felt this sort of joy when you talked about how the Star City Games employee announced the name that you prefer to be called by over the loudspeaker. All this stuff may not have happened were not for the initial welcome, warmth, or acceptance that you felt in the Star City Games events, right?

Emma: Absolutely. Kali Anderson—she is—oh my God, she is one of the best people I know. I cannot say enough nice things about her. And in a lot of ways, I feel like I directly and indirectly owe her a fair amount. She's just—I don't know if she'll ever realize the impact she's had on my life. She's easily my favorite person in Roanoke. One of the people who indirectly convinced me to move here. I got some strong feelings for that woman.

James: And then the other thing I picked up on is really-- you crushed. You were living the full grinder life-style, and you were killing it. You were doing so well that people had to notice you.

Emma: For whatever it's worth, I don't think I was necessarily crushing it, in terms of Magic results. I have only top-eighted one Open my life. I've top-sixteened a bunch, and I've come in ninth in two of them. But I am very good-- I would say I am one of the most consistent players on the SCG tour. Almost any tournament I enter, I will do something between 9-6, and 11-4 [in terms of an overall win-loss record]. I'm good for [winning] 66% of my matches in every tournament I enter. And that did enough to get me on the leaderboard and cash events, so I can keep coming to events, and still get feature matches because you don't get to [a] 10-5 [record] without at least making a semi-deep run. But I would not describe what I did in tournaments as crushing it. I think my theory is very good, and I'm very good in writing about the decisions I make, and I'm very good at talking the talk. But I do not necessarily think I'm the best tournament player.

James: As you said, we can't all surpass Jon Finkel. You found your way to be consistent within this framework, and I think that's admirable.

Emma: Thank you. I do think it's important to note-- my goal in Magic is to end up in coverage. So it is more important to me to be able to talk the talk and play a lot of different decks in order to know how they all work, intimately, than it is for me to have the most Open trophies.

James: You told me that you are less of a grinder and you're a self-described mail buyer for SCG. Was there something that led you to go to tournaments less frequently, and have more of a consistent job in that area?

Emma: Yeah, sure. It's not a secret that I am vocal about social issues. Particularly ones in the Magic community. There were a few things towards the end of 2017 that happened. One where Christine Sprankle quit over harassment that she received from a Magic YouTuber. And I was pretty vocal about speaking up against the YouTuber. And I got a lot of hate, as a result. I got messages in my inbox threatening me, I got harassment, I got called every name in the book, I learned slurs that I didn't know were slurs, and that was pretty rough. I got some death threats around an event where-- they were serious enough for security to be raised at the event. But I figured, you know, this will die down. Especially with anxiety issues, and things like that I deal with, it was rough, but it's not hard to assume that there is a light at the end of the tunnel, right? This can't go on forever. But then, there was another thing where there was a "Women in Magic" draft in a private Facebook group.

James: Oh man, yeah. I heard about that.

Emma: It was private, but this private Facebook group had over 3,000 people. And I was able to get in within a minute of finding out the group existed.

James: That doesn't sound very private.

Emma: That's kind of where I'm at. The Facebook setting is called private, but really? I found the draft, and it was basically nine women in Magic and a bunch of people in the comments, pack one, pick one... based on their fuckability. There are a bunch of shitty things in the comments about the women themselves, there was one who was a trans person in the community...[who] got called an "it" a bunch in the comments. There were other women who weren't in the picture that ended up getting brought up in the comments and dragged a bunch, myself included. And I kind of posted it on Twitter. I took screen caps of the entire thread and all the pictures, I reached out to the women in the picture first and said, "Hey, I found this, and it's pretty fucked up, and I want to post this publicly. Are you comfortable with me posting this? Because it has some raunchy stuff about you in it." It included-- it doesn't matter what it included, I don't want to bring that kind of attention to the people.

But I posted, and it exploded. It absolutely exploded, and it ended up getting about a half dozen people, some three-month bans, and I think it was a year-long ban, 18-month ban for Travis Woo, because he was the moderator of the group, and there was evidence that someone had tried to bring to his attention the existence of the thread and he basically said, "Yeah, I'm busy, I'll deal with it later," and then just didn't.

After that happened, the harassment got a lot worse, because I was the original poster of the thing on Twitter, got 100 retweets, and I was at the point where I was getting 10 to 12 messages a day. I think the worst I ever got was, "I'm going to chop your cock off and choke you with it." That's like, as graphic as it got. Well, that's as graphic as the words got. There was one where one guy was like, "Oh, did you turn into a girl because you have a little wiener like me?" And then sent me a picture of a small penis. There came a point where I had two options. I could either lock my messages, or I could take a step back from Magic. Or at least from Magic in the capacity that I was participating in. That being coaching and grinding full-time, and because of coaching, I had to be accessible publicly. So I couldn't turn off my DMs and not get out of Magic, because then I wouldn't be able to communicate with clients, or new clients.

And a job opened up at Star City Games that I was interested in, and because of my background in Yu-Gi-Oh I felt like I was a natural fit for. It was buying cards that people sent in through the mail. We have a buy list where you can put in all the cards you're selling us, their conditions, their languages, whether they're foil or not, et cetera. You sort them, you send the package to us, we verify that the cards are correct, we make any changes as necessary. Like if you send us played cards and list them as near mint, we'll downgrade them and adjust the prices accordingly, send you an email to make sure the price is okay, and then we give you your money.

And that is the job I have now. But it's been absolutely fantastic, just having a normal job where I'm not required-- if I need to take a break from social media, I can close the Twitter app, and I won't get on Twitter for the rest of the day.

James: It saddens me to hear about the abuse because I don't think many of us who started playing Magic were the cool kids in school. To me, it feels a little bit like—to use a generalization—the nerds turning on the nerds. Now this tough macho bullshit is coming out, and you're getting death threats. And these are people who are probably not the coolest kids in their school, either, so I'm just really saddened to hear all this stuff. That's all I can say.

Emma: Yeah, I don't know. I have a theory where a lot of the people who act that way might not have been ostracized for being nerds, and that was just something they clung to. And when we see things like that draft thing exposed, that they thought was entertaining previously, they're faced with this truth, right? They see all these other nerds saying, "Wow, this is shitty," and this is punishable, right? So that forces players with the reality that maybe they weren't popular in high school because they were assholes. And no one wants to be told they're an asshole.

James: Yeah, I mean, nobody is going to look in the mirror and be like, "Yeah, I need to change something about myself." It's always the other person's fault, right? That's kind of how the world is, unfortunately.

Emma: Exactly, and we're all guilty of it. I've been guilty of it. And am still guilty of it sometimes. But I think that a lot of the people who are lashing out were upset at the fact that they were being told that something that was entertaining to them is wrong, and they don't want it to be wrong.

James: Again, it doesn't fit their script of how life should be, right?

Emma: It just sucks, in a lot of ways, it feels like there are a lot of extra hoops that women and non-binary people end up having to jump through to play Magic because of a vocal minority.

James: Is there any possibility, you think, of going back and competing? Or do you think that period of your life is in the past and you want to work on doing commentary, coverage, or something else now?

Emma: I don't know. I think that I need to do more in Magic to end up being a shoo-in for a coverage position. I don't know if that makes sense, but I have demonstrated that I can talk in front of a camera, and I've demonstrated that I can be marketable, and that I am charismatic, right? I've said it a dozen times already, that I'm not where I am today because of my results. It's literally because of myself as a personality and as an entertainer. But to be great at commentary you need to be good at Magic, right? I still need to demonstrate that I have the knowledge to talk about high-level Magic.

James: Have you thought about the steps that you're going to take to get there?

Emma: I'm taking Magic tournaments more seriously than I used to, in that I'm trying to stick to decks that are the best deck for the tournament, rather than decks that are the best for me to learn with. I'm focusing a bit less on learning and a little bit more on my tournament results. And even if I don't get to coverage ever, I'll be fine. That's not my biggest goal in life. I care a lot more about other things. The parenting thing I mentioned before is a much higher priority, and it's not conducive with the traveling Magic lifestyle. Today, I still go to one or two tournaments a month. Here is me being a shill for myself, but I have a Patreon for people who are fans and want to help me succeed if they have a couple of extra bucks to throw my way to make it easier for me to still go to events, because now that I have a 9-to-5 job, I have to fly more than I can drive, so it's more expensive for me to go to these tournaments. I'm not able to step up to the plate as frequently, so I'm trying to make my swings count more.

James: It sounds like you accept your current situation and you're trying to maximize the opportunities you get.

Emma: Exactly. I don't know. I'm not sweating it, I'm just trying to enjoy a time in my life where I'm fairly comfortable. There's a difference between problems and "real problems." And other than some trans related stuff, my list of "real problems" is pretty close to non-existent.

"Success to me is understanding my limitations, trying to overcome some of them, and trying to set small goals for myself. I want to experience as many interesting, unique, fun things as I want to go for.

—Bob Huang

CHAPTER 7

BOB HUANG

Bob's reputation precedes him. He's a hugely talented Magic player and has been known for notable innovations in the Modern and Legacy formats. Although he's been playing the game for a long time, Bob first gained notoriety in 2013 with a top sixteen finish in Grand Prix Washington DC. Since then, he's continued to brew and play all kinds of different decks.

Bob's measured takes about Magic cards and strategy typically turn out to be right. He is the man who almost broke the Legacy format on multiple occasions due to his keen eye for what works, and refining the best ideas into strong decks.

Bob is a regular contributor to the Channel Fireball website and a regular co-host of the *Everyday Eternal* podcast. He writes about Magic strategy and conducts analysis of tournament data that is awe-inspiring in terms of its attention to detail. Bob is deeply analytical, both in his approach to life as well as Magic.

I picked an interesting point in Bob's life to conduct an interview. He had just taken a long sabbatical from work to backpack around the world. Now that he was back in the United States, and resuming his "normal life," I was intrigued. I wanted to talk to Bob about more than just Magic.

Bob and I ended up having a very honest conversation. I learned about his Magic origin story, but also about his mindset and where he was going in his life.

As a Magic player of Asian heritage, I could also relate to some of the difficulties he had in pursuing non-traditional career paths that deviated from the expectations of his parents. As Asian kids growing up in North America with immigrant parents, there was an experience there that we collectively shared.

There's definitely a lot more to people than meets the eye, and Bob fits that description.

Recorded in October 2016.

James: You just got back from a big trip. How's life been?

Bob: Pretty great. I was backpacking in Southeast Asia for about two and a half months. That was from June through early September. I just got back—kind of getting back into the swing of things, which has been a little bit of a transition.

James: I saw that you recently resumed writing articles for Channel Fireball. Is that something that you're looking to do more regularly?

Bob: Yeah, I took a big hiatus. I don't even know how long it's been since I wrote an article—it's been a while. I always felt if I had something interesting to write about, and could deliver, or teach my readers something, then I'd go for it.

I've always felt that there are some writers out there, who, well it's not their fault that they have to write every week. But if you do have to write a weekly article, sometimes you need to stretch it out and find things that might not be as interesting. I enjoy that I get the freedom to write when I want, and I also think the Legacy community has been lacking in good content for a little bit.

James: You mentioned that it used to be better in terms of Legacy writing. There's more content out there, but it also feels like the quality perhaps isn't as good as in the past. Why do you think that is?

Bob: A couple of different things. One point is that I don't think Legacy is necessarily less popular. The peak might have been Grand Prix New Jersey, where there were over 4,000 people and was still featured as the second format on the Star City circuit. I think in many parts of the world—Europe most prominently, and also Japan now—Legacy is super popular.

          But I do think the coverage has shifted. Most notably, Star City has shifted to Modern. In my view at least, Modern is the most popular format. I would say it's even more popular than Standard. People I talk to are always super excited about Modern, so I think it has usurped Legacy's throne in terms of the most popular constructed format.

James: I know you play Modern and Legacy, but you have played just about all the formats. Is that still the case?

Bob: There was a period where I was like, "Alright, let's go deep. Let's play all the formats, get on the Pro Tour circuit, and see how I can do." I've since scaled back and now I'm only playing Legacy. I haven't touched Modern in about five months.

James: Having said that, half of that time you were travelling. It's hard to play Magic while backpacking.

Bob: Yeah, and that was on purpose. I needed a little break from Magic. I wasn't playing much before I left, but I was still thinking about it a lot. I needed a little bit of a break.

James: We'll get back to the trip you took because I think that's fascinating. Let's start from the beginning. Tell me a little bit about your background, where you grew up, and how you started playing Magic.

Bob: I was born in China, but moved to the United States at a young age. Family has always been a heavy influence for me. My grandparents lived with me when I was young. We moved around a lot, but since age eight I've been living in the Boston area, which is where my Magic career started. It was elementary school in fifth grade. I had a best friend at the time. We got to know each other—I don't even remember how, but somehow we talked about the video game Myst.

It was an interesting puzzle game and we were both super into it as fifth graders. Then my friend is like, "Oh, I play this other game that's really interesting. It's called Magic." So my friend Clint taught me how to play and it was a super fun game. I loved buying booster packs, and I was competitive, even at a young age.

I would say even in elementary school and junior high, I started going online, reading forums, and finding deck lists. All my friends would come with these casual decks, and I would look stuff up. "Looks like this Goblin deck is really good. I'll build it." So I would build it, just without the money rares. My friends would get destroyed. Ever since I was young, I've always been a person to do research to try to get an edge.

James: Why do you think that is?

Bob: I guess that's part of who I was. I have a younger sister, but she definitely doesn't play Magic. It's some part of me that enjoys competing, and that's one reason I got into the competitive scene as well. All through my life, I was the classic type-A Asian student. Studied hard, got good grades. Then once I hit a certain point where I needed more than beyond just doing well in school. I wanted to do well in Magic, and competing was the next logical extension for me.

James: What was it like growing up with your friends in the Boston area?

Bob: I grew up in a town called Acton, a suburb of Boston. It was the prototypical New England suburb—very sheltered. I grew up very privileged, and from that comes a lot of good and bad. Acton has been in the news lately due to some suicides. In many ways, it is a high-pressure environment where success is seen as getting in an Ivy League college.

It taught you how to work hard, which I value. But it also put some undue pressure on a lot of people living in that community. With my type-A Asian upbringing, my dad was also hard on me. It definitely shaped who I am as a person, but I don't know if it necessarily shaped who I am as a Magic player.

James: Did you have that pressure, growing up, to get into a good college and all that stuff?

Bob: Yeah, and I did do all that. I went to Dartmouth, which is a wonderful school. I attended the same school as Jarvis Yu, actually. So I did do all that, but now that I'm more "free," I've come more to terms with myself. I realized that what I need isn't necessarily that, and I've been happy in the past year or two of my life. I saw through some of the pitfalls that I used to fall into.

James: When did you first move into competitive play and the actual tournaments?

Bob: I first got my DCI number when I was studying abroad in Paris with other Dartmouth students. I didn't get to meet that many locals, but I really wanted to do so. When I first got my DCI number, I didn't know what I was doing. I had read some articles before and built some decks, but I never went to tournaments to compete.

When I first started out, I had no expectations of trying to win. I was like, "I'm going to get a DCI number, meet some French people, and play this thing I really used to enjoy." The more you get into it, the more you want to get good at it. Not great results by any stretch, but it made me want to play more.

At that time, I was playing a little bit of Standard, but I also played Legacy. I got to play my sweet Affinity deck, which I grew up playing against my friends back in junior high. It was cool being able to use those cards again in Legacy. I was performing decently with it, and as you win, that addictive feel of winning snowballs, and I got into it more and more.

James: What year was this that you got your DCI number and started playing in tournaments?

Bob: It was 2011.

James: It wasn't really that long ago.

Bob: My first booster pack was back in elementary school. I think it was Odyssey. It wasn't until Mirrodin Besieged that I got my DCI number. However, I did play semi-competitively before 2011. There was an online league.

It was super cool. It was called Magic League, and I know a lot of good players from there. I think Jarvis [Yu] used to play there. I know Paulo Vitor Damo Da Rosa used to play there as well. I used to play against them when I was a little kid, they were probably just teenagers. It's kind of crazy.

James: You're playing tournaments in Paris, you get to know some of the locals, and then you head back to the United States. Can you tell me about the American scene when you got back home?

Bob: Paris was my sophomore year of college. When I went back to the States, I put Magic on hold. I did pick it up again in my senior year when I graduated early, but for the most part I put it down. I didn't have that many friends at school who played. At the time, I also saw it as a nerdy thing to do. I wouldn't go out of my way to hide it from people, but I wasn't trying to—

James: Not going out of your way to tell people you played.

Bob: Exactly. I mostly put it down. It wasn't until I graduated from Dartmouth that I moved to Northern Virginia ["Nova"]. Dan Signorini lived there, so I reached out to him on The Source. He was like, "Yeah, we play at this store called Curio Cavern." That's where it really got started for me.

James: Is that when you got into Legacy? Dan's a pretty hardcore Legacy player.

Bob: Well, before that, I did have some decent results when I was playing in Paris. I studied abroad there, and then I interned in London. I was playing a little bit of Magic there and had some pretty good results playing Legacy.

That was when I decided I wanted to focus primarily on Legacy because it was the coolest format. I enjoy playing with the older cards. So, getting to meet Dan and going to Curio that first time, I think there were thirty-seven people. I was like, "Wow! This is awesome!" There were so many cool people, and it's a big, highly competitive crowd. I love all of that.

James: At that time, you've already graduated. I assume you moved there for a job?

Bob: Yeah, that's right.

James: Then what happens there? Did you continue to meet more people and get more exposed to the scene?

Bob: The Nova crowd was so welcoming. Everybody goes way out of their way to help friends in need, whether it's rides or decks. The community was so incredible and I got to know all the competitive players there because I was also competitive, and I learned so much from them. It was watching them win, and learning from them, especially Dan. He played so much Delver. I picked it up myself, and that's been the deck I've been known for since.

James: Were there specific generalizable lessons that you learned? Do you remember what were some of the key things you learned that allowed you to level up to where you are now?

Bob: That's a tough question. I feel like everybody improves at Magic in their own way. I don't think it's necessarily a linear path. For me, I understood the concepts well enough. It was getting the practice through repetition, and then talking to other good players about card choices, deck ideas, and so forth.

James: Discussions and the grind, as it were. Just playing games and watching others.

Bob: Exactly. It's hard to put my finger on "when I got good," if such a thing can even exist. I still think I have a lot to learn, even in terms of playing Delver well. So, I think it's a slow and gradual path. There wasn't one secret, by any means.

James: Were there people that helped you improve your game, and how you look at it? Maybe mentor figures?

Bob: I would say one big thing I learned from that crowd was how to treat people. I talked a little bit about how welcoming everybody was. A lot of people who compete are strong, but there are a lot of players in that community that I deeply respect. For example, Jeff Mcaleer is a name that you probably haven't heard, but he is the community dad—the host. He does weekly cube drafts, Legacy play testing, and he goes way out of his way for people. Have you heard of David Gearhart?

James: Yes.

Bob: Gearhart used to be an old-time Legacy player. He's in our friend circle and was seriously injured in a motorcycle accident. Jeff was like, "Hey, it's not really convenient for you right now, so why don't you live with me and my wife for a few months?" It was way above and beyond the call of friendship. They took care of him. Seeing things like that moved me a lot more than playing cards ever could.

James: It sounds like people like Jeff were extremely generous on a personal level.

Bob: I think Jeff definitely stands out, but it wasn't just him. There were a lot of others like that.

James: That sounds cool. I would imagine that a lot of Magic players, myself included, are not part of scenes where people are mature and hang out. It's more than just a "I play Magic with them" kind of thing.

Bob: Yeah, and that's what was appealing to me about Legacy in general. You find more people who are relaxed. For the most part, Legacy can be competitive, but still, you're not really playing for the money. You're playing for the good times, for the friendships, and for the competition.

James: You'd mentioned that Magic is not a binary thing. It's not like, "Okay, I'm bad at the game. Now I'm good." You keep getting better as a player, the more you play. But if you could look back a few years ago, can you think of a turning point, or a particular tournament where you felt like you "got on the map"? I'm wondering how you made that ascent into a Magic grinder and writer?

Bob: I can tell you the story of four key tournaments as milestones in my Magic career. The first one was Star City Games Baltimore. I don't even remember what year it was. It must have been 2013. I got to the very last round and I was paired against Brian Braun-Duin [BBD]. We thought we were playing for ninth place, but it actually turned out that we were playing for top eight—so we played it out.

He was on Storm, I was on Blue-White-Red Delver. This was one of my first tournaments playing Delver. Before I had played Affinity and Show and Tell. In my mind there was this mental block of, "Oh, Delver is for the good players who can do everything well. You should just play Show and Tell." But Dan kept winning with it and I was thinking, "You know what? I'll try Delver this time and see how it goes."

I picked up Delver and got so close to making the top eight. BBD and I drew—I was going to beat him in the next turn of extra turns. He wanted the points and we thought we were playing for ninth, so we just drew. He didn't concede to me. Afterwards we both found out that had he conceded to me, I would have been in the top eight. It was weird because it was so upsetting. I was really happy, but at the same time I was upset that I didn't get into the top eight.

In my head I was also like, "Well, I basically got there." That hit me as, "Alright, I can do this. I can do this. I can do this." That was one key experience.

James: That's pretty good perspective. I think most people would be extremely pissed to be so close to the top eight, especially with a concession. Maybe you were, too, but it sounds like you got over that.

Bob: Especially now, I never get too upset at any given tournament. I feel like I've gotten my fair share of good luck. I think luck is even in the long run. There's no such thing as someone who is *always* luckier than someone else. The ultimate thing that matters in the end is play skill. It's about focusing on what you can and can't control.

James: What was the second milestone for you?

Bob: The next tournament would have to be the one you mentioned, where I finished in the top sixteen out of 1,600 or 1,700 people—Grand Prix DC. That got me a gig writing for Channel Fireball, so that was the next phase. I did well with that deck at several other tournaments as well.

James: Which deck was that?

Bob: That was BUG Delver with Hymn to Tourach. To this day, it might be my favorite deck that I have played in Legacy.

James: Top sixteen is pretty darn impressive. How did you feel in Grand Prix DC as you were playing in it? Had you played the BUG Delver deck a lot, did it feel familiar to you?

Bob: I did practice extensively for it and prepared well. I think it was one of the best decks at the time that nobody else was really playing. In particular, it had a great matchup against Blue-White-Red Delver due to Hymn to Tourach and Liliana of the Veil. You just out-carded them. They were playing True-Name Nemesis, but you had Golgari Charm and Liliana of the Veil. It was a next level deck. I'm happy to do really well with it.

Another key point in the tournament—I beat a well-known pro, Eric Froehlich. He's known as a pretty salty player. He was pretty salty when he lost to me. But I felt great because it was like, "Oh yeah, I beat this pro who was way better than I am at this game." I also thought, "I'm better than him at Legacy." That may or may not be true. But I felt that at the time.

James: The badge of honor. You've bested him.

Bob: So, that happened. That was super exciting and it catapulted me to the level where I started writing articles. I became a little bit more well-known. People started adding me on Facebook and asked me questions like, "Tell me how you sideboard with BUG Delver," that kind of deal. That was cool. Then the next tournament after that was amazing. It was the Star City Games New Jersey Open, with Blue-Red Delver.

James: We have got to talk about that. This has got to be the thing that you're best known for, right?

Bob: I would put my next tournament above this, but this one was the absolute best, in terms of—well my friends and I, we built and designed this completely new strategy out of the blue. Not only was it awesome, it was literally the best deck in the format for several months until it got banned. It was crazy that we built this new deck, and it was so good.

James: I read that you were playing online and then you played somebody who had the idea for what later became this deck. But you developed it into something that was fully fleshed out.

Bob: That's exactly right. I play a lot on Cockatrice. Not as much anymore, but I did used to play on it a lot and I would take random decks. At first, Carsten Kotter wrote an article about playing four copies of Treasure Cruise in Delver. I was like, "That's kind of interesting." I started messing around with it myself and then I was playing on Cockatrice.

This is when the spoiler was released but the cards hadn't come out yet. Then I ended up playing against a guy who was on Blue-Red Delver, and he had the idea. He had four Treasure Cruise and four Monastery Swiftspear. When I first saw Swiftspear, I was like, "That's pretty funny—I thought we were playing the good cards in the new set."

My opponent was like, "No, this card is insane." I don't remember who won, but it ended up being impressive either way. I asked him for his list and he gave it to me. We started messaging back and forth about the deck and I started playing it. The main deck, from when I played it and when he showed it to me, didn't change too much—maybe four cards at most. Then the sideboard I helped to refine with the help of the Hatfields [Alix and Jesse, pioneers of the Legacy format], and my other friends at Curio Cavern.

James: So it was one of these things...the moment you started playing with it, you knew it was the real deal?

Bob: Yes and no. I felt it was super strong, but at the time, there were so many people who were telling me Treasure Cruise is not playable in Legacy. "It's not a good card." It's laughable to think about it now, but I had some strong players who were my friends tell me, "That card is not good." I thought, "Well, I think it's pretty good." But I didn't have enough faith in myself, and my testing results, to say: "No, you're dead wrong. I'm going to be laughing at you."

James: You didn't want to be the guy who said this would break the format. Just like Temporal Mastery would break the format, right? [Laughs]

Bob: Well, I don't know if it was that. I was unsure and I was like, "Well, I think it's good. I'm going to play it and see what happens." Then I ended up winning the tournament, which was a combination of having a great deck, but also some good luck. Especially in the finals, where my opponent had a Griselbrand out. This is how good the deck is—that my opponent had a Griselbrand, but because I had Treasure Cruise in my deck, I was able to draw six cards and keep pace with him.

James: Oh, geez. [Laughs]

Bob: It was a crazy tournament. Part of the reason why the deck took off so much was it was so damn cheap. There were no Wastelands. You only had four blue dual lands, so it was cheap compared to the other decks. Then everybody started playing it, which is how it got so big.

James: That was right before Grand Prix New Jersey, right?

Bob: Yeah, so that was SCG New Jersey, and I won that tournament with Blue-Red Delver. It was crazy how quickly the deck took off and became one of the absolute forces in the metagame. Then, following up from that, Grand Prix New Jersey happened.

By then, Blue-Red Delver was the most played deck in the room. To combat that, we found a deck that was really, really good against it. I believe I played against Blue-Red Delver six times in the tournament. I beat Seth Manfield, Ari Lax, just these awesome pros who were on Blue-Red Delver. I was playing Blue-Red-White Delver.

It was pretty cool to see. I built something great, and then I really understood it, and was able to find a way to beat it as well. That led me to another top sixteen finish at Grand Prix New Jersey. Once I had these subsequent notches on my belt, I felt more and more comfortable with my play testing and deck building skills. So, yeah, it was slow increments of building confidence and improving.

James: It must have been a huge validation for you. What was the formula for beating it?

Bob: There were two key cards. There was Stoneforge Mystic and Counterbalance, and both of those things were insane against Blue-Red Delver. This Grand Prix New Jersey idea of running Stoneforge and Counterbalance was from my friend James Pogue. He said, "Why don't we play the old trump to Delver mirrors—Counterbalance in the board?" Then we tested it and it was super good. So I wasn't the first one to come up with these brilliant ideas. I just happened to be lucky enough to win with them.

James: You had people who helped you to refine ideas.

Bob: Exactly. That's one thing that's so important, is having a good network to bounce ideas off of, and learn things like this.

James: Did you have another tournament that you said was instrumental to your Magic career?

Bob: I guess I should have counted GP New Jersey because it did qualify me for the Pro Tour. But the key tournament I had in mind was when I won Eternal Weekend. That made me happy for months and still makes me happy just thinking about it—that I'm a Legacy Champion.

James: Yeah, that's an official title. [Laughs] Tell me how that tournament went down for you.

Bob: That tournament was totally different because I didn't prepare for it. [Laughs] I got lucky in some other ways. I guess we can go back a little bit for some context. I hit up one of my friends, Dylan Donegan. I was like, "I saw you top-eighted with this Grixis Delver deck. How good is it?" He says, "Bob, you should definitely play it. It's super good. Just literally play my list." I took his list, which I never do. I always think in my head that I want to make a list better and change all these things, but here I literally just took his list. I changed exactly one card.

In round one, I played against Grixis Delver or Grixis Control, I can't recall. The game goes super long and I think, "I don't think I'm going to win it. Oh well, I'm just here for fun, I guess." It was turn four or five of extra turns. I drew the card that I changed from Dylan's list.

Dylan had Sulfuric Vortex in the fifteenth slot of his sideboard, and I replaced it with Izzet Staticaster. I drew the Staticaster while my opponent had a board full of Elemental tokens for blocking. I play the Staticaster, kill all his tokens and then attack for the win on turn four of extra turns. That was the first match—the turning point. The rest of the tournament was smooth sailing from there.

It was crazy that I won the tournament. I was so happy because I went there with some of my best friends, and it was a surreal experience. You just don't expect to win a tournament so big and so important. The first prize was incredible. It was a painting of a Tundra. I was floored. It was an incredible experience.

James: In the photos I saw, you had a very large smile on your face.

Bob: Definitely one of the best days of my life.

James: You're looking to defend your title this year, right?

Bob: Yeah, I want to make the trip out to Columbus this time and we'll see how that goes.

James: You've just recounted four or five tournaments and they're all Legacy related. At this point, would you say that Legacy is the format you're most skilled in?

Bob: I would definitely agree with that. I consciously made the choice recently to, in many ways, give up on competitive Magic. I've decided to only focus on Legacy because I know I have my strengths there, and I know the format really well.

The reason I'm giving up on competitive Magic is because there are other parts of my life that I find lacking, that I want to work on. I was so addicted to Magic for two whole years. I did many of the things that you wrote about.[12] That's why I was excited about this interview. I need Magic in my life. I love it. I love competing, but it needs to not be the only thing in my life. I'm trying to find more of a balance, and I've come to the realization I only have a finite amount of time. When I go to play in a tournament, I'm not there to mess around. I want to win. So this is the best path for me—to have that life balance while also being able to compete. I've given up on Modern and Standard. I honestly don't think I'm talented at all. I do decently in some of these formats because I put in the work, but I no longer want to put in the work, and I've come to terms with that. I don't expect to do nearly as well as I have done in the past, and I'm just taking it as it is.

James: First of all, I think you're being very humble when you say that you're not that good of a player. Clearly

---

[12] In my first book, *Magic: The Addiction.*

the results show that you are. Maybe you put in a lot of practice and a lot of hard work, and that's why you're successful. But the fact is there are a lot of scrubs, like myself, who put in the work and still didn't get there. So I think you're underselling yourself.

Secondly, how much time did you put into Magic? Was it basically your life? Did you feel like other parts of your life—personal and professional—were suffering as a result of focusing on Magic?

Bob: Yeah, in many ways. Definitely. I can't deny that at all. In terms of my professional life, I would put it this way. I always grew up being told things like, "You need to work hard. You need to work hard to get into a good college. Once you're in college, work hard to get a good job. Go to Wall Street and make a ton of money."

At some point I thought to myself, "When does the rat race end?" So I sort of gave up on that life. I let my work life be as it is. I didn't really try hard. I worked in investment banking and the hours...let me tell you, just getting out of the office, and it's daylight of the next day. I couldn't handle it. I had given up on that aspect of my life.

But because I was such a competitive person, I looked for another outlet. Magic ended up being that. I had tournament success and I did well with it, so it kept snowballing. I almost used it as a form of validation for myself. I mean, it is what it is. It can be good or bad. I'm trying to move to the next level. Still don't quite have it figured out yet, but we'll see.

James: Was that the reason why you took your two-and-a-half month trip?

Bob: Exactly. Getting a break from Magic wasn't the only reason, but it was a big reason. Then the other big reason was—I love travelling. I love meeting new people. Understanding them and their stories. Much like you, I suppose. For me, that was a once-in-a-lifetime opportunity. I don't know in the future if I'll have this chance again. So when I saw the chance, I went for it.

James: What was it like? Can you describe to people what it's like to do a two-and-a-half-month backpacking trip, in a part of the world that you're not normally in?

Bob: I learned so much. I think the biggest takeaway was that everyone is on their own journey—on their own spiritual path. There are so many different ways that you can live this life. I was always locked into the "Type A" lifestyle that I didn't see that there was much more out there. I met many people who were farmers, and they were happy with where they were.

For me, just understanding that you don't necessarily need to be "successful," or seen as such by society, to feel that gratitude. You don't need to be seen that way to feel happy and live a good life—that was my main takeaway. It was just so interesting to have new experiences. I learned how to scuba dive, which was extremely challenging at first, but I absolutely loved it because it's like being in nature with the animals. It's way cooler than being in a zoo.

I also did a lot of mountain climbing. I climbed an active volcano. I met many amazing travelers and learned their stories. It made me think about how I'm living my life. Just seeing that there are many more possibilities out there. I can do whatever I want. I just need to figure out exactly what it is that I want. [Laughs] I'm still working on that part.

James: Were there any specific moments or conversations you had with people, that made you feel a sense of gratitude?

Bob: You know, it's a curious thing—gratitude. Some people might say, "Happy people are grateful." But in many ways, it can be the other way around. Or at least it is for me. Once I realized how absurdly lucky I was—I mean, my parents grew up in a small rural village in China. If they hadn't studied hard and made it to the United States, I would probably be a poor villager in China with very limited options as to what I can do for my future.

Instead I came to the US. I went to an Ivy League school. I have the brains to pretty much do whatever I want, so I feel so grateful for the opportunities that I've been afforded. That has made me want to seize the day—*carpe diem*. To not be afraid and go for what I want in my life. If I'm looking for something—just fucking go for it, you know?

James: That's a great observation. On the flipside of it—did you encounter people who were "less fortunate" than us, but were still feeling grateful and happy?

Bob: Yeah. Okay, so, I mean almost all the people, all the locals, that I met would be jealous of being able to live in the US. That was definitely touching. But learning a lot of their stories, too, it gives such a good sense of perspective on where you are in the world that I wouldn't trade it for anything. I'm already making musings about my next big trip, so, yeah, I hope to keep it as part of my life going forward.

James: You mentioned scuba diving and climbing an active volcano. Is that something in your personality, or did you confront yourself to do that?

Bob: Now, you wouldn't guess it because for the most part, it's weird. It's almost like there's a couple of different sides of myself. That's true for everybody, I suppose. There's a certain aspect of myself that longs for that adventure—to do something exciting, special, and out of the ordinary. Then there's another aspect of myself who is happy living the day-to-day and being comfortable. I enjoy both.

James: Do you feel a noticeably different "before" and "after" Bob Huang, when it comes to taking this trip?

Bob: I do. I don't think it's in any way that I can necessarily put my finger on. "I was like this before, and now I'm not." But life is a journey. It's like improving as a Magic player. It comes in small increments. I think going on this trip pushed certain realizations harder. I might have advanced towards them a little bit quicker, but I don't necessarily feel like I'm a completely different person. I have a wider sense of gratitude and perspective. So I try to bring that to Magic and other aspects of my life.

James: Now that you've come back to North America, when do you think you're going to be doing another trip?

Bob: It will probably have to be a couple of more years. I talked about how I wasn't career focused. Now I am somewhat career focused. I found a new role that I'm engaged in, so my next two-year goal is to do well in my job and get promoted. That will hopefully afford me the freedom if I decide to move on. Hopefully I will be able to find a job more easily. So yeah, I don't know. I'm focusing on my professional development for the next year or so.

James: Have your interactions, or relationships with people, changed now that you've had this experience? Possessing gratitude or certain learnings about yourself—does it change the way you interact with your family and friends?

Bob: Yeah, definitely. I would say the biggest one is my relationship with my dad. I talked briefly about how he was very hard on me as a kid. But now I've seen past that. Obviously, I know that he wants the best for me. But for him, happiness is leading a successful life and making a lot of money. That's what matters for him.

I realized it's not what matters to me. I have other goals that I want to focus on. Seeing how so many different people chose a different path than the straight path to success has given me more freedom. Now, I'm definitely going to go my own way.

James: Do you think he's understood that a little bit more over the years?

Bob: No. I think he's still struggling with it because he grew up in a small rural village and this is what he knows. Everybody is in their own prison, inside their own head, in so many ways. You don't realize what's possible. You put constraints on yourself and have these ideas for "how society should be," and "how things should work," and "how life should be lived." These ways of thinking can narrow you down.

He's disappointed in me that I don't seem to be as focused on material wealth or success as he is. But I don't think that I can change that about him. So I need to go my own way, and hopefully one day he will accept it.

James: What does it mean to you to be successful, or fulfilled? I'm curious how you define it.

Bob: That's the thing. Everybody has their own definition. For some people, being successful doesn't even matter, which is fine. You need to come to terms with yourself and what you want in life—and then not make any bullshit excuses for yourself and go after that. That's one approach I have for Magic as well—is that I never make excuses.

At least, I try not to make excuses, because no matter what, one big lesson I learned from Magic, is that no matter how well you can do something, there's always something you can do better and improve upon. So many pros have said this—that they don't feel like they're good players at all. They feel like they make a lot of mistakes. Honestly, it's the straight truth. Even the best players in the world make mistakes, but theirs is on a magnitude lower than the rest of us.

So tying back to the original question, there's always something people can do better. That's one philosophy I have, is not to make excuses for myself. Going back to your question, which is "how do I define success?"—I'm still figuring it out. I don't know the answer.

For me, I think the next big step in my life is that I haven't been in a serious relationship for a long time, and that was because I was mildly depressed after my last one. That's one thing I'm focused on. Hopefully, knock on wood, it works out. I'm interested in meeting someone and having that serious relationship.

There are a couple of different aspects to my life. In those two years where I was super addicted to Magic, I wasn't going out that much and my life was one-dimensional. Now, it's much better. I have a lot of friends outside of the Magic community and we do other fun stuff. We go hiking, rafting, out to bars. I went to my first music festival earlier this year and loved it, and I plan on going to a festival every year. But it's just broadening other aspects of my life.

James: Just experiences, it sounds like.

Bob: Yeah, exactly. Just life experiences. That's what matters to me.

Success to me is understanding my limitations, trying to overcome some of them, and trying to set small goals for myself. I want to experience as many interesting, unique, fun things as I want to go for.

James: You touched on something—and I'm not sure if you feel comfortable talking about it—but you said that you were mildly depressed at a certain point in time. What happened there, and how did you get out of that mental state?

Bob: This was in Paris in 2011. Maybe I didn't know it at the time, and I guess maybe I didn't go into Magic as a reason to take my thoughts off things, but it is what I ended up doing. I had gotten out of a messy relationship and was not feeling good. I wasn't enjoying anything out of my day, despite the fact that I was in Paris of all cities, which is one of the most amazing cities in the world.

Then I thought, "I used to play Magic. Oh, I guess there were a bunch of stores. You know what? I'll go out and play." I traded my mild depression in some ways for this Magic addiction. Thinking back, that is probably what happened.

James: Do you think about forks in the road and how you could have done things differently? Maybe a small choice could have changed your life in big ways.

Bob: Definitely. There's a word for that. It doesn't necessarily encompass that specifically, but the word is *ruminate*. It's when you endlessly think about things in the past that you maybe could have done better, or things that you regret. I definitely used to have that habit.

I'd think, "Why did I say this and this—I lost a friend because of that." I don't know how, but I don't do that as much anymore. I accept things as they are and I'm way more at peace with myself. I'm happier. I don't know how I got there, because it's not something you can try to do or not do. It's just who you are if you happen to ruminate a lot. I used to, and I don't anymore. That still ties back to being grateful for where I am right now—having that wider perspective on how other people in the world are living. So that's good.

James: I get the sense that you've matured a lot, and have a level of self-awareness, which not everyone has.

I'm trying to understand how you made these conscious decisions to re-examine your life. I played over ten years of Magic without ever thinking about this kind of stuff, and you're way ahead of the curve. [Laughs] How did you manage to do that?

Bob: I don't know. Winning at Magic was super satisfying, but then—

James: Because you're winning at Magic. You're taking more time away from Magic...but if I were in your position, I would keep playing *more* Magic because I'm winning. So why stop? [Laughs]

Bob: Right. I was doing well in Magic, but I still wasn't fulfilling those other aspects of my life. I think moving to Richmond was great because I live with two roommates outside of the Magic community. They are the most outgoing—in many ways, just wild and crazy—people that I never would have met otherwise. We just happened to be roommates together. For the first six months or so, I was still in my little shell. I didn't hang out with the masses much.

Then I thought about taking a hiatus from Magic. That was the timing. I started hanging out with these two roommates more and going out. They opened my eyes. There are things in life other than this card game. That definitely helped. Having conversations in my travels, having conversations with other people on how they lived their lives and how they saw through things. How they went through their own sorts of family troubles or heartbreaks. Learning all of these stories, really. I've been fortunate to learn so much from so many different people. That has given me the chance to break out of my pattern of just doing Magic-Magic-Magic.

"When I get a challenge, I want to be the best at what I do. Every time I get a challenge, I try to get more and more information about how to be the best in the role that I'm put in."

—Michael Bonde

CHAPTER 8

MICHAEL BONDE

My friend Julian introduced Michael to me as a "soldier, teacher, and Magic player." Now that was an unusual background, and something I wanted to explore further.

Michael is a Danish Magic player, and as outgoing, friendly and extroverted a person as one could imagine. He is intelligent, creative and hardworking – attributes that have translated to a consistent stream of appearances at Pro Tour and Mythic Championship events.

Michael's deep understanding of the game, and his willingness to innovate at key spots, has translated into a solid Magic career. At MC Cleveland in 2019, Michael finished in the prestigious top eight for the first time in his career.

Prior to Cleveland, Michael celebrated two 17th place finishes in previous Pro Tours – no easy feat given that these events are filled with the best players in the world.

When the Cleveland top eight finishers were announced and the tournament coordinators called out his name, Michael unleashed to the world what became known as the "Michael Bonde dance." The dance entered the pantheon of Magic memes and is readily available on the Internet in GIF format. It's a great example of the sheer exuberance and zest for life that permeates Michael's personality.

Curiosity leads to good conversations. I'm pleased to be able to share this conversation with one of the wunderkinds of Danish and European Magic.

Recorded in September 2016.

James: Michael, what made you want to qualify for the Pro Tour, and stay on it?

Michael: I've been playing Magic since 2008 on a regular basis. I started in 2004, but it became serious in 2008. And then the time I invested in Magic—online and in real life with my friends—eventually became a quest to qualify for the Pro Tour. Just to try and beat my own records and beat the best players in the world. My entire mentality changed towards trying to become the best Magic player in the world. Through learning new aspects of the game, meeting new people, and trying to see how other people perceive the game. Trying to adapt and see if I can be as good as the best players in the room.

James: Your goal is to become one of the best. Is that your sole focus?

Michael: Yeah, but it could be anything. It literally could be any game. The mental part that you have to focus so much on, in every single game. The deck building and the strategy in general. You have infinite information in Magic. You can always read something. You can always try and do something to improve. And I think that's super stimulating, to break your brain down and focus 100% on Magic. When I am not in school or working a job, I relax by using my brain towards Magic.

James: Let's rewind. Tell me about where you grew up and what your childhood was like.

Michael: I grew up in Denmark, in a really small town with 2,000 inhabitants called Funder. Funder is located near a bigger town, Silkeborg, which is still [a] really small town. I grew up in Funder with my two siblings and my mom and dad.

James: Your mom and dad—what did they do?

Michael: My mom started studying because she hurt her arm, but she helped elderly people at a—I don't even know the English word for it. But she went to this house for elderly people to [help take care of them]. Like an elderly home. My dad was, and is, a driving teacher. We are a regular Danish family in a really small town with 2,000 inhabitants. I went to a regular school and hung out with my friends. We played some sports. Nothing too interesting from those early days. It was just a bread and butter family in a little small town somewhere in the middle of nowhere.

James: Did you have any particular memories of that time?

Michael: There's always been this sibling rivalry. I have one brother. We're almost the same age, and we're the same height and weight. [Laughs] We always had this rivalry no matter what we did. He's super competitive as well, so we always played these random games—Stratego and Danish Monopoly. Just trying to beat each other all the time. And eventually he started doing some martial arts and I started playing a Danish game called handball. It's not Danish, but it's very common in Denmark. It's not very common in the United States, or anywhere else.

James: Although—handball is an Olympic sport, right?

Michael: Yeah, yeah. It was on the final day of the Olympics, I think. And I started playing that. I tried to play different sports like badminton and football, to see what I was good at and what I liked. And eventually handball was the thing I picked up. And then my competitive spirit led me to attend all these extra seminars of handball and trying to be the best. Later on I started practicing rifle shooting. My dad is a hunter, so he was happy that he could do something with us—my younger brother and I. Once a week, we went out to the shooting range and had our family time together—practicing with the rifle.

James: Did you hunt as well?

Michael: No. You need to be sixteen years old, and have a paper from the state to be able to hunt.

James: So you didn't accompany your dad to his hunting trips?

Michael: No, no, no, no. We just went to the shooting range and participated in all of these tournaments. We had Danish nationals in rifle shooting, like you see in the Olympics. My brother and I were competitive, and my dad—he wanted to hang around with us. He was used to shooting the rifle when he went hunting, and so we adapted well to the competitive shooting part.

James: You must still be a pretty accurate shooter, right?

Michael: Yeah. I went to the military, and you have all this rifle training and gun training. I went to the Sergeants' Academy as well—I should say, Sergeants' School. And I finished in first place out of 120 people. Over the course of eight months, I was the number one shooter in every single discipline. I guess I'm still pretty good at it.

James: Wow. Was that just a lot of practice, or do you have some natural talent for it?

Michael: I think I probably have some talent, but we practiced a lot, too. When shooting the rifle, it's about how you look through the optical sight. If you're 100% natural in the way you're holding the rifle and looking through the optical sight, it's easy for you to shoot straight. In that sense, there is skill involved. And if you're good at holding still and aiming, that is also a skill. But other than that, it's about practicing and knowing what to do. It's like Magic or any other sports. It's just practice, practice, practice. The grind. If you grind, you get better.

James: It's about the grind, and putting in the practice.

Michael: Yeah. Definitely true when it comes to the shooting range, and when I played handball. Also true later on in my life, when I started playing Magic. I'm good at grinding and gathering empirics [knowledge about a specific Magic format] for specific situations that I want to be better at.

James: At what point did you make that transition from general gaming into Magic?

Michael: Pretty much everyone played or collected Magic cards when I went to school. But we didn't really know how the game unfolded. We just traded the cards because the art was beautiful. Then I went to the gymnasium [seventh grade to ninth grade]. People were playing Magic in the common room and I said to them, "Wow! I used to own these cards. It looks fun. Can I join?" And they said, "Yeah, we have this sweet Soldiers deck from Legions.[13] You play it like this. You can hang around and see if you

---

[13] Quite a coincidence that Michael's first Magic deck was a Soldiers deck, and that he later went on to become a professional soldier. I did not even recognize this connection until I was editing this book.

can decipher the rules." And eventually we started playing every single lunch break. Every single time there was a lunch break, I went down there and they were playing. And I started going to this club and drafting and playing—just having fun with Magic.

James: Do you remember your initial impressions of the game?

Michael: My initial impression of the game was that it was a wonderland of mental challenges. When I looked at my classmates playing, they played in a specific way. I could decipher what was wrong and right with how they played, and I could try and tell them how I would play out their hand. My first impression was that there are different ways of interacting with your opponent. There are different ways to play the cards in your hand, so the game must be super complex. And when something is super complex, it's more fun to dig into it because you know that you will face good challenges relative to the time you spend. I was already playing a lot of chess at this point, and I thought that was super challenging. But there are not many chess players around, and if you play against the same people and you keep winning, then eventually they don't want to play against you anymore.

This was a whole new level of competition because people really wanted to play. There was luck involved as well. It's a lot of skill and then there is some luck, which eventually will give worse players than you a shot at winning. That's variance.

James: That makes the game more popular, right? More people want to get in.

Michael: I think so. The same goes for League of Legends and Dota. You play in a team, so you don't know if it's 100% your fault or if it's your team. And it's easy to start another round and see if it goes well.

James: Magic for you started in the Danish equivalent of high school.

Michael: Yeah, it's called a gymnasium. But you go when you're 14 or 15. You attend a three-year educational program, which eventually leads to college.

James: And then what happened to you after the gymnasium? Did you go off to college and continue playing Magic?

Michael: I was this restless soul. I canceled my gymnasium after the first year and tried something else. And then I tried something else again for a half year. I also canceled that. And then I started in the military in 2004, I think. Or 2005.

James: What made you want to join the military?

Michael: I thought that I needed some discipline. I thought that it would be a cool place to test yourself. A whole new setup that was away from everyone's day-to-day life…I don't know. I thought that it would give me some good human abilities, and some reflection on what is right and wrong. Discipline in general.

James: Did you feel, as a kid, that there were parts of your life that felt undisciplined? Was it part of your role in society, or some interaction, that led to that?

Michael: No. I felt restless because I did what I wanted. And I was lazy because I wanted to game all the time. I wanted to play World of Warcraft and Warcraft

III on my computer. I wanted to play Magic cards in my spare time and school was not a priority for me. When you're younger, it's hard to wake up in the morning. I was super lazy and it was a downward spiral. I thought to myself, "How can I change this?" And eventually I found out that attending the military would be both a good mental and physical challenge. To test yourself and see if you're good at it. A new challenge in another form.

James: That's impressive. You made it sound like you needed more discipline, but it takes a lot of discipline to *realize* that you need more discipline, right? [Laughs]

Michael: Yeah, but I figured out that I was not good with school. There were a lot of things I wanted that didn't involve going to school and sitting in a classroom. Even though I loved getting new information and learning, it was not the right time for me. It was so hard to get up in the morning and so hard to drive to the school. It was physically tearing me apart. I had to do something else. So yeah, maybe there's discipline there. Maybe not even discipline, just self-reflection that I needed to try something else.

James: Okay. You enter the military. What happens next?

Michael: It was like going to school, but with a gun hanging by your side. There is gun training, but it's such a small part of the overall Danish military institution. They don't even try to brainwash you. They just try to make you a better human being. It's mandatory to go to the military in Denmark, but they don't have that much space. Therefore, every 18-year-old attends something called "the session" where they do a lot of tests. Eventually, they pull a number out of the equivalent of a hat. If you get a number between 1 to 5,000, you have to join the military. If you are any other number, up to 36,000, you don't have to.

James: It's kind of a lottery, and most of the people don't have to go.

Michael: Yeah, it's basically a lottery. You could put it that way. But it's written in our constitution that every 18-year-old has to serve in the military. They circumvented that with the lottery system.

James: Did the military experience match your expectations?

Michael: It was harder than I expected. The problem is that there are a lot of things that don't make sense. The big picture is that it's an education in discipline. Every day you have to put all your gear on the bed and it has to be clean. You have to count it. The sergeant comes into room and he's looking at your room. Is it clean, and did you put all your clothes in the dresser in the correct way? There are all these stupid things. Over time, I didn't think they were stupid. But initially, it felt stupid.

James: Just at the time, right?

Michael: Yeah. It seemed so stupid that you had to put in all your clothes into the dresser in the correct way. It had to be perfect and you had to show all your gear every single day. It's what the leaders expect, as a form of control. But eventually you get into the routine and you became better at it. I thrived there. I'm not in that good of a shape, but it wasn't the hardest part of the military. You eventually whipped yourself into shape. About halfway through, I was thriving 100% in the educational system of the military. I thought that my friends were nice. I thought that every single day was joyful. I woke up in the morning and went out to eat. After that, I went to my bunk and cleaned it up. We had adventures every single day.

James: What kind of adventures?

Michael: There's a routine that you have to follow: clean up all your things, show all your gear, gear up, go out to the woods. Out there, you have to learn all these basics because the mandatory military stay is four months. Every single day is about getting a new education about radio techniques, or how to use a gun, or how to camouflage yourself in nature. And all sorts of basic hunting or military skills. Every single day was basically a brand new day, being out in the woods and part of nature. I liked that because it was something that I didn't do much as a child. It was fun to go out, sleep in the woods, and do random things with the people that I liked.

James: It was like organized camping.

Michael: Yeah, with a gun by your side.

James: [Laughs] With a gun by your side.

Michael: What I'm describing is basically this camping experience where you learn how to be one with nature. You learn all of these skills, and you become a better person. No violence, though. They don't preach violence—quite the contrary. The Danish military is an institution for discipline, where you just happen to have a gun by your side.

James: How long were you in the military?

Michael: I was there for five and a half years.

James: Is that a normal length of time, or did you extend your stay?

Michael: No, it wasn't normal. I was handpicked to attend the Sergeants' Academy and got educated as a sergeant. Over the course of eight months, I had two teams of soldiers. After that, I was stationed out to Kosovo for half a year. I came back from Kosovo and then I went to the Officers' Academy and tried my luck there. Eventually, I realized that I had to do something else in the military to evolve as a person.

James: It sounds like you grew into a significant leadership role at quite a young age. Is that right?

Michael: Yeah, that's true.

James: What was that like—learning to lead and having other people follow your orders?

Michael: I was 19 when I had my first team. I had to lead 10 people, and occasionally 30 people, who were all older than me. And in the beginning, I was nervous. The first day I went and met with all these people. I was kind of nervous, but eventually you do grow with the role. If you're good at what you do and you know a lot of things, then eventually you can be creative. You can tell them what to do and why they have to do it. And a lot of people will accept your instructions if you have reasoning behind your leadership.

James: The reason why they picked you for the role, and subsequent roles, must have been because you were doing something right. What do you think you did that was effective?

Michael: When I get a challenge, I want to be the best at what I do. Every time I get a challenge, I try to get more and more information about how to be the best in the role that I'm put in. And it's also through grinding, trying out all sorts of different things. Wanting to become better, to exercise more, to read a lot of books about a specific topic. Teaching myself, leading, and eventually figuring myself out. The thing about leadership is—if you're not yourself, and you're not comfortable with being yourself in a leadership role—it's hard to lead. But if you look at it as a game or challenge—making people do their best, and have fun at the same time—then that's the best way to do it.

James: Did you feel that you earned the respect of those that you were leading?

Michael: Definitely. I am still in touch with some of them. We still socialize, even though it has been 10 years since I was their sergeant. It's the same with people I went to Kosovo with. We have a lot of mutual respect for one another. I can feel it when we talk. It's hard to know exactly if someone has respect for you, but I get the feeling when I talk to my old military buddies. And in the moment, when I was their sergeant, I definitely felt that they had respect for me.

James: You can still feel the bond, right?

Michael: Yeah, it's hard to explain. But I think there is a bond. And when you're a leader, if someone is not following what you're saying, or if you don't have a good dialogue with them, you feel it instantly. If they don't have respect for you, it will be hard to work together.

James: Sure. They will hesitate to do something.

Michael: Yeah, exactly.

James: Tell me what it was like to go to Kosovo—that whole experience. You said it lasted about half a year?

Michael: I went there for five and a half months in 2008. I went to work. And prior to this, I was this lazy teenager who wanted to game. But in Kosovo I was a sergeant. It was very interesting. The most interesting thing was that every single day we worked from seven in the morning until seven at night. It was a huge change, going from not doing anything to working twelve-hour days. I don't even know how much work it was—maybe 100 hours a week. It was a change from a typical daily life. But when you're stationed out there, people are super professional. There's always these random incidents and all sorts of work duties to attend to. Eventually you develop a routine and get to work. You make some good friends, people that you trust 100% and you can talk to them about everything. It's this special feeling. You're away from everything. You're away from your family. You miss a lot of people and then you are surrounded by people that you have complete respect for. And the respect is mutual. You just have to make the best of it.

James: It's like having a new family.

Michael: Yeah, exactly. I had a family there. There were a lot of people that I talked to in Kosovo that I still have a lot of respect for. I try to follow what they are doing now, even though I don't see them much. I think they're fantastic people.

James: That sounds like an amazing experience. For someone like myself, who's never been in the same situation, the closest analogy I can think of is being part of a sports team. But it sounds like much more than that.

Michael: I think a sports team is a good comparison. When I think about the feelings that I got when I was stationed out and when I played sports, it is basically the same. You're part of unit that wants to perform well, wants to have a good time and would do anything for each other. And I think that's a very good comparison.

James: When you were stationed there, were there any particularly memorable experiences?

Michael: What stood out was that even though people have a hard time in their local area if there is war, they are still nice people. I don't find anything bad in a random person on the street, unless they have been taught to be bad. So every time you met up with locals—with new people from different countries—everyone was super friendly and outgoing. They wanted to know about you and where you're from, and they wanted to help. And I think this goes for almost every community, including the Magic community. If you're open and friendly and start talking to people, then eventually people will want to talk to you. They will want to help you, and you will want to help them. It will rise into something bigger than two people in competition. Basically, people are nice to each other if you put them in the right situation. And that's what I got from Kosovo.

James: And that was a new feeling for you?

Michael: Yeah, with the media it's like…when you read about war and about people in general, you read that they are not outgoing. People try to tell you that other people aren't operating with the best intentions in mind. I don't even know how I would explain it. But when we went to Kosovo and talked to a lot of the locals, we knew the real story. The locals were super unhappy with the whole situation, but they were not bad people. They wanted to talk and be friends with us, and they wanted help from us. I treated them as my neighbors. They were not bad people. Some people can force other people into becoming bad, but in general I think everyone has good intentions.

James: Now that's a powerful observation. If I may jump ahead—what was it that made you decide that you had to get out of the military? You said that after five-plus years, you wanted to move on. What was the motivation behind that?

Michael: I knew that I wanted to work with people, and I knew that I didn't need to be the leader. I wanted to work with people in a different setting from the military. Even though it had been good for me, it still had its restrictions. I wanted to either be a social worker or a teacher. That was why I ended my military career—so that I could attend towards those other goals.

James: Was it around 2008 that you left?

Michael: It was actually in 2011. I started in 2005 and I stopped in 2011.

James: In the life of Michael Bonde, what happened in 2011 after you left the military?

Michael: I left. I quit my job. I left the school. I moved away from the nation's capital, Copenhagen, and moved back to my hometown with my best friend at that time. And we moved into this nice apartment in the middle of my hometown. I came back, started going to school, and went back to being non-military Michael. Just hanging around with friends from my younger years and having a good time. Not having all this stress surrounding me, that's been there since I was 18. It was nice to sit back and focus more on hanging out with my friends and going to school. Getting smarter in some ways. And that's when I picked up Magic cards.

James: Did it feel strange, though? To have been in the military and adopted that, for years, as a way of life—and then moving back to your hometown and leaving all of that behind. What was the adjustment like for you?

Michael: It was hard in the beginning because when you work in an institution like the military—or anything that's driven in the same way—it's hard to go and do something else. Everything now worked in a different way and you developed habits. You have to reinvent your whole way of thinking—how to go to class, how to talk to someone. It was hard. There was a transition period, and it's still ongoing, even though it's been a long time since I went to the military. For example, I got to school and realized a lot of things. About discipline—it's not something that everyone is accustomed to. When I go to school now, I want to get the most out of my hours spent at the class. That clashes with someone who's just there to hang out. And I want to be friends with all of my classmates, so we have to find a common ground. "Yeah, I know that you're just here to hang out and I'm here to study, but we can still be friends because we're still interested in the same things." There's this clash of the disciplined mindset versus the non-disciplined mindset.

James: In a classroom setting, not everyone has the same common ground.

Michael: Yeah, but it applies to everything. For example, learning and perceiving the world around you, trying to understand the world. You can't make everyone adopt the same thought pattern as you. But in the military everyone is always wanting to do their best, and they're there. If they're not doing their best, they're probably going to get fired. So academic life was very different from what I was used to. I'm not struggling with it, but I have to work on not bullying people around. I'm not sure if bully is the right word—

James: You have to be aware of it.

Michael: Yeah. You can easily bully people. "You should do better because we're here to get better." I need to be aware that there is socializing and other factors at work. You can't force people into wanting to go to school if they don't want to. I just have a different mindset than the peers in my classroom. And sometimes you get into interesting situations when you have to work together. Because I have been in another very different culture before, I have to be aware of this mindset. It can make collaboration in the classroom difficult, I think.

James: Are you still studying today, or have you completed it?

Michael: No. I studied sociology and then I figured out that I really wanted to teach. It's divided into two different schools—if you want to be a social worker or a teacher. And eventually I found out that my calling is to teach. I simply love it, and it gives me a lot of energy when I am teaching. I'm studying it in my third year, or my fifth semester, in the Teachers' Academy.

James: Your goal now is to be a teacher.

Michael: Yeah. I'm trying to balance the whole going to school to become the best teacher that I can be, with playing as much competitive Magic as I can. And also being a good boyfriend and family member.

James: It's ambitious. But given your background, I'm sure you could do it.

Michael: I seriously hope so, but it's challenging. There are only 24 hours in a day, so eventually you run out of time. And it's hard to balance these two or three different aspects of your life.

James: Oh, I wouldn't worry about it. I mean, sleep is overrated, right? [Laughs]

Michael: Yeah, as you get older you sleep less. So that's good, I guess.

James: Going back into the Magic part—as you resumed civilian life, you started playing Magic again. What was that like?

Michael: I knew how to play Magic when I started in the military, but I wasn't that good. I thought I was good, like everyone else feels when comparing their skills to the local area. But as time moved on, I figured out that every time I went to regional tournaments in Denmark—these bigger tournaments—people were way better than I was. That was a hard thing to cope with. I thought I was good, but I was really just the best of the worst. I started to focus more on the whole "how can I become better at Magic" question, because I felt that I had unexplored talent. I teamed up with some of the better Danish players and learned from them. I wanted them to tell me everything they knew, which amounted to these huge grind sessions. We would sit down and grind Magic for three days straight. And eventually I became better, attended Grand Prix, and started getting better results.

James: Can you talk a bit about that grinding process?

Michael: We took our laptops to our friend's house. During release weeks on the old version of Magic Online, there were these queues that would fire every time 16 people signed up. We played three Sealed queues at a time. So you would start deck building. Then when you submitted your deck, you started a new queue again. You would build a deck while a match was going on. Play the match, start another Sealed queue, repeat. We would get our grind on, and grind empirics.

James: You were exposed to a lot of different things, in terms of competition. Why specifically Magic?

Michael: My opinion is that people don't do things if they're not good at it. Some people can play football just because they like it, but they won't invest a hundred hours in football if they're bad at it. If they're not getting better. Eventually, when people pick something up that they have a raw talent for—not saying that they're necessarily good, but at least better than someone else who's picked it up [and doesn't have any natural ability]—they become curious. *Can I become better at this?* And that's how I thought about Magic. I knew I was good at it without any practice. So how could I become better? It was this whole curiosity to try and become a better Magic player. And when I played against people who were better than me, it was super frustrating but also enlightening. *How could I become better?*

I thought that I could try and ask those people if they would teach me what they knew. So eventually I sat down with these good players, and they taught me a lot of different aspects of the game. Then I became better. It's always an evolution. Every time you play against a player who is better than you, you become enlightened. Using your brain 100% when you play Magic and applying it to all the different aspects of the game...I really love it. I love the game and its mechanics. But I also love to be able to focus 100% on how to become better in the Multiverse, be a better player, be a better deck builder. There's all these different aspects of the game that you can put a lot of mental focus on.

James: Yeah, absolutely.

Michael: I simply love to play Magic. First of all, I love the game. Whether it's casual or competitive, as long as I'm matched up against a person who is the same skill level, it's super challenging. But eventually you'll get, as you say, knocked down. Instead of attributing it to variance, I always want to see if I could have done anything else. If I could become better. When I'm not at school, working, with my girlfriend or friends, I just want to do something enjoyable. Thinking about Magic, and playing it, is something that I enjoy and get a lot of energy out of. Not trying to become better is not something that I can do. I want to know if I can flourish in the competitive scene.

James: Regardless of situation, if you're *in that moment*—you want to learn and do the best you can, right?

Michael: Yeah, I think learning is an ongoing life process. If you stop wanting to learn, I think you will miss out on a lot of things. If there's a good documentary, I want to see it. If there's a good book, I want to read it. If someone has an interesting point about didactics, or the universe, I want to see if I can understand it. To see if I can become smarter, more knowledgeable, maybe pick up some new interests. I think knowledge is super fun to obtain.

James: That's great. Once you started grinding Magic, is that when you met your friend Thomas Enevoldsen?

Michael: In the beginning, he was good friends with a lot of people from my local area. From the town I live in now called Århus. But I didn't know him that well at the time. But I knew that he was a very good player. Same with Martin Dang, who was his good friend. Martin's also from my local town. They were good friends and they were grinding a lot. And then a guy called Lasse [Nørgaard], who won Grand Prix Madrid in 2008.[14] He was around and is a strong Limited player.

---

[14] https://magic.wizards.com/en/events/coverage/gpmad08

Eventually, when I started hanging around with them—we had the same interests in terms of going out and having a good time—we could apply the stuff in Magic to everything. Eventually Thomas and I got to know each other. We had the same goals and wanted the same things. We had a good chemistry.

James: Yeah. I don't know if you listened to that recording with Thomas that I did with him...but his first impression of you in that fateful tournament was quite interesting. [Laughs]

Michael: I know that he said something, but I can't 100% remember it.

James: He said the first time he played you, he thought that you had no idea what you were doing. That you were some kind of scrub.

"Here is this guy, Michael, that I just met. He's looking at playing the game completely differently from conventional wisdom."

Michael: Yeah.

James: "But somehow he still did really well in that tournament, so he must have been really lucky or something." [Laughs]

Michael: [Laughs] Yeah, this was my first PTQ, so my first leap into competitive Magic in Denmark. I played this stupid Naya control deck, which was so awkward. I had Goblin Assault, which would make 1/1 tokens. I had a lot of mass removal and planeswalkers. It was a weird deck. I actually went to the top eight of that tournament, beating Thomas in the Swiss. But this was before I knew anyone. And he was part of the "good" Danish Magic players, the second generation. That's when [Svend] Geertsen was around. Thomas was second generation, along with Martin Dang and a lot of other really good players. And I knew that he was strong from reading tournament reports, but I didn't know him as a person. I was intimidated playing against him. But I loved playing Magic, even at that point. I had my own deck and wanted to see if it would do well in the tournament.

James: Clearly you had something. You top-eighted and managed to defeat Thomas in your match.

Michael: Yeah, but then we played against each other in the quarters and he won that, so justice was made in that tournament. [Laughs] Eventually I got looped into the whole secret society of good Magic players. When I moved to Copenhagen, it just took off. I got a lot of new friends from the Copenhagen Magic community, and eventually I knew everyone. Thomas and I started traveling a lot and became good friends.

James: Was that the turning point, or the thing that made you more serious about Magic than before—was being part of this group and traveling together?

Michael: I was already the most dedicated in the group. I knew that I had something to prove and also something to learn. I had been grinding since 2010. Attending almost every tournament that I could, putting my capital on hold and seeing how I could grind more money just to be able to get to go to all these tournaments. And eventually when you start traveling a lot, you start a trend and people want to join. They think it's fun and they want to join you. We eventually became this huge group of people and formed a team, Team Rocket. We had a lot of good players that all wanted the same thing—to go out, have a good time, and play Magic. When people had enough of it, after one or two years, I kept on going. I wanted to keep getting better, all the time. And Thomas stayed on, too. He said, "I really enjoy this, so let's just keep on grinding." He was one of the dedicated few. When he got off work, he wanted to attend these GPs and talk about Magic.

James: You've been to a lot of tournaments over the years. And you've traveled a lot. If you were to look back at the past five or six years, was there a particular moment that stood out for you?

Michael: I went to the United States for two months— one month with Joel Larsson, and then Thomas Enevoldsen and Christoffer Larsen came and stayed with us the next month. We traveled the U.S. and just grinded.

James: What year was this?

Michael: This was in 2013. Or maybe it was 2012. We just booked the trip. I asked on Twitter, "Does anyone want to go to the U.S. for two months and just play Magic?" And Joel Larsson had just come out of the Finals at the Pro Tour. He said, "I would love to."

And then Thomas got off work, and Christoffer got off work, and we met up in different parts of the U.S. We hung out and went to Roanoke to play the Star City Games events. We hung out with Brad Nelson, Todd Anderson, and all these super nice guys and girls in Roanoke. And we became part of this huge community where they played every day. They wanted to invest a lot of time in it, and Magic was part of their daily life. We woke up each day and had a great time. We walked around, talked about Magic, and played with some of the best players. That was the first time where I thought, "I need to go to the Pro Tour. I need to do this even more." Because hanging around with some of my best friends, as well as my best friend, and having a great time in the Magic community—it doesn't get any better than this.

James: What were the American players like—people like Brad and Todd? Did they have the same kind of dreams as you, such as, "I want to be on the Pro Tour"? Or did they have something else in mind?

Michael: They were already on the Pro Tour, but we met them on different occasions during the grind. They asked us if we wanted to go down to Roanoke and hang out with them and do the prerelease weekend. It came as a shock to us, as we wanted to go to New York to get the feel of the Big Apple, so we rearranged our plans and went down to their place. And we thought that was an amazing invitation. It was huge to be welcomed to a whole new community of people who loved the game as much as we did. Todd was writing so much for Star City Games. So was Gerry Thompson and BBD [Brian Braun-Duin]. And Brad Nelson was already a really good player at the Pro Tour. We united on the common goal of playing Magic and having fun. And that's pretty much what we did for the entire ten days that we stayed there. We had fun with new friends and had an amazing time. They were some of the best moments in my life and Magic career.

James: What were your impressions of America?

Michael: Everyone is super friendly. Some people say that it's a hollow friendliness because everyone wants to have a good appearance on the outside. But I think in general, it's great. And when you're welcomed into a community, it doesn't matter how big it is. As long as you're smiling, being friendly, being happy, and wanting to talk to people and become friends with new people, I think there's almost no better place. Attending random tournaments and meeting new people all the time. Everyone's friendly, so you need to be friendly too, to flourish in the U.S.

James: That's great. It seems like you were an ambassador for your country. I don't know if your American hosts knew much about Europe. I wonder if you changed their perception of Denmark, or other European countries.

Michael: I would like to think that, at least in a positive way. I think people liked having us there because we were hardcore grinders. Both Joel and I are nice people. It's cool that I am calling myself a nice person, but—

James: [Laughs] You are.

Michael: Yeah, thank you. We tried our best to be open-minded and wanting to understand who they were. Not every Magic player is similar. Some people are shy, while others are extroverts—but it doesn't make them a worse person. So, just trying to understand these people that you grind with. And if you see them on a weekly basis, eventually you'll get to talk to them and become friends with them. And that was what happened here. We were basically behaving as if we were at home. And I think that being true to yourself and not trying to be someone else eventually pays off. I'm good friends with many of them now and I love hanging out. I love seeing them when I go to the U.S., and I love it when they're visiting Europe. I hope that they saw us as good ambassadors, and as good human beings.

James: I think the second part is more important—just being a good human being.

Michael: It was such a great trip to the U.S. Everyone was so supportive. Everyone was helpful and it gave a whole new meaning to the grind, in terms of why I should do it and what the fun part of it was.

James: That sounds amazing.

Michael: Yeah, and how the community in general interacts with both foreigners and friends. People just want to help each other.

James: What about your Magic game? What was the competition like when you were in Roanoke, or some of those New York areas? How was it compared to what you were experiencing back home?

Michael: You get a lot of more games under your belt that's not part of Magic Online. You get to interact with people. Every time there's something that you don't understand, you ask. Gerry Thompson was hanging around Todd Anderson's place a lot and he literally wants to play Magic all the time. And the same goes for Thomas. Thomas wants to play all the time. This wasn't like me, because sometimes I want to talk about it and do something else instead, even though I love Magic. But eventually I picked up the whole habit of playing all the time. Every time we had a spare moment, we would sit down and grind the game. Even if it's Legacy against Modern or some bad matchup, we'll still play 20 to 30 games. You take all the opportunities you can get to play to try and understand Magic even more. So, people wanted to play all the time and people were so good that you could spar with literally anyone and you could get value out of it. That was such a great opportunity for me because I was way worse than they were at the time. I just came out of Strasbourg where I top-foured with Death and Taxes with Thomas, so I had this understanding of how to play Legacy. But I leveraged Thomas's information and knowledge about Legacy, and the deck in general. I had this knowledge coming in and I wanted to try to understand the Standard format and Magic in the same way.

James: What are your goals for Magic in the next one to three years?

Michael: I've been traveling a lot. I think I played in 80 GPs since 2008 and now five Pro Tours. I have come to the conclusion that playing Magic just for the sake of playing it is not always that great. You need to be traveling with some friends to ease the whole process. My personal goal is to obtain Gold status again and qualify for all the Pro Tours. And to do well in at least one Pro Tour. But my secondary goal is to see if I can help my friends qualify for the Pro Tour. That way, we can travel together and I can help them level up their game.

James: What does it mean for you to "do well" at a Pro Tour?

Michael: First of all, I really want to be a part of the Danish National Team. That's a dream come true if I can win my WMCQ [World Magic Cup Qualifier]. That is my goal at the moment, to try and get on the Danish National Team within the next year. If not this season, then next season. But doing well at a Pro Tour…now I'm qualified for all the Pro Tours. I wouldn't have even dreamt of this goal last year. I did well at Pro Tour Madrid with a 17th place finish. I felt like, "Wow, all this time invested in the game really paid off." My non-Magic playing friends understood how well I did at the Pro Tour. My dad and the rest of my family understood that I was getting somewhere because of this result. It felt like this huge personal victory, playing against the best players in the world. I tried to stay focused and play my best, and eventually it worked out. It was an insane feeling.

James: But what did you have to do to get that Pro Tour finish? How did you improve your game over the past couple of years – you spoke about grinding, but can you elaborate on the process?

Michael: I can analyze new formats with time. I'm decent in Limited, but I don't win that much in the beginning. But after I play a lot of games and grind empirics, I become better and stronger. I can see my own improvement. People do this all the time. When they practice, they become better. It makes sense. But I need the grinding aspect. Prior to Madrid, I got in contact with Martin Jůza and I teamed up with him and his friends for two Pro Tours. They went to the shop and they played three drafts a day for seven days. And this was an environment that I thrived in—playing, talking about Magic 24/7 prior to a Pro Tour. Spending 100% of my time on grinding and empirics. And playing a lot of Magic games with a lot of Belgians, Netherlandians, the whole team. Playing from when you woke up till bed time. That stepped up my game over the course of the last year.

James: Was there anything else, other than just putting in more time?

Michael: I got the opportunity to talk to players that were better than I was, that understood different formats in a better way. People like Petr Sochurek, Martin Jůza, Lukas Blohon, members of the Cabin Crew team that I tested with. I put in time playing against some of the best in the game and talking to them. They helped me perceive Magic in a different way. I don't know if I've leveled up as a player, but I got a new perspective on Magic. You're always evolving when you talk to better players.

James: Having been exposed to that, and being successful on that level, do you feel that you still have room to grow?

Michael: There's room for improvement. When we play—my best friend Thomas and my good friend Christoffer—we often Skype. Same with some local guys, like Stefan and Samy. Every time we play a Limited match, if the others are on Skype, we screen share. And we talk through everything as if we were streaming. The way I perceive and talk about Magic—I have to be able to make people understand why I think the way I do. I need to get better at forming a game plan and all these different aspects of the game. And I think when you put words on what you want to do, and why you want to do it, you become better.

It goes for everything that you know—all your knowledge. As soon as you can form words around why you're doing it and others understand you, that becomes the next level of evolution. Then you can discuss your mindset with people who are trying to understand it, and eventually you'll come to a conclusion that a new approach might be best.

And it's difficult, but Thomas, Christoffer and I are all working on it. We are so different in our ways of playing the game that we want to understand each other. We want to see if we can understand each others' points of view. We're winning in different ways, and that's interesting. Trying to understand why the other person would think the way they do gives you a whole new way of interacting with your opponents. That way, you can shift gears or next-level to beat your opponents, when you assume another person's mindset.

James: Right. Not to say that you end up playing exactly like they do, but being aware of different options or different lines of play.

Michael: Yeah, exactly. There's a difference between control versus aggro versus midrange players. I think this difference in play style is super fascinating, and it's something that I really want to dig into.

James: How would you describe your game?

Michael: I would describe my game as...I'm pretty good at understanding the game states and dealing with a lot of knowledge on the board. I tend to like these super long, grindy, midrangy matches, especially in Sealed. Eighteen lands on the draw and grinding them out on turn 21. Things like that. That's really where I think Magic is the most fun. When I played those kind of decks and they were good in the format, that's when I was most successful. For example, Death and Taxes in Legacy does this. There's a lot of information available to you all the time and you have to manage your resources. I play a lot of Jund when I'm able to. I played Jund in GP Lille. I think those games are super fun. Knowing your opponent's hand, knowing what to play around, and playing good matches. That's Magic in its essence for me.

James: I've often heard from people who stream that the reason they do it is because they're forced to explain their thoughts. I suppose that explaining your thoughts will make you a better player, because critical viewers would have to buy into what you're saying.

Michael: Yeah. I think you can always work with your intuition. If you have muscle memory and you also play Magic with your intuition, it is hard for other people to understand why you're making a particular play. It can be hard for you to put words on it. As a teacher, the most important thing is to know what you're talking about. If you know 100% how and what to do, it's easier for other people to understand it. And I think that spreading the word makes you even more professional. It makes you understand it yourself, and then you can reflect on it and eventually grow. And I think this applies to more than Magic. This goes for everything in life, basically.

James: Going back to your goals—you mentioned that you'd like to help other people get on the Pro Tour. That's a noble goal because I don't often think of Magic players with goals like that. Goals that aren't individual goals. Is that part of who you are?

Michael: I have some friends here in my local town that are good players, but they feel intimidated about the whole traveling to GPs and attending major tournaments. It's hard to play a large tournament with nine rounds on day one when you're getting started. Statistically speaking, you will do bad. I try not to push them, but I'll Skype them and talk about Magic. We try to hang out in our spare time when we're not attending school or working. We'll play and talk Magic, and I try to make them better players. Eventually, I hope they will attend GPs with me. I'm trying to push that for GP Rotterdam because it's a team GP. I even arranged a team for two of my friends to play in, because they are good Magic players but haven't attended a GP yet. I think that if they would attend GPs, they will get more competitive and eventually do well on the Magic scene. So I'm trying to inspire and influence them into trying competitive Magic, because I want to travel with them. I want to hang out with them because they're fantastic people.

James: I can make an association to your military days, when you were in a leadership role. When we talk about Magic teams these days, you're not really a team. You're playing together, but at the end of the day, the matches are still individual. So wanting to lead people there and help them grow—that really does feel like a true team. It's great to hear that.

Michael: Yeah. Martin Dang, Thomas Enevoldsen and Christoffer Larsen took me under their wings when I started playing Magic. They liked me as a person. I think that if I can do this with my friends who are not into competitive Magic right now, I should. I know what Magic did for me and I love the way that I improved my game, and the way I improved as a person. I want to make people feel comfortable in that competitive environment and make them feel better. Others helped me and I love it. I would like to share some of that knowledge, wisdom or whatever. Basically giving others a way to do it by helping them with the framework. And then let's see if they can flourish in the same environment.

James: If there was a Wizards of the Coast brochure for why you should play Magic, I think your face should be on it. [Laughs] If you could look back, have you ever thought about whether Magic has been detrimental to your life in some way?

Michael: If it changed my way of living, or if it did something bad?

James: You can interpret the question in several ways. You can interpret it as, "Do you have any regrets? Are there any negatives from playing Magic? Is there an opportunity cost, where you lost the ability to do something else while you're playing?" Being a very self-analytical person, I'm going to assume that you thought about these questions at some point.

Michael: I think the hardest part about it is the time commitment. I talked about it a bit earlier. If I have to become better at Magic, I need to dedicate even more time to it. And in doing that, there are other things that you simply can't do. I want to hang out with my friends that aren't playing Magic, but sometimes it's just not possible. I might be traveling, and when I get home, I want to hang out with my girlfriend because I miss her. And then I have family events. I don't have to go to those, but I want to because I want to see my family. And some people would be left out. And I think that's the sad part of it. There's not enough time for everything. So if my friends don't play Magic, it's hard to dedicate that much time to seeing them because either they don't have time or I don't have time. And then you have to try and talk to them on a daily basis to be good friends, even though you don't see each other. Sometimes that can be kind of hard.

James: Oh yeah, absolutely. But like you said, there are only 24 hours in the day, right?

Michael: Yeah, and then you make new friends along the way. If you can see one of your good friends twice a year, and if that's good enough for both of you, then you should go for it.

James: Have you had some good friends that you've lost contact with over the years because of your commitment to Magic?

Michael: Not really lost contact, but not talking as much anymore and not being able to see them. I have a good friend called Kim. He plays casual Magic, but he's not that dedicated. He has a job and girlfriend as well, so he has a lot of time commitments too. But every half-year we try to do something crazy with each other, like go to a festival or something. Just try to get the most out of the time we have together. And this has become something that I'm looking forward to every time it happens. And I have some of my high school friends...actually tomorrow I'm going to play board games with them in my hometown. We really need to focus on trying to get together when we have the time for it.

James: And what about Magic itself? Is it going to be a life-long thing for you? As you become more dedicated in teaching as a profession, how do you see Magic playing out?

Michael: My goal is to try to incorporate Magic, or just gaming in general, to my teaching classes. It has so many good aspects that you can easily put into the learning environment. But I would like to become a better Magic player and try to balance work with playing Magic. Eventually, it will become more of a "GP every second month, a Pro Tour once a year." I don't know yet. At some point I'll have a child as well and I'll dedicate 100% of my time for the child. But I think Magic will always be part of who I am. I don't see myself putting it completely on the shelf, but I see myself not putting as much time into it once I have other obligations.

James: Different degrees of involvement, but not ever completely gone, right?

Michael: Exactly. It gave me so much personally that it will be too hard to put it on the shelf. It would not make sense for me as a person to put it on the shelf. I can't see a situation where I would do that. But I tried to put everything else on the shelf—handball, shooting, all of these things. The time invested in those activities didn't give me as much pleasure as Magic did. Eventually, Magic overruled all of those other things. And it's not easy, but it's easier to balance your day-to-day life with Magic specifically. I think Magic is the place where I want to be, and where I want to get my energy from.

James: Any final thoughts?

Michael: I have some fantastic friends within the Magic community. Thomas and Christoffer are some of the people that I love the most. And I think that when they helped me, that was the best thing that's happened to me in Magic. The same goes for Lasse Nørgaard and Martin Dang helping me when I moved to Århus. I would like to tell people that they should take people under their wings. It's a way of becoming a better human being, I think. Magic is a game for people of all personalities. Helping others in the Magic community is great, and no one is judging you. And I would like to say thanks to Frank Karsten, Martin Jůza, Lukas Blohon, and Petr Sochurek. They are amazing players who took me into their teams. Same goes with Brad and Todd. They took us in and helped us stay in the U.S. for 10 days without asking for anything back in return. The Magic community in general is so wonderful and I love being part of it. So I would like to say thanks to the entire Magic community.

"*I realized that what I like about Magic is the freedom it gives me... I've kind of accepted that I'm where I want to be.*"

—*Paulo Vitor Damo Da Rosa*

Chapter 9

Paulo Vitor Damo Da Rosa

Paulo Vitor, or PV, is a Brazilian Magic player and a member of the prestigious Hall of Fame. With 12 Pro Tour top eights and nearly half a million dollars in career tournament winnings, PV has proven himself time and time again in high-level play. He easily belongs in the conversation of "top five Magic players of all time." Consider the fact that PV is still in his early 30s, and he may very well finish his career at the top of the ladder.

What's more, PV isn't just one of the great Magic players of all time – he's also one of the best theorists in the game. The remarkable thing about his written work is the consistency and quality of the output. PV constantly one-ups himself on a weekly basis. Many of his articles have become classics and allowed players at all skill levels to improve their outlooks on the game.

PV's standards for content are so high that he made me think about how I could raise the bar for myself and improve my podcast. When I initially approached him about recording an interview together, PV was adamant about knowing what we were getting into. He made me pitch him on why he should do the podcast, who it would be for, and what sorts of discussions we would get into.

This was in the early days of the podcast, and I hadn't formalized the format into the way things are today. For a podcasting amateur, I had to dig deep and articulate my vision to him. I had to sell him on the why.

It was a valuable lesson, and something I needed to do. And bless his heart, PV knew that I cared about improving and was open to feedback. Upon hearing my responses, he agreed to do the podcast with me.

And so, we were all ready to go...until, in a cruel twist of podcasting fate, I lost my voice a few days before we were slated to record.

To this day, I'm not exactly sure what happened. Some kind of bacteria or virus, probably. Of course, the irony of a podcaster not being able to speak was not lost on me.

Fast forward two weeks later, and we had a decent conversation. We covered some things that PV was incredibly passionate about outside of Magic, that he doesn't normally talk about in his Magic writing.

It was a lot of fun to be exposed to PV's brilliant Magic mind, and I'm honored to be able to share it to a wide audience.

Recorded in July 2016.

James: Tell me a little bit about your family background and where you grew up.

Paulo: I was born in Porto Alegre, in Brazil. It's a big city in the south with about two million people. I've lived there all my life and I'm 28 now. My mom is a biologist, but she doesn't practice, and my dad's a retired economist. They don't live together though, as they split up when I was a little bit younger, and I live with my mom.

For some people in the US, it would be weird—you're 28 and you're living with your mother—but for Brazil it's quite common. Normally, you only move out if you're getting married or if you go to study somewhere else.

James: Do you have any siblings?

Paulo: I have two brothers. They're only half-brothers, though—my dad's kids. We have three different mothers, and they're both older than me because my father is much older. One is 45, the other is 33, and we have a good relationship. We're not super close like most siblings are, but we're still close enough, I would say.

James: What about your dad?

Paulo: Not a lot. I'm very close with my mother, not as much with my dad. It's not that there's anything wrong, specifically. I just don't talk to him that often.

James: How did you first get into gaming?

Paulo: Most of it was my own initiative in terms of Magic. I started playing when I was young, about eight years old. But even before that, I've always liked games with my friends. They were kids' games, and my family used to play cards too. They would play—I don't know the names of the games in English—but it was stuff like gin, and I'd watch.

I would want to play, so they taught me, and I really liked it. It was obvious that I liked it more than they did. For my family, it was, "Oh, let's do that," and then, "Yeah, let's stop doing that." I really, really liked it. I wanted to do it all the time.

So, I found this game, and it was a card game, which I already liked. It had to do with dragons and sorcery, which was appealing. I read about it in a magazine, asked my mom about it, and then she called the magazine and found out where I could buy those cards. That's how I started playing.

James: That was about 20 years ago. Do you remember what Magic set was out at that time?

Paulo: Homelands was the latest set. I remember that I bought a booster pack of it.

James: How did you go from buying the cards to playing the game?

Paulo: Well, my mom took my friend and I to the store and we bought the cards, and then we played against each other. At some point, we taught our other friends to play at school, and eventually I started going to the store and meeting new people who played. My friends from school quit playing, but I continued.

James: Was it common for people that young to go to the card store and play Magic, or other games, at the time?

Paulo: No, not at all. I was by far the youngest person there. My mom would always go with me and wait because I was so young, and she had no idea who these people were. She barely knew them. She'd just go to the store with me and stay for hours, so I owe her a lot when it comes to Magic. It was a very long time before I found someone who was younger than me, or the same age as me, playing Magic.

James: Did you ever feel that if you were the youngest person there—did you feel anything when you played your opponents, or feel that they perceived you in a certain way?

Paulo: I feel like in Magic there's not that much difference. You can't really notice it. Our PT team for example, has people that are 35 years old, and it has people that are 20 years old. It doesn't feel like you're dealing with two people that are in radically different phases of their life, which I guess they're not, but you'd feel that in any other place.

I can't even imagine another place where a 20 year old and a 35 year old would be equal. In Magic, you do have that, so I don't think that's weird.

There was only one time when a guy tried to cheat me in a tournament, and I'm sure he tried it because I was young. He succeeded, but that's the only situation I can remember.

James: How did you feel when you got cheated? Did it change you in some way, or change your vigilance towards cheating?

Paulo: I don't think so. It was a very frustrating experience. It wasn't only that I was younger, I was also from a different place, and that guy was from the main city. He thought he was going to get away with everything, and he was right. He did get away with it, and I guess it made me feel frustrated and powerless. It didn't change my feelings towards anything, though.

James: How did you make that transition from playing Magic to your first tournament?

Paulo: The first tournament I went to, I didn't know there was going to be a one. I went to the store to play like I normally did, and they told me, "Oh, there's going to be a tournament in this different store, this different location. Do you want to come?" I said, "Yeah." So they fixed my deck.

They removed some cards that weren't legal for that tournament and I played. But it didn't really change anything, it was fun. I started playing more and more tournaments and eventually there started being tournaments with prizes. I think that was when we started having PTQs, so it was like, "Oh, this tournament is really worth something."

Then we would have a schedule with – there's a Block PTQ in two months that people would prepare two months for. It was very different than the US where you have, or used to have, 50 PTQs or whatever. It wasn't a big deal. But for us, we got three tournaments a year, so those were all big tournaments that we prepared for.

James: When did you have success in tournament Magic? Did it happen for you right away? Did it happen as the PTQs came around, or before that?

Paulo: It was definitely not right away. First, I lost constantly. The time I started doing well was around Invasion block, which was in 2000. That's when I started playing in Magic League. It was an online league that we played on Apprentice, and we used IRC[15] to play.

Then I started talking to other people in different countries, and it gave me an outlet because we didn't have anything going on here. I didn't follow the Internet, or whatever, and so that was when I started getting competitive. I started going after tournament results in other places, finding out what kind of decks were good, and that's when I started doing well in local tournaments.

James: The implication here is that the local scene didn't have much to offer you personally in terms of leveling up, or learning to get better at the game.

Paulo: It definitely helped me because I was so bad when I started. It got me to a point, but I also feel like it maxed out very quickly, because there weren't that many people and the tournaments weren't that

[15] Internet Relay Chat – a precursor to chat rooms and instant messaging services.

serious. There was one guy who also played a lot, and he'd come to my house.

We would play in these online leagues and prepare together for tournaments. But other than [the guy who played a lot], most people didn't take it that seriously or weren't good enough. There was definitely a cap on how far I felt I could advance playing with the locals.

James: Did you have a strong desire to get better?

Paulo: It wasn't so much the desire to get better. I enjoy being better, and I think this game is more fun when I'm better. So, I don't know, I'm not driven by some desire to be the best, you know? I just want to be happy, and at the time doing well in these tournaments made me happy. Having a better deck and beating people— that made me happy, so I wanted to do it.

James: Other than the friend who was playing the league with you, were there other people, either online or offline, that helped your development as a player?

Paulo: For sure. Even after I became a Pro player there were a lot of people that helped my development. I don't feel like I peaked and then stopped learning. There was a guy who was the son of the store owner, and he helped me a lot. Then there was this friend who I played with competitively. There were some other people I practiced with that also helped. A lot of the people in Magic League, the online league, were instrumental. There were a lot of people who were super important.

James: Can you give me a few examples of—not the people specifically, but—what are some of the things that they helped you with?

Paulo: The store owner's son, he helped me with everything logistically. He was a little bit older, so when I went to my first tournaments, he'd take care of me. He would stay with me in rooms, talk to my mom about it, lend me cards, that kind of thing.

The people online, especially those who didn't live in Brazil, they'd tell me, "This was the tournament. This was the deck that won in a GPT in New York," or whatever if they lived in NY, for example. It was something I wouldn't have had access to if it wasn't for those people.

I would look at those decks and try to change some things. There were other people who would play test with me on Apprentice and we would talk about Magic, and this kind of thing. A lot of different types of help.

James: So it was information exposure, but also practice and getting more experience, right?

Paulo: Yeah. They also helped with my English a lot, which I think is important if you want to be a Magic player.

James: I was wondering about that. Your English is quite fluent and it comes through in both your speaking and writing.

Paulo: I've been talking to people who speak English for so long, and I've been reading, talking to them and getting my English better. When I say talking, I really mean writing. We used IRC, but basically, communicating with them made me able to read pages that were in English that not everybody else could read at the time. I was able to read even though I was so young, because of these people in Magic League.

James: As you play Magic League and you start getting more into that, was there a point where you realized that you were "on the map" when it came to Magic?

Paulo: There are a lot of different thresholds that I feel I've reached. One of them was when I was invited to my first Pro Tour. It was Worlds 2003 in Berlin. Back then, you could get invited by being one of the top Latin American players, and I did consistently well enough in my home town that I was sometimes the first, second, or third ranked player in Latin America, even though I had never done well in a major event.

I didn't win Nationals, but I was qualified anyway. People had no idea who I was because I was a kid from a different city, and a lot of people thought I faked tournaments because they're like, "How can this person get such a high rating playing in this town where no one knows anybody or whatever?"

The core of the Magic players in Brazil were from Sao Paulo and Rio, which are the two major cities. I was from a different city and people thought that is just not possible. That was the first time that I would say I got on the map, because I went to the tournament with those people, and I top-sixtyfoured this tournament, so that was cool.

After that, I would say probably my first PT top eight which was Charleston in 2006. It was a team event, and that was probably the point when I was on the map for everybody, not just Brazil. I remember I watched the coverage of those matches, and the commentary would be like, "Oh, you probably don't know who this person is, but he's done well in this, this, and this tournament." The commentators didn't know who I was, but when they went through my story—my history—they found that I had three or four PTs, GP results, and whatnot. That was when I became known.

James: I would assume that for many people who have a European or North-American-centric view, they don't know much about players coming out of your region.

Paulo: They still don't. I mean, I would say what put us on the map wasn't me. It was Carlos Romao. Carlos won Worlds in 2002, so he was the first Brazilian to have a big result. Then one of his teammates from Argentina also top-eighted the same tournament. That was really when our region was put on the map. But, yeah, the fact that we did well in the team event definitely helped.

James: That must have been validating.

Paulo: Yeah.

James: Going back a moment, when you played in your first Pro Tours back in 2003, did you ever feel nervous playing in them?

Paulo: Oh yeah, for sure. I feel nervous right now.

James: [Laughs] Oh, really?

Paulo: It's the kind of thing that you're so excited about it, you don't sleep very well. I used to feel like that for pre-releases too, but obviously it's different when you're in a major tournament. You want to be the best you can be, but you know it's very hard.

So yeah, I get nervous. I get less anxious now because my life doesn't depend on how well I do, but in the first tournaments I went to, I thought, "If I don't do well in this tournament, I'm just not going to come to another one."

I got to play against all these people that I only knew about. Nowadays, I know everybody and I've talked to those people. Some are my friends, some aren't, but I still know them. They're real people to me now. But before, the first time I saw them, they were just names that I recognized. It's very intimidating.

James: Right, and they didn't know who you were in the beginning. They thought you were some person who made up tournament records to get there or something.

Paulo: Yeah, those were the Brazilian people. The foreign people just had no idea who I was.

James: It's interesting because you said that in the beginning you didn't know if you were coming back if you didn't do well. Did you really think that, "I need to top-eight this Pro Tour, or top-sixteen that one," or you would stop?

Paulo: It wasn't exactly that. The first time I went, the company that distributed Magic in Brazil—they offered to pay for it, for everyone who was qualified. Not just me—everyone. They paid for our plane tickets and our hotel. It was something that I thought, "If it wasn't for them paying, I wouldn't be able to do." I didn't have the money back then. It was very expensive and I was very young.

I didn't have my own money and my family couldn't afford for me to start travelling to Germany to play a game. But, since the distributors were paying, I went. And I did well—I top-sixtyfoured and got $500, which was a lot for a 15 year old Brazilian kid who wasn't doing anything.

It showed me that there was prize money to be won. It's possible for me to do well, so maybe I can go to another one of those things, even if they don't pay.

The first time I went, it didn't feel like it was the beginning of something big. It just felt like, "Okay, I'm going to this tournament, and that's it, because they're paying." Once I made money and started doing well, I realized, "Well, I can actually go to those things on my own because I can justify doing that." That's what changed.

James: It's more of a practical consideration because you're effectively being sponsored in the beginning.

Paulo: Yes.

James: I guess it worked out. You were winning and then you got to go to another one and you were able to fund that.

Paulo: And it was very important too, because back then Pro Tour Qualifiers didn't give you plane tickets, they gave you a $500 appearance fee or two boxes of cards. Most of the time, where I lived, players just took the boxes because $500 was simply not enough. You'd pay over twice that just for the plane ticket. United States dollars are worth a lot in Brazil too. We're not a poor country, but right now for example, $1 is 3,5 reals, which is our currency. Some things are much more expensive when you're paying in dollars.

James: Sure.

Paulo: The fact that they paid for that was huge, and that I would get prize money in dollars was also huge.

James: Was there a particular point here that you felt like, "Okay, I'm feeling committed to Magic as more than a hobby and it's going to be more than just something I do on the weekends"?

Paulo: I don't think there was ever a point where I had to consciously make that decision. Since I started playing so young and it was such a huge part of my life, it was a very natural transition. Magic started being my job before I got to the point where I had to have a job. I didn't have to decide—do I want to do this for a living or not?

I was doing it because I didn't need to do anything for a living at that point. I was studying and I was very young. Then when I got to the point where I needed to do something for a living and I needed to make my own money, I already had that.

I guess I never really thought about it. I did what I liked to do, and it happened to be a job, which at the time I didn't need. I didn't stop my life for it. I kept studying, went to college and stuff like that. It all worked out, and it's what I like, but I never felt like I had to commit. I was just doing what I liked to do, and it was enough.

James: Why Magic? Because you strike me as someone who has a lot of interests in different hobbies and are quite well rounded.

Paulo: Well, Magic was the first game that I played seriously and because of that, I think it's the one I'm best at. I had other games that I feel I'm good at, but it's different. I feel like in Magic I've already worked to the point where, you know when you're starting a job, you're an intern. Then you start going up and up and eventually you become a manager. I feel like I went through the internship phase in Magic without even realizing it.

That was just where I was supposed to be. I was so young, and then I followed the natural progression of my Magic career with my life before I was supposed to be [a professional player] at that time. For other things, I discovered them when I was much older, so I would have to go through that intern phase, while already being a partner at something else.

The fact that Magic was the first—it made me accustomed to a certain lifestyle, to having such rewards for my preparation— which made it harder to commit to other games. With them, I would have to start in the beginning, and I wouldn't be as famous, rewarded, or as good as I am in Magic.

I don't really want to go through that process again when I'm already good at something. Now that I know the difference between the two stages, and when I started, I didn't—so it didn't make a difference. Does that make sense?

James: It does make sense.

Paulo: Yeah, it's like saying you are a top doctor. You have a clinic. You have all that experience and resources, but then you can also become a lawyer, which you like a lot. However, you would have to start as an intern in a law firm, and it'd take years to get to that point as a lawyer.

You are a doctor already so you don't want to do that. Even though you like practicing law, you're not going to make that your career because you already have one. You don't need to.

James: I'm wondering if there are particular points for you in your Magic career where you felt doubtful about continuing to play?

Paulo: It happened about three years ago. It was a point where I wasn't doing well at all. I'd been Platinum for six to eight years, or equivalent, which is the highest level you can get in Magic. Then I was Silver in next year, then again the next year. Going from Platinum to Silver is hard. When you're qualified for everything, it's hard to at least not reach Gold. I had to do particularly badly, which I did.

I thought, well, maybe this isn't what I'm supposed to do. Maybe I should be trying to do something else, I'm not good anymore, or maybe being good doesn't matter anymore. It's very hard to be unlucky for two years. There had to be something going on. That created a spiral where I felt like what happened was that I got unlucky for a certain period of time, and that demotivated me.

I thought, "Oh well, I'm practicing, but I'm not winning anyway. I'm losing to people who are worse than me, so why am I spending my time practicing? I'll just show up like those people and hopefully I'll get lucky like them." Then I lost more and more because I became worse, which created a snowball effect where I kept doing badly. At the same time, though, I didn't want to practice because I thought I was doing badly and I thought I wouldn't be rewarded for practicing.

So I didn't, and I did worse. At the end of those two years, I thought maybe this isn't what I'm supposed to do. But, then I started doing well again.

James: How did you end up doing well? You said yourself you spiraled into less than ideal habits because of some bad luck. How did you climb out of that?

Paulo: I think it was the opposite and I got lucky. It was PT Brussels, where we had the Esper deck. I felt like I played well, but not particularly well. My result was good— I top-sixteened, and then I immediately did well at a GP after that. I think I was lucky then, just like I wasn't lucky before.

But it showed me that I liked doing well. For two years, I had only dealt with failure for the most part. I was like, "Well, I feel really bad when this happens. I don't want to do it anymore." But getting lucky again showed me how good I feel when good things happen. It made me realize that it's worth dedicating time to, because I really like how I feel when I do well.

James: Would you define failure as losing more than winning?

Paulo: [Laughs] Well, not necessarily losing more than winning. Just losing in general. The way I feel is that I have a cushion, because I know Magic has luck in it, and I'm not the best player. I still make mistakes, so I don't expect to win every tournament. But, I would expect to do well in some tournaments based on how much I practice and how good I am.

I have a cushion. For example, I've done well in the last year. So, if I were to do badly for the next couple of months, that wouldn't make me feel bad because I think, "Well, you know, it's just my average. I will do well [at] some things and badly [at] other things." But I felt like after two years I lost that cushion.

I was kind of, "Okay, is this the time I do well again?" It was just never that time, and it kept piling up—defeat after defeat. That's why I felt like a failure. I had all of the bad parts with none of the good. Right now, I'm having just the good parts. So, when the bad parts come—and I'm sure they will eventually—I'll have a big cushion of happiness.

James: You have a happiness quota, or balance that you can draw from.

Paulo: Yeah, so I'll be able to withstand it. If the defeats last for a whole year, then maybe that cushion will disappear again.

James: You really thought about stepping away when you had that bad run?

Paulo: I did. I thought about doing other things, and sometimes you see other people transition into playing other games. I feel like Magic has a ceiling and you can only climb so far. I felt like I hadn't reached that ceiling yet, but for a lot of things I have. I mean the company example from earlier—if I'm already the president, there is nowhere else to climb.

Then I see people around me who are actually climbing greater heights and having other things. For example, I see people playing Hearthstone and playing in tournaments that give you more money. Then those players stream for 30,000 people. When I stream, I stream for 300 people.

Sometimes I think maybe I'm supposed to be doing something else. Maybe I should get a normal job and try to climb the ladder in that—and eventually become super rich. Or not. Maybe I should play something like Hearthstone, which is newer, but gives you other possibilities.

I realized that what I like about Magic is the freedom it gives me. I don't think any other job gives me that, and I've kind of accepted that I'm where I want to be. Even if I can climb higher, I live a good life, and I feel a big part of that is because I can do whatever I want. I practice when I want. I can play League of Legends for ten hours if I want, or I can watch TV shows for ten hours, or absolutely nothing.

The only thing I have to do is write an article a week and practice for the PTs. It's something that, when I started looking at other people who work, they don't have that luxury. Even the League of Legends players—for example, Soren Bjerg streams for 30,000 people.

He's super rich, and I'd like to be super rich too. But, at the same time, do I want to stream for ten hours a day? I don't think I do. So I'm actually in a very good place with Magic right now, but at the time, after those two years, I was thinking, "Wow, Bjerg is super rich and I'm never going to be super rich." That bothered me.

But I didn't realize how much he worked—the way I don't want to. So I feel like I've made my peace with Magic, you know? I understand it has pros and cons, but the pros are very good for me, because it's exactly what I'm looking for. I'm not going to find that in another job.

James: I know you play other games as well. Can you walk me through what are some of the other things that you're into right now?

Paulo: I play a lot of things, most of them for fun. I play and watch League of Legends a lot. Actually, I watch it a lot more than I play. I know who everybody is, a lot of champions, I'm into it even though I'm not very good. I also play a bunch of single-player games, such as Baldur's Gate II and Heroes of Might and Magic III, which are old games, but I still play because I have fun.

I also play bridge, another card game, semi-competitively. I went to the Junior World Championship once representing Brazil, but it was the only big tournament I went to. It doesn't feel like it's ever going to be a profession for me, but it's something I do for fun. I go every week to the club and play.

James: Why do you feel like it could never be a profession?

Paulo: I feel like I would have to dedicate so much, and I can't because of Magic. It's not that I wouldn't like to live as a bridge professional, it's that I don't feel like I can be both a Magic and a bridge professional. I'm already one of those things, so there's no point in trying to change. The people who are playing bridge have been playing for a very long time. Some people have been playing competitively for over 50 years and I would have to work very hard to be as good as them.

James: How did you start playing bridge?

Paulo: A friend of my mom's played bridge, and she knew I liked card games, so she introduced me to it. I watched a tournament, took some classes, started learning it, did some research, and I started playing.

James: Are there any similarities or parallels you would draw between bridge and Magic as games?

Paulo: Some things. Bridge is very different because, well, in Magic you work with incomplete information— you don't know what the top card for a deck is for example, so you can't prepare for everything. In bridge, all the cards in the deck are in play. While you don't know who has each card, you know they're all there. You know all the possibilities.

No one is going to surprise you with something that you didn't think of, simply because it's all there. Bridge is also a partnership game, so you play with someone else. That makes it very different, because you have to consider what the other person is trying to tell you from the way they play.

But some of the things are similar. For example, when someone comes up with the concept of tempo in bridge, where people will be like, "Oh, you lose tempo if you play that." I already know what that means and understand what you're saying from the way you're saying it. No one else around me understands because they weren't exposed to this term.

Stuff like—should you play to win, or not to lose—you can also apply in bridge. You know, percentage chances and hedging. When you have to make an aggressive play, when you have to make a defensive play, and trying to take inferences from what people are doing. These are all concepts that you use in Magic. It's not the exact same, but it's similar.

James: Is it a specifically skill-based game, or are there elements of luck and variance in it as well?

Paulo: It's extremely skill-based. The way bridge works, to give you a quick overview, is that teams are four people. Say there's A, B, C, D and 1, 2, 3, 4. Those are the two teams. You play in two different tables. There are four positions—North, South, East, West.

So, in table one, A and B are going to be North-South. And 1 and 2 are going to be East-West. In table two, 3 and 4 are going to be North-South and C and D are going to be East-West. The teams reverse positions.

What you do is you play and you don't shuffle your cards. You pass them to the other table, and they're going to play the same cards you just played, except someone from the other team is going to have my cards and someone from my team is going to have my opponent's cards.

Your goal is to score more points than the other team, holding the exact same cards. There's no luck in the sense that—I had all the aces in my hand, so I'm going to win, because when the cards go to the other table, your opponent is going to have all the aces. They're going to have the exact same hand that you did, so you have to do better than them with those cards. In this regard, there is no luck.

The only luck that exists is that you can make a bad play and be rewarded. For example, you make a play that is 20% to work, and it works because that's the way of the cards in this particular hand, and so you win. At the other table, the team is going to make a play that is 80% to work, but it doesn't work in this particular game, so you were rewarded for making the worst play.

Overall it's very skill-intensive, and you play a lot of boards, so the better team is always going to win.

James: That sounds really interesting. I've only played it recreationally, so it wasn't two tables or anything like that. But that sounds really neat.

Paulo: That's the best part in my opinion.

James: I'm wondering if it's the enjoyment that keeps you going, or if you have any specific goals around bridge.

Paulo: It has definitely been enjoyment. I have no goals… It's something that I could do if I wanted to dedicate myself—but right now I don't want to dedicate as much as I'd have to, so it's just for fun.

James: What about for Magic? Do you have any goals for Magic as far as what needs to happen in one year, or even what needs to happen in five years?

Paulo: There are two main goals. The first goal is always to be able to play Magic professionally, which usually means hitting Platinum. I don't know what's going to happen to organized play in the future, but the goal is getting to a point where I can go to these tournaments and play Magic for a living.

I can still do all the things that I want to do— I don't think, "Oh, I can't do this because I don't have enough money." This is the point I'm at right now. I can do basically everything that I want and fund myself going to these tournaments, so I'm self-sufficient. That's the goal. I don't have to pay to play Magic. It pays for itself and for everything that I want to do.

The secondary goal would be to win Worlds, which is the one thing that I've never done in Magic. I've won a Pro Tour, which back then was harder than winning Worlds—but no one knows that. If I talk to my uncle and say I won a PT, it means nothing to him. However, if I tell him I'm the World Champion, that means so much more.

This is what I want, you know? I want to be able to say I'm the World Champion. I've never been able to say that in my resume.

James: It's being able to tell people outside of the game something, right?

Paulo: Right now my close family knows, but outside of them, they don't know how good I am. I tell them that I do well in these tournaments, that I'm one of the best players, but I don't feel like they truly understand. If I won Worlds, they would, because everyone understands what World Champion means.

James: Right.

Paulo: They think it means the best in the world, which in Magic, it doesn't, but—

James: You'll take that label.

Paulo: —It's something. Yeah, because say I get third or fifth, I'm not as good as I would be getting first, you know? Maybe I just drew a land that I needed, as opposed to not drawing a land. So it gets blurry inside the game, but outside it means so much to be a World Champion in anything, really. You know, "I happen to be the World Champion in this game." They're like, "Wow! That's impressive!" Then you tell them, "I won a PT." They're like, "Yeah, whatever." So, I would like that.

James: Paulo, on this note, how important is it for your legacy to be known outside of your friends and family?

Paulo: I don't know exactly how much it means, but it definitely means something to me. I would like to be a celebrity, but it's very unlikely to happen. Even if I win Worlds, I'm not going to be a celebrity. But I'd love if a newspaper did something with me, to inter-view, or whatever—something that is not Magic-related. That would be really, really cool. It hasn't happened yet. Maybe it never will, but when some-one outside of Magic recognizes me, that's a goal.

James: It's interesting to me hearing you say this because I know there are probably—I don't know how many thousands of people in the world right now—who would love to just be in your position. Yet, you're still hungry for more. You know what I mean, right?

Paulo: I do, I do. I mean, I enjoy being a personality in Magic. It means a lot to me that I have a column, that I write something and people read it and pay attention to it. Or, I'm in a tournament and people ask to take pictures with me, they want my opin-ion, to say hi, or they tell me they're a big fan. This means a lot to me and it's very important. It would also mean a lot if someone who doesn't play Magic would have the same thing, you know? It's unlikely to happen, but it would be cool.

James: Absolutely. I also think it's—not to make fun or any-thing—but it is really interesting that you said, "Oh, I want to be in the newspaper or something." But in fact, you're so well known on the Internet. I mean, there are going to be much more eyeballs looking at Reddit's MagicTCG section and seeing your name, than most newspapers, you know?

Paulo: Let's say TV then, not newspaper.

James: So the really mainstream media channels.

Paulo: Yeah, I would really like that...

I like that people care about what I'm doing, they listen to what I have to say, and they like me even though they don't know me. Someone who's hoping that I win, or even hoping that I lose and they haven't even met me before—it's very different than anything else I've had in my life.

I have a way of interacting with people that I don't personally interact with, and I don't think many people have that. If I think of the people I know, they affect everyone who's immediately in touch with them. But for me, if I play a PT and I do well, then next week there's going to be someone in Malaysia who's playing a different deck because of me. I'm affecting people from the other side of the world, who I've never met and probably never will. I think that's really cool.

James: Even indirectly, you're making someone's life more interesting or enjoyable, right?

Paulo: Yeah, I like it.

James: What's the weirdest place that you've been recognized, that you were surprised that someone came up to you and said, "Hey, you're PV"?

Paulo: On the bus. Once, I was going to university and there was some guy who was, "Oh, you're PV, aren't you?" I'm like, "Yeah." He says, "I'm a big fan."

There were some classmates of mine on the bus too, and they were like, "What just happened? Do you know this person?" "How the hell did he know you?"

"From Magic." Stuff like that. Once I was in New York with my mum and we were on the street and a guy said, "Hey, I'm a big fan. You're PV from Magic." That was cool, too. We were in another country, not in the Magic scenario at all, and this guy knew me. Those were two things that imprinted in my mind—I thought they were cool situations.

James: Just by those two stories I can tell that you have reached the mainstream. People recognize you on the street. That's pretty cool.

Paulo: Still Magic players.

James: [Laughs] So you're the youngest person to have reached the [Magic] Hall of Fame. Can you tell me what it was like? In terms of what went through your mind when you found out that you'd entered the Hall of Fame?

Paulo: I found that cool, but wasn't really surprised. Ever since they announced the Hall of Fame and I started getting close to being eligible I thought I was going to get in. So it wasn't a moment—it wasn't like you went to [the] Hall of Fame like, "Oh my God! I'm in the Hall of Fame!"

I was getting used to the idea for years before I went into [it], so it wasn't mind-blowing or anything. It was still pretty amazing though, because it's something that I'm never going to lose. It's going to stay with me forever, regardless of what I do. In 30 years, maybe I haven't played Magic for 20 of those years, I don't even know what Magic is anymore—and I'll still be a member of the Magic Hall of Fame.

I think that's huge. There are very few things in life that you take with you forever. Maybe my university graduation, or a child, something like that. The Hall of Fame is one of those things that I could get, so I felt very honored.

James: That was in 2012, right?

Paulo: Yeah, in Seattle.

James: Did you feel that your reputation changed dramatically before and after you joined the Hall of Fame?

Paulo: I don't think so. People say, "Oh, he's a Hall-of-Famer," or whatever, but before the Hall of Fame, I had the same results that put me in. People already knew that I was quite good, so I don't think it changed anything.

James: What about being able to tell your family that you're a Hall-of-Famer? Does that mean something to them?

Paulo: I don't think they know exactly what it means. I don't know if I even told them that—my near family—because it's never something that comes up. They know that I travel to all those places and I'm gone for months at a time, but when I meet them, they're like, "How did you do in this tournament?"

"Oh, I did well." Or, "I got third, fifth, last," or whatever, but that's the range of the conversation. It never goes any further. My immediate family knows—my uncles and aunts. But, I don't know. It's still not being World Champion. It's still very cool, but I don't think they understand exactly what it means.

James: So switching gears a little bit, we had touched on your writing a few times. Can you tell me how you started writing Magic articles?

Paulo: It was something about wanting to be known, not very different from what I've always felt. It was a way for me to get known, so I talked to the Brainburst editor. At the time it was Brainburst, today it's TCGPlayer. I was like, "Okay, I'm this kid who plays Magic in Brazil and I had this good result," or whatever. "Can I write a report for you?" And he was like, "Yeah, sure."

I wrote it, enjoyed it, and then I went to tournaments the next year and people were like, "Oh, do you write for this website?" I'm like, "Yeah." and that's where they would know me from. Writing made me happy, you know?

Being able to put those things into paper or into a computer helps my thought process. It helps me understand if what I'm thinking actually makes sense. So, this is how I started and just kept going.

James: What have you learned over the years from writing articles?

Paulo: I don't think anything very specific. But for example, when I wrote about putting your opponent in certain situations so that they make the play that you want, it made me understand the thing that I was actually doing. All the people in Magic do things, but not everyone understands *why* they're doing the things that they do.

If you do things that work, but when the situation changes a little bit, you're not going to be able to adapt because you don't know what changed and what needs to adapt. I feel like I've always done those things, but writing about them, thinking—okay, I'm going to write this, but then the reader is going to ask, "How about this?" I want to have an answer.

So I have to think about it, and it helps me understand why I'm doing these things so I can replicate them, or adapt easily. All the strategy articles help me adapt, even writing about mulligans, for example. Writing about sideboarding, playing to win versus playing not to lose, tempo, aggro, the resources and how they interact—all those strategy articles help me become a better player because they force me to think about why I'm doing the things I do. I can understand when I'm wrong and also when I should change something.

James: It's making you better—making you personally better through the process of reflecting and writing.

Paulo: I think so. It definitely helps.

James: How important is the feedback from the articles? Do you ever gain any new insight as a result of others talking to you about what you wrote?

Paulo: Sometimes. In a topic like [play to win versus not to lose], usually not. But in a topic—for example the "Keep or Mulligan" column that I do, yeah, definitely. I get to read other people's thoughts. "I think you should mulligan for this reason." Actually, that makes sense, so I learned something, and I got better.

When I write about new cards or decks in general, sometimes I'd write something like, "Oh, I don't think this card works because of A, B, and C." Then someone else replies, "Actually, I think it works because of G." So, now this card that I thought was bad, I now think it's good. There's definitely a lot of value. It changes depending on what kind of article it is.

James: What articles have you most enjoyed writing over the years? Do you have any favorite articles?

Paulo: I have a couple. One of them is the "My Story" article I wrote for Star City many years ago. It was me telling my story of how I started playing Magic, went to my first PT, and what I was thinking at the time. It was very impressive because I didn't expect it to be popular. I didn't know what I was going to write about that week, so I thought—I'm just going to write about me.

Then it turned out to be hugely popular and people wanted more of it. They told me it was the best article they've read. I was like, "Wow, I didn't think people cared." So, I really like that one.

Strategy-wise I like the resources one that I've written, which is about how you manage tempo, life, and cards. I also like the sideboarding one, which is general sideboarding, mulligans, and general strategy. I like this kind of general timeless article.

I'm usually not a fan of the, "here's what won last week and what I would play this week" article, which is a bit awkward because it's what a lot of people want to read. But I'd say my favorites are the big timeless strategy articles, and the one about myself.

James: I always feel that the evergreen stuff is the best. You can read it three years from now and it will still be relevant.

Paulo: That's exactly how I feel. I feel it's something that I am more equipped to write about than other people. I like when I write an article and people think, "PV wrote that," because it looks like something that I wrote. I also like when they think, "PV wrote that, but no one else would have."

When I write about a deck that won the tournament last week, anyone can do that. You don't have to have some deep understanding of Magic. You just write about it, play test a little bit with the deck, then you practice with it and you'll have some general knowledge of Standard or whatever, so then you write about that.

But for people to fully communicate how to approach strategic decisions in the game of Magic, I think you really have to understand what you're doing and what's going on. I don't think many people do. It's the kind of article that I feel, "I wrote this article and I don't know anyone who would've written a better article." for this particular topic—you know?

Because I never see it. Whereas when I write an article about the deck that won last week, I think, "Well, anyone could've written that."

James: The articles you put out about inducing bluffs, or making the right plays around that—I really enjoyed them. I felt like they had your unique voice, like *that was PV's article*. Someone else couldn't have written that. I think what you've done recently is among your strongest, in my opinion.

Paulo: Thanks. I try to do this "PV Article."

James: Have you ever thought about how to improve as a writer, or just the experience itself is enough?

Paulo: I'm definitely trying to improve. I don't have any particular goals, but I do want to get better and better at it. A lot of it for me is trying to understand what people want, because usually when I write, I write what I'd like to read. Most of the time it works, but sometimes people want to read something else, which is why a lot of the time you see me asking on Twitter and Facebook—what kind of articles do people want to read?

I know what I like isn't necessarily what everyone likes. Sometimes I try doing something that people asked for, that isn't necessarily what I'd like to read—my public readers are not necessarily all the same as me. I pay a lot of attention to feedback in my articles. It's much more important for me that people see me as a good writer than as a good player because I know my value as a player is not fluid.

I'm as good as I am good, and if you don't think so, then I don't care. Right? I'm either good or not. But with writing, being good at writing means that people like your articles. Feedback and people's opinions is much more important. You can't be a good writer in a vacuum. If you write great articles, but no one likes them, then you're not really a great writer. So it's important to me. I read everything that they write about me. I read all the comments. I read all the Reddit threads, and I'm always trying to get better because I like being a good writer. Ideally, people like what I write so they keep reading it. I'm always listening to feedback.

James: Has there been any feedback that's surprised you?

Paulo: When people who I know personally, and I know they read a lot of Magic and are really good, when they tell me my articles are great, that's surprising. I'm like, "What? You don't know all those things already? Why do you like it? Do you need it?" Then they'll respond, "Yeah, I read your articles." I'm like, "Oh, wow! That's super impressive to me."

Also the reverse, when sometimes people are very mean. They take it very personally. For example, when I write something like, "This deck is bad." To me, I'm talking about a deck, but to some I'm talking about the person who built the deck, and they get offended.

It's something I've had to deal with in my writing. I have to change a little bit, because if you say bad things about something that I played, I'm not going to be offended at all. To me, that's two completely different things. I realized that this is not the most common point of view...The first two times I got this type of comment, they're like, "Wow, you're a jerk," I didn't understand it. I was like, "Why am I a jerk? This deck doesn't have feelings." It turned out that the people who made the deck were taking it more personally. So, yeah, that was surprising to me.

James: Have there been examples of topics that people have asked you to write about, that at first you think, "Oh, I don't know if that's going to be a good thing to write about." But as you wrote it, it ended up being engaging for you?

Paulo: I think that about a lot of the topics that I write about. [Laughs] I mean, a lot of the time I ask people for suggestions and they give, I would say, all kinds of suggestions. Most of them are just not big enough to make an article for. The biggest problem is, A, no one would like to read it, or B, I can cover it in a tweet. I think those are the two biggest issues with the suggestions I get.

Sometimes there's something that I feel, "This is an interesting topic, but I don't know enough to write about it," so I don't. Then in a couple months, I feel like something happened. I'm like, "Oh, wow! That's actually a really good example for this thing that someone suggested three months ago." So I go and write an article and it turns out being great. [Laughs] I don't remember any specific situations or articles, but it happens.

James: It sounds like you have a strong point of view as to what you want to write about—what's good, what isn't. I think that's key.

Paulo: One of the suggestions I got once was, "Write about the importance of shrines in Standard." Like Shrine of Burning Rage. I'm reading that and I think, "That's just not important at all." How am I supposed to write about their importance? It would be a very short article.

James: Right.

Paulo: You can tell that this person is passionate about this topic or they wouldn't suggest it.

James: Do you have any particular writers that you're fond of?

Paulo: The first writer that I was a fan of was Zvi Mowshowitz. Zvi is a guy that used to play a lot—he's in the Hall of Fame as well. He has like five PT top eights, but hasn't been around lately, so people might not know him. His articles were my inspiration, you know?

When I read Zvi's articles, I thought he always answered the things that I was going to ask. To me that was very important. I read a paragraph and I thought, "But what about this?" Then next paragraph was the answer. So I was like, "Wow! This person really knows what they're talking about because they understand what someone couldn't understand from what they've just wrote—and they explained that immediately."

This is what I try to do with all my articles. I read them and I think, "I'm reading this. What am I thinking?" So I try to answer. In a lot of articles—I read something and I think, "So what?" There's no "so what." People will say something, but they don't conclude anything from it. Zvi always did. Every time I would think "so what" he immediately followed up by explaining why what he said was important.

James: You're saying his writing is essentially complete.

Paulo: Yes. You understand why he picked a certain topic. You would read it and he'd start by telling you why you should read this, and why he's writing that. Then you would read it and, yeah, it would be complete. I think that is a good way of saying it…He wrote general articles, too. He wouldn't write about a specific deck. He wrote about how he thought, which is what I try to do. I would say he's my main inspiration.

I'm also a fan of Patrick Chapin. I think he's had some incredible articles, where he goes super in-depth. That's what I love about his pieces. For example, a new set is out. Let's build a deck with this card. Then you have 35 different deck lists with the card, in every possible context that you can think of. I'm like, "Well, that's impressive. The card has been out for two days. I haven't even thought of one deck and this person already has 35 decks here."

It may be good. I don't know, but he has thought of all of it. For example, he wrote a 10,000-word article on a card that was released yesterday, so I think that's super impressive.

I also like Luis Scott-Vargas a lot because he also understands that he's supposed to communicate what he's thinking. He's a smart person. He thinks a lot of things, so I want to get inside of what he's actually thinking—

James: Can you clarify that?

Paulo: When I'm reading a tournament report—if I'm read-
            ing a report by a random person, they'll say, "And
            then on turn two, I played Lightning Bolt." Or,
            "Then on turn two, I didn't play Lightning Bolt."
            And Luis would say, "On turn two, I thought I
            should play Lightning Bolt because of X, Y, Z, so I
            played it."

            He communicates thought processes a lot more
            than just actions. Or when he writes set reviews,
            he was like, "This card is good because of *this rea-
            son*. This is what I'm thinking." You can really
            see his thought process because he communicates
            everything, which is important.

James: You're saying that he doesn't try to shortcut it.
            Maybe other writers just assume that the reader
            understands something, and—

Paulo: Not necessarily that. It's that he knows why he's
            thinking the way he's thinking, and so he can repli-
            cate the process in writing.

            A lot of the people don't know why they played
            that Forest on turn two. They didn't even think about
            it, but LSV knows, and he remembers. Then he'll
            write about it and he'll tell you why he played that
            Forest on turn two. No one else would—because for
            other people it's not a very interesting moment. But
            for him it was interesting because he thought some-
            thing, and he told you.

James: Got it—and that's something that you try to apply
            to your writing as well, right?

Paulo: Yes. Then you also have people like Mark Rosewater,
            who's insanely good at what he does. He's also very

good at writing. So even though it's not a topic I'm as passionate about, I enjoy reading his articles because they make things interesting.

Mark will [write out] the thought processes. "We created this mechanic because we thought this," as opposed to just, "We created this mechanic." I like reading what people think and reading their thought processes. This is true in basically anything.

James: You reminded me about something that Ben Friedman told me, that the best advice you could give to players is, "Think for yourself." Don't do something because someone said, "This is the card you should take, or this is what you should do."

If people understood the thought process behind why people said certain things, or if writers did that more, I think the overall Magic skill level in the community would improve.

Paulo: I definitely agree with you because I feel like if someone tells you something, and you don't understand why, you cannot adapt it. For example, if I do "Keep or Mulligan" and then I just say "Keep," then— when are you ever going to get that hand again? It's going to be slightly different.

You have to know why I kept it, because then you can see if what's slightly different next time changes anything. If you don't understand why, you can replicate but you can't adapt. I feel like in Magic you never get the exact same situation—it's never the exact same metagame, same draw, or the exact same opponent. You need to be able to adapt rather than copy.

James: Changing gears again—you played in a lot of Pro Tours competitively, made a lot of friends, and met a lot of people over the years. Are there particular people in the Magic community that you would be proud to call your closest friends?

Paulo: Yeah, there are. There are people I've been close friends with, others I'm not close with anymore. I would say that the Brazilian crew—like Willy Edel, for example, is a very good friend. Even if he never played Magic again, we'd still talk. Thiago Saporito, probably the same thing. They are people who are involved in my personal life. Like, I know Willy's wife and kid. We've been through things together that are not inside of Magic, so he's a good friend.

I think there are Brazilian kids that you probably don't know, Thiago, you probably know. Internationally, I think—for example Luis [Scott-Vargas] is someone whom I'm involved with on a personal level, not just on Magic. If I never played Magic, I'd still talk to Luis. He's my good friend. A lot of the Channel Fireball crew from when I tested, like Josh [Utter-Leyton] and later met Matt Nass.

There are people I still talk to from time to time, even if they're not involved in any Magic thing. The new people from my new team, Face to Face, like Alexander Hayne—those are all people I would consider my friends. Jacob Wilson, Sam Pardee, these are all people I consider my friends even outside of Magic.

James: If you stopped playing Magic tomorrow, how do you think your relationship changes with Luis and some of the other names you mentioned?

Paulo: It's going to change a little bit. It depends on what I...if I stop playing, but I still understand what's going on, then we can still talk about Magic. In this part it's not going to change much. But let's say I forget that Magic ever existed, or whatever—I think we'd still be friends.

I would see those people that much less. That's the big difference. I get to see Luis ten times a year, which for someone who lives in the United States, is a lot. Then maybe I would see him once or zero times in that year if I didn't play Magic. That would be the main change, but how I felt about them wouldn't change.

You know, I would still talk about personal things or whatever. I'll talk to Thiago about personal issues, or things that we like to do. Right now, for example, we're going to the PT in Australia. There's a group of us—it's Ondrej [Strasky], Jacob [Wilson], and Shahar [Shenhar]. We're going to New Zealand for a week to sightsee. We don't have to do that, it's not related to Magic in any way. We're just friends, so we're going to go and have fun. I don't see why I wouldn't be able to do that, except that I'd have to travel all the way to New Zealand as opposed to being in Australia.

James: You've mentioned in the past that you want to do Magic coverage. Why?

Paulo: There's no pressure to do well. Obviously, you want to do well, because you're doing a job, but it's different than playing Magic. There's no luck. Your mood is not going to depend on how well you do. Sometimes I just don't want any pressure.

I want to go to a tournament and meet my friends and talk about Magic, but I don't want to care so much about how I perform. I don't want to have to choose a deck, for example. Choosing a constructed deck for an important tournament is an excruciating process for me because if I don't find something I like, I feel awful.

If I'm doing commentary, there's none of that. It's very light in comparison to playing the tournament, but I can still be involved. That would be my main motivation—being involved with Magic without having the pressure to perform constantly. This is what coverage is to me.

James: Could you see that as potentially something in the future that gives you the freedom you want, and allows you to still be involved in Magic?

Paulo: Yeah, for sure. I'd still like to play from time to time—because of all the things I'm thinking that I can talk about doing coverage, that's only possible because I play. If I were to suddenly stop playing, then I would probably be a worse commentator. So I think it would be less rewarding in general.

But yeah, I could see myself doing it. In theory, I could see myself doing commentary at a PT instead of playing the PT for specific situations. Like in Sydney—I don't have to do well in Sydney. I'm already locked for Platinum, and very likely locked for Worlds. So this is one tournament where I would be able to do commentary if I wanted to. I can see myself doing that in the future, if they want me.

James: There are so many more things I want to ask you about that, but I'm going to end with one final question. Let's say that there was a young player who wants to start playing competitively and get good at it. What advice would you give him or her?

Paulo: There's no perfect way to get better, but I think the best you can do is compete. Because a lot of the time people don't want to go to a tournament if they don't feel they're good enough. They're like, "Oh, I'll just play side events." Or, "I'm not going to attend because I'm just going to lose." I don't think that's the right approach if you want to get better.

If you want to improve, you have to compete. Even if you're going to lose, who cares? Playing in a GP and going three, four, or seven rounds is probably going to make you a better player than just practicing with your friends for a week, or even a month because it sticks to you. It puts you in contact with other good players, and you can see things that aren't around you.

That's the most important thing. Don't be afraid that you aren't good enough even if you aren't. It doesn't matter. Playing in these tournaments is how you get good enough. That's it. Just putting yourself out there and competing.

"And while Magic has flowed throughout my entire life, it's always been there. And I think it will always be there, I never see it going away. For a game to have that kind of grasp on you, it has to be something intensely special, right? And it needs to be shown as that to a new generation of players."

—*Bryan Gottlieb*

CHAPTER 10

BRYAN GOTTLIEB

Bryan wears many hats. He is a Magic player, lawyer, husband, squirrel lover, and co-host of the hit *Arena Decklists* (formerly *GAM*, pronounced 'game') podcast. Over the years, he's held jobs as a full-time poker degenerate and bartender.

Bryan tends to excel in whatever he puts his mind to, has an 'aw-shucks' sensibility about him, and undersells the massive difficulty required to achieve things. He possesses extremely high EQ (emotional quotient) – I suspect this is due to his law background – and this comes across in all his interactions with people.

There is a quiet confidence about Bryan, bordering on but not *quite* in the realm of irrational cockiness, that I admire. When he says something about Magic strategy or theory in his usual understated way, you tend to believe him.

I had known about Bryan's solid work in Magic podcasts for quite some time. Before he joined *Arena Decklists* as Gerry Thompson's co-host, he was a regular on a Canadian Magic podcast called *First Strike*.

What compelled me to interview Bryan – and propelled him into the I-absolutely-have-get-him-on-*Humans-of-Magic* category – was one particular *Arena* podcast episode that he recorded with Gerry Thompson. The episode, named "Greatness, At Any Cost" – was an examination into what it meant to be great at Magic, or any competitive pursuit.

They referenced the plot of the movie *Whiplash*, which is about a drummer who does whatever it takes to excel in his craft – whether it be taking extreme emotional abuse from his teacher, or abandoning his romantic relationship because he didn't want to put any energy into it. As a big fan of the movie, I identified with the discussion and found their musings on mindset and self-improvement compelling.

After hearing the episode, I asked Gerry to introduce me to Bryan. The rest is history.

In particular, I'm especially happy about this conversation because it involves exactly zero discussion points about Magic. I was so caught up in listening to Bryan's backstory, and how he went from a poor rural boy in New York to where he is today, that some of the topics we had planned to discuss didn't come up.

This was the interview equivalent of 'deep work' or 'flow state' – I was completely immersed in the conversation, and it was as natural as any discussion between two friends. I lost track of time, and one question naturally transitioned into the next.

It was super easy to have the conversation with Bryan, which also speaks to his abilities as a podcaster and communicator. And it exemplifies the *Humans of Magic* ethos – discussions with Magic players about topics, and themes, *other* than Magic.

Bryan is great and I'm honored to have this opportunity to highlight his story.

Recorded in April 2018.

James: Tell me what was going through your mind when Gerry asked you to step in and be the co-host of *The GAM Podcast*.[16] Did you have any doubts about getting involved?

---

[16] In 2019, this podcast was renamed to *Arena Decklists*.

Bryan: So I don't know that there was ever a time where I wasn't going to accept. Obviously, I recognized the opportunity. And quite frankly, if I just had the opportunity to chat with Gerry about Magic for an hour and a half every week and no one ever listened to it, I would still sign up for that. He has a great mind for the game and is a friend who I enjoy talking to on a regular basis. So it's nice that we have this excuse to get together and chat every week.

But while I knew I was ultimately going to accept the offer when he came to me, there was some trepidation on my part because I was taking over, I was stepping into the role of two Platinum Pros, Andrew Brown and Michael Majors, my predecessors on *The GAM Podcast*. And I mean, I'm not stupid. I know when I stepped on *The GAM Podcast*, everyone was like, "Who?" Nobody really knew who I was when I was doing it, and you could argue, rightfully so.

I don't have this huge swath of finishes in Magic. I have a Pro Tour top twenty and a GP top four. I think another Pro Tour top fifty, but I've never been a Platinum Pro, I've never been a Gold Pro, I've never been a Silver Pro, quite frankly. And there's a lot of people around the game who absolutely had no idea who I was. While I desperately wanted to take the opportunity, I was concerned. I didn't know how people would react to my presence on this show, I didn't know if they would accept me as a replacement for Majors and Andrew, who are both great hosts.

So there [was] definitely some trepidation...I started talking to Gerry about it [saying], "Look, how are we going to position this? I don't know if people are going to accept me. Do you want to do this where I'm posing as a quasi-pro who wants to level up and you're guiding me through it? Or do you want to do some other kind of structure where I'm interviewing you almost every week and I'm just kind of a host and you're the one spewing the information?" And he's like, "No, you know a lot about Magic, just talk about Magic. Why would you do all this stuff?" And I'm like, "Well, is everyone going to accept me?" And he says, "Yeah, just talk like we talk, back and forth. Be yourself, talk about Magic, people will understand very quickly that you know what you're talking about."

And I don't know if I buy that. I don't know if I always know what I'm talking about. But I will say that he proved to be right. People ultimately accepted me in the role, and I think my fears were totally misplaced. Our community surrounding the podcast is incredibly supportive, I interact with our friends over in *The GAM Podcast* Discord all the time.

And basically, from day one, it's been like, universal support. I can think of maybe two people on the Internet who said mean things about me. And if you only have two people on the Internet saying mean things about you, you're so far ahead of the curve. I mean, the Internet is the meanest place on the planet. So two people, I'll absolutely take it, I have no objections to that whatsoever.

James: In the Magic community, it's almost like your opinion doesn't matter unless you're a Platinum or a Gold Pro. You're only as good as your finishes, right?

Bryan: I totally get what you're saying. I would say it's a mixed bag. There is some of that, what you're describing. There's a lot of information presented about Magic, an incredible amount of information. There's websites, podcasts, people voicing their opinions on Twitter, then you go to Reddit, then there's a million other subforums that you could go to, and everyone has a say about Magic.

And quite frankly, a lot of the information is just noise and you need to learn how to filter a lot of it out. And one of the easiest shortcuts we can take as consumers of this media is to put a threshold that someone has to qualify before we're willing to accept their opinions. And the cleanest ones, the easiest ones to default to, are things like Pro Club status. Or you're a Platinum Pro? Then I'll listen to you. If you're not, well, there's a lot of information, I don't have time for that.

But I do believe that where you're willing to put yourself out there and face that barrier, and work for acceptance, and you know, let your words prove your knowledge, there's opportunities as well.

And also, there's this kind of weird subset of Magic personalities who, while they don't necessarily sit in the forefront of most players' minds, when you start talking to people who really know the game, their names will come up. And they've either stepped away a little bit from the game, or they are split between a focus on Magic and their careers, so they haven't taken those forward-facing roles.

[Someone like] Ben Lundquist. I think Ben Lundquist is one of the all-time great Magic minds and deck builders. And a lot of people now probably don't even think of Ben anymore. But there's this whole host of old-school players, theorists, and deck builders who-- people who are really in the know, if you bring up their names, they'll go right away,

"Oh yeah, that guy knows what he's talking about, that girl knows what she's talking about, I definitely listen to everything they have to say."

So while there's this kind of elitist structure to where we get our information from, there's these backdoor opportunities to present your information and have it taken seriously. And we've seen a lot of people come up that way as theorists more than players. It's a harder out, don't get me wrong. You do have to prove yourself a little bit. But I guess in some sense, there's the fact that you have to prove yourself through results too, which is extremely difficult to get.

I don't want to diminish the accomplishments of the Platinum Pros. Obviously, they had to do an incredible amount to get that credential, to be able to have people respect their opinions. I'm just saying there's another plausible, though difficult, way to get your voice out there.

James: That's one of those things where the podcast medium, for example, is exceptional. Because through listening to you and Gerry on *The GAM Podcast*, I can get inside your minds and really understand your thought process around deck construction and other things having to do with the game.

Bryan: Right, it takes a lot of the filters down. And that can be both problematic and super helpful at the same time, because it takes off all the checks that you have on yourself. You don't have any choice but to take chances when you're podcasting. At least for me, I never know what my brain is going to put out there, I never know what kind of corners I'll back myself into with my proclamations or my theories on the metagame that week, but I need to be able to assert them confidently, knowledgeably, and it really allows me to tap into-- I guess I would say almost an innate sense of the game.

I have to rely on that sometimes and be comfortable putting myself out there, and occasionally, looking like an idiot, too. You don't have the time to edit your thoughts over and over. For me, I know if I'm writing a Magic article, which I haven't done in quite some time, but when I was, it took me forever to write an article.

And this is how I write legal briefs or legal articles. I'm a heavy editor, I'm not comfortable putting words out there until I'm sure they're expressing exactly what I want. So it was hard for me to take that hand brake off and just let my ideas flow forth. But I think you're right, that it lets you get to the essence of the content creator much quicker. You get to know them better, you get to understand what they're about and how they think about the game much faster than through the written word.

James: Absolutely. I see your podcast as having Magic-related topics and general life topics, such as the one covering "what it means to be great." That was one of my favorite episodes. How do you and Gerry figure out what you want to do every week?

Bryan: A lot of it is timing, what's going on in the Magic world. Often, a lot of weeks, the answer to what we're going to talk about just presents itself. Like, "Here is this interesting Modern tournament. Or there were bans this week, or the entire Dominaria set spoiler got leaked ahead of time." And you know, we have this whole new flush of cards to talk about.

The pacing of the Magic world really shapes our cast at a week-to-week basis. And it becomes very clear, to us anyway, having done it for a little while now, what we should be talking about, each week, what people are interested in.

When we tend to go a little bit off the rails, do stuff like the greatness episode[17] [GAM E67 – "Greatness, at any Cost"] or other "level-up" episodes that we've done before, it's often when there's a slowdown in the Magic world. Like, Standard is a dead format that no one cares about anymore, or there were no tournaments because it was pre-release weekend or something like that. It seems like the opportunities just present themselves and we like to seize them…

James: So it's topical, generally speaking, and you guys find where the gaps can be filled with these non-timely topics, right?

Bryan: Right. Because I think first and foremost, our listenership relies on us to be on the cutting edge of the metagame. That's not to say that we don't get more overwhelming responses to the level-up episodes. Because by far, the most resounding response I've ever gotten was to the greatness episode. I've heard from so many people that they appreciate it, and it seemed to connect with a lot of people.

But at the same time, I think if we were doing that every week, we'd lose a lot of our credibility. The number one thing we have to provide to our listeners is an edge at their tournament that weekend. They need to have the level-up, they need to know

---

[17] https://soundcloud.com/user-121566285/gam-e67-greatness-at-any-cost

how to get ahead of the metagame, what to expect at their local tournament, what to expect at the GP, what to expect at the RPTQ. Whatever important tournament they have coming up, it's on us to give them the tools to succeed, first and foremost. And once we've taken care of all that, then we can look at the other topics.

James: It's almost like a responsibility to the listeners because that's sort of the mission of the podcast, or the mission statement of the podcast, as it were.

Bryan: I think so, that's how I view it. And I think Gerry would feel the same. Look, there's a lot of times that I would rather do free-flowing pieces, quite honestly. I like getting into the psychology of the game, talking about learning, talking about self-improvement outside of Magic. But like I said, we have a responsibility and we have to check when we go down those roads.

James: Which comes easier or more naturally to you? Obviously, you're doing an awesome job on the strategy part or the metagame part, but it sounds like, from what I'm hearing, that this kind of learning or self-improvement thing drives you as well, and I can definitely hear the rapport that you and Gerry have when you're going through it.

Bryan: I am very comfortable with the topic, but I would also say that we often don't sound stilted or forced because we have a great editor, so shout outs to Conor for that. He's the man behind the scenes making us sound good every week, cleaning up our silly mistakes. But you are right, we do have a natural rapport and we're comfortable talking with each other on these topics. And for me, there's a deficit I have to make up. And it will always be there, and I'm appreciative of that deficit.

But when it comes to metagaming and being a week ahead of the format, Gerry is the man. Gerry is who I learn that stuff from. When I was reading articles, when I was coming up as a competitive player, he was the one shaping my perceptions of metagames and teaching me how to adapt my deck for the SCG meta at the time. He is certainly going to have a leg up on me on that regard.

And I think by the same token—and this is not at all a diminishment of what Gerry has done in his life, because I think his accomplishments as a Magic player, and not only as a Magic player, but as a person—if you've known Gerry for a while, you know he's grown a tremendous amount as a person over the years. So this is not me downplaying any of that. But I do think that my experiential background is wider than his. I've done more things, be it going through law school, going and bartending all across the country, in Las Vegas, or being a professional poker player for a few years. I've done a bunch of different tasks and I found some success in the academic world, some success in the Magic world, some success in the bartending world, as weird as that is.

My background is a little wider. And I'm able to draw on all of that stuff when we're talking life lessons. And I think we come a lot closer to a point of parity on our life stuff than our metagaming stuff. Not to say I don't contribute to the discussion... the two of us working together get to the end of a metagame much more quickly than either one of us working alone would.

But I'm always going to give him the lion's share of the credit. He refines my ideas. I'll bring very broad ideas to the table when it comes to metagaming, preparing, and thinking about what decks to play. But Gerry is good at honing them down to a fine point. He provides all of his lists to our Patrons every week. Take his list over mine 99% of the time. He gets to a much cleaner place.

He has the hours to put in to really figure out those last few slots in his deck where, a lot of times, my decks won't be quite at that level of refinement yet. Not to say there's not potential there, and I've certainly brought my share of great format-defining decks to a metagame before, but he does it all the time. You've got to give credit where credit is due.

James: And that is the essence of a great Magic partnership, where two people have different backgrounds, they're coming from different places. One person might be more "skilled" or have better results, but Gerry is always willing to pick up ideas from everyone and be respectful of those ideas. It's very much unlike the typical Magic discourse where people will say, "This card is garbage" or dismiss ideas outright. I think you guys are willing to go down certain paths that I don't usually see.

Bryan: I think that's a great observation. It comes from a place of trust, I think we both trust each other a lot. Obviously, for Gerry to bring me in to this podcast that he had already worked so hard to establish, along with Majors and Andrew, I think he showed a tremendous amount of trust in me, which I am incredibly appreciative of. And obviously, I trust his opinion on the game, I have for years and years, and that's what's being reflected when we have those back-and-forth conversations, is we don't dismiss each other's ideas out of hand. We'll give each other time to come to conclusions, and sometimes we'll end up dismissing our own ideas as we talk through them.

But there's so much more value to be gained in open and receptive discussion than the kind of almost nasty dismissiveness that a lot of Magic players take on in their discourse. It's strange where we embraced a little bit of a culture of negativity to shoot stuff down a lot. And look, you have to mitigate your flow of information, I get it. You can't explore every possible idea, there's too much out there. But if you're able to approach new cards, new decks, new formats with a more open mind, you're exposing yourself to more possibilities. And I think Gerry shares that belief as well and that's why we have that free-flow of information. And we don't throw ideas away out of hand, we give them their due course before we move on to the next topic.

James: Now I'm going to switch gears slightly. Tell me a little bit about your childhood and where you grew up.

Bryan: I don't know how interesting my childhood is. It was a little weird. I was born on Long Island in New York State, lived there until I was about six, when we moved to a small town in upstate New York called Richmondville. You've probably never heard of it because nobody has, there's one traffic light and way more cows than people. And I lived in the absolute middle of nowhere. We were in the woods, there was no cable TV in my house, so I didn't have cable TV growing up, and we were also very poor. Very poor. I'm always hesitant to use that descriptor because, in my work as a lawyer, I work with impoverished people now, and I see some horrific poverty. We ate every night, we always had a roof over our heads, and the heat was always on, so we have it better than a lot of people in this country and around the world for sure. So I don't want to overstate things. But at the same time, there was not a lot of money, I'll just leave it at that. And I stayed in that town until I graduated high school. It was a weird place to go to high school, not very culturally diverse, just a bunch of white people, a lot of poor white people, some middle-class white people, and a very almost sheltered childhood, it's how I'd describe it, not a lot of exposure to bigger things.

James: At what point in your childhood did you realize that you were "poor"? Do you remember what was the event, or events, that led you to realize that?

Bryan: I actually do. And it's kind of a funny story. I remember being very young and watching *Roseanne* with my parents. And if you've ever seen the show *Roseanne*, which has, in recent times, unfortunately become controversial. But my innocent self just appreciated it as a show. And a lot of the show is based around their struggles as a very poor family. But their house was like, four times the size of mine.

James: It was a sitcom set, yeah.

Bryan: But I remember being like, "Mom, if they're so poor, how come their house is so much bigger than ours?"

And she answered something in the effect of, "What do you think we are?" And that's when I realized that we also did not have much. But it's funny that it took me-- obviously, that's not the best representation of wealth, it's based on nothing, it's just a TV set, like you said. It's kind of like the *Friends* problem, where they work in a coffee shop and have the $10,000 a month apartment in New York City. TV doesn't always account for proper distribution of income. But that was my "a-ha" moment, when I realized we didn't have all that much money.

James: You had mentioned that your family was putting food on the table every night, so from that perspective, the needs were met. But were there things with your friends or people outside of your family that made you realize there were certain things you did not have access to?

Bryan: I knew there was a lot I wasn't doing. So many things I wasn't being exposed to. We didn't go on vacations. I think I only flew maybe once the entire time I was living under my parents'. And that's when my dad's family flew us somewhere, so it wasn't even something born of them. It was the little experiences that I realized, at some point, I wasn't having access to. And then as I got older, and I was in high school, I spent a lot of time with my friends and not at home anymore, and obviously, the differences become very obvious at that point. My friends have their own cars, their own rooms, more video games, and things like that. It becomes clear as time goes on, I think.

James: Can you tell me a little bit about your parents?

Bryan: They're fine people, that's how I'd describe them. They generally always mean well, and we have a fine relationship. But they're very, very different from me. My mom worked in convenience stores growing up, behind the counter, and she ended up eventually working for one of the school systems up here as a special ed aid. And my father worked behind the counter at a tire shop and did that for a little while, and he doesn't work much anymore. But they're kind of-- I'm not trying to say anything bad about them, and if this sounds bad, I don't mean it that way. They're very simple. They don't look to do a lot or learn a lot, they like TV, my mom likes gardening. They're good people, but they're very different from me in that they're not that into learning, they're not that into culture or experiences, they just want to do their thing.

James: Are you close to them?

Bryan: I guess I would say I was forced close to them because we lived in the woods and there were a lot of times that I was hanging out at home. But I think in terms of a typical relationship, I'm not really close to them. I see people that have relationships with their parents that are more friendship-based, there's a lot of commonality, they share experiences, and they do things together. And that's just not something my parents and I share. It's gotten better as time has gone on because I was also an extremely, extremely difficult kid. I feel bad for them, I wasn't easy to raise, I was in trouble all the time and I hated school more than anything else, so I didn't want to go to school. I didn't make things easy on them. But as time has gone on, we still see each other all the time, we go out to dinner, we go out to lunch. So things are good, but not super close, that's how I'd describe it.

James: And what kind of troubles did you get into as a kid?

Bryan: Let me think carefully about that before I say anything. Well, like I said, I hated school. I hated high school more than anything. The only thing I loved was football. So I would generally attend school through football season, and then after that, I'd maybe go once or twice a week, at best. That was always a point of contention. I partied a lot when I was in high school with my friends, I wouldn't come home for long periods of time. So you know, nothing particularly salacious, but stuff that kids who are general never-do-wells get into, that was what I was into.

From a very, very early age, I didn't feel like I was learning anything in school. It was not useful for me. Either it wasn't challenging enough, or the topics discussed were things I didn't care about. Or I felt that if it was something I did want to learn, I would teach myself on my own, I didn't feel like I needed the curriculum. And a lot of that is hubris, you know, thinking there's nothing these people can tell me. And trust, me, I've dealt with—

James: I'm better than them, kind of thing.

Bryan: I've had a lot of that surrounding my personality for a very long time, and it's certainly something that still pops in from time to time, that I really dislike about myself. And I try and improve and get rid of it. But when I was a teenager, it was unfiltered and brutal hubris all the time. So there's a lot of that, that played into my resistance to education. And I have ADD, like a bunch of people who play Magic for whatever reason, we seem to default at this game, so it was hard for me to sit still throughout a school day and to have that structure, have that very defined curriculum and learning pattern. It didn't work for me at all, and it led to me clashing with the principals, and teachers, and all that kind of stuff. But when football season was on, I was a model student. I was there every day, I showed up because if I didn't go to school, I couldn't practice. That was the one exception. But as soon as football season was over, all bets were off.

James: What position did you play in football?

Bryan: I was defensive tackle.

James: Are you still close to the game? Do you still follow it?

Bryan: No. I find it kind of reprehensible, to be honest with you. Something clicked for me one day where it was like, these young primarily black men are being exploited to such a huge extent. And granted, they're making a lot of money, but I think one theme that I'll probably keep coming back to in the course of this conversation is you get one life to live, and these people are doing irreparable harm to their minds and bodies for the entertainment of others. And I did irreparable harm to my body. I couldn't even tell you, it was high school football, but my knees are shot, and I have back issues, all from just working out too much and lifting too much. So I don't know, the gladiator combative stuff doesn't do it for me anymore. And I can't tell you specifically what turned me on it, but at some point, I was just like, this is not for me. And it was overnight, where I watched every single football game and had DirecTV Sunday ticket one year, and the next year I was like, I'm done with this, this doesn't do it for me anymore.

James: Can you ever imagine this happening for Magic? Maybe one day you're playing Magic online or you're in a tournament and you're like, "What am I doing here?" And you walk out and never play Magic again? It's fascinating to me that you have this life experience at a young age and you're so different from that. It strikes me very much as—we have the agency to make our own life decisions and decide what we want to do. And we don't have to be trapped into a certain thing.

Bryan: Right. And I think that agency sometimes takes time to develop. And I think, with a lot of things, it's not like—agency doesn't apply to you as a whole, it applies to each individual thing in your life. And only at certain points where you have moments where you're like, "Actually, I have agency over this." One of the things I talk about with Magic a lot, people ask me all the time, "Do you ever get burnt out on Magic? What do you do if you're burnt out on Magic?" And I'm like, "Well, I don't play Magic." Isn't that obvious? If I don't want to play Magic, why would I keep playing Magic?

But I do remember a point and time in my life where I would just play more Magic when I didn't want to play Magic. In a retrospect, that's kind of insane, and I think that's why I don't see myself ever leaving the game at this point, because I do love it so much, and I also developed some of this agency around the sometimes negative aspects of Magic that can creep in. And I know when I need to back away from the game.

And I also think that if there was something driving me to play when I didn't want to play, it would be my podcast, my content, I would feel a debt to people that I have to play to be able to present them with relevant information. But I actually don't believe that to be the case. I need to stay informed, I need to stay thinking about the game. Neither of those things have ever been an issue for me. I love keeping up with the game, I love thinking about the game in my spare time, I can't see myself ever not wanting to do that. But sometimes, the act of playing can be detrimental for me, either I need to focus on something else in my life, the time is just not there, or I just-- you know, the weather is nice, and I don't want to be in the convention center at a particular weekend. But I think that's okay. I think I can do that and still be able to create good content for people who listen to my podcast. I don't think I can do that and be a Platinum Pro, and this is a lot of the reason why I haven't had those kind of Pro Player's Club accolades is that I will back away when it's best for me. But I'm comfortable with that. I like the place that Magic takes in my life right now and have for a few years now. It's been going well. So I think it will continue in the future.

James: That's great. And if I may go back to your high school days, tell me what happened after that. Because you were quite a rebel, you didn't like going through the school system. What did you do after graduating from high school?

Bryan: I did graduate from high school, I was pretty solidly middle of my class. I think I had a 78 average or something like that, but I took the SATs, and my SATs were 99% percentile SATs. So I was able to go to a good state school. Obviously, most elite colleges would not have looked at me, given a 79 average in high school. But good SAT scores were enough to get me into a very good state school. I went to SUNY Albany and was there for a couple of years.

And it turns out I also did not like college very much. Well, maybe that's not fair. College was fine. And I appreciated some of the learning opportunities there. However, what I appreciated much more than the learning opportunities were the partying opportunities. And I took full advantage of those opportunities, partied a ton, but thankfully, with college, it kind of worked out fine because college was mostly, "Just take this test at the end of the semester and that's what your entire grade is based on." And so, I was able to do fine in college. For the most part, I was on the Dean's List, just showing up and taking the test. It worked out much better for me than high school, where they expected me to be there every day.

James: What was going through your mind as you were studying for the SATs and deciding to go to college? Because you must have had to really apply yourself to be 99th percentile. It doesn't just happen.

Bryan: I didn't prepare. I just took the SATs because I thought I was supposed to. And then I went to college because I thought I was supposed to. None of these things were conscious decisions where I'm like, "This is what I want to do." And when I went to college, I had no idea what I was going for. It was just one of those things where your guidance counselors tell you, "You have to go to college." I hadn't taken agency in my life choices at that point yet. All my friends were going to college, this is what you did.

James: Are you naturally introverted, extroverted, are you a very social person? Is that why you get involved into the partying scene and all that? I'm trying to understand.

Bryan: I'm trying to understand, too, because it's so funny to me, looking back now, that I think I developed into an incredibly introverted person. I don't go out, I don't go to bars, I don't party. I'm very happy staying at home with my wife and my dog. But I guess back then, I did like going out. If I'm being honest, I think I really liked girls, that was my main thing. I liked being around girls. And so, that comes with the socialization, the drinking, and the partying. That was a huge part of my motivations back then. I don't really know how to answer that question. If you wanted me to answer it now, I would say I'm very much an introvert, which also clashes somewhat with the fact that I am doing a podcast and putting myself out there to a bunch of people. But it would still be my answer to that question as of right now. But I guess at some point, I was very much the opposite person. At some point I became a bartender, which is the most extroverted position you can have, right? You're in charge of keeping everyone interacting and happy.

James: You got into bartending as you were in school or after you graduated from school?

Bryan: No, so my path is essentially-- I go to college, right? And things are going well. I'm making Dean's List, not at the top of-- I don't have a 4.0 average or anything like that, but I'm doing fine. And this is in about 2001. And if you're about my age, I'm sure you remember 2001 was the time of the poker boom. And all of a sudden, everyone on campus was playing poker all the time, and like everyone else, I started playing poker all the time. Unlike most other people, I was like, "Huh. I think you'd probably learn a lot more about this game and not be stupid about it, and I wonder what would happen if I put some time into it."

I started learning poker and I started reading about poker, studying poker, I was on 2+2, Party Poker, Empire Poker, 12, 24 hours a day, and I started making a lot of money. Enough money that I couldn't see any more use for education in my life. I was like, "Why would I do anything else?" And you have to keep in mind that this all comes from a lens of having grown up very poor. And now I'm 19 and I'm making a lot of money for a 19-year-old. Especially one who has never had money in his life, who has never seen money, and things escalated very quickly. And I didn't even drop out of school, I just stopped going to classes. Because I was like, "Whatever, I have enough money to pay off these loans, it doesn't really matter." And I just played poker for a few years. Mostly online, a little bit live, but I started to do really well for myself, and that became my job for a while, and I thought it might always be my job going forward.

James: Were you very disciplined about it? You had a proper bankroll that you managed? I remember at the time, the games could be rather soft if you knew what you were doing.

Bryan: My bankroll management was good. I wouldn't say great, it was good, in that I always made sure there was enough reserved to keep me playing. Money management was not good. Everything that pulled off the top of my bankroll was spent incredibly quickly. But there was enough to go around. Like you said, games were soft, so it didn't really matter. There was enough for both proper bankroll management and wasteful spending. And I'd certainly never hit nosebleed stakes, I wasn't at the very top of the poker game, but I was making a comfortable six-figure living for a few years. I guess I would say I was half-disciplined. My bankroll management was pretty good, my money management was horrible.

James: What were some of the craziest things you spent money on? Was it like a Lamborghini or something?

Bryan: No, it wasn't anything that-- so like we discussed, lots of partying, and you know, buy the whole bar drinks. Buy ten kegs for a party. But the dumbest stuff I bought was clothing. I bought so much Gucci, Armani, just the dumbest shit you could ever buy.

My face is red right now, I can feel it. It brings me so much shame to think of the money I wasted on this stuff. I again implore everyone to please try and understand that I was a really dumb 19-year-old kid who had never seen money. And I was so into conspicuous consumption that it brings me pain to think back on it. It's crazy how silly I was with that stuff. Tons of fancy clothes. I bought some nice guitars, some nice computer equipment. I was very into home theatre stuff, so I had very early high-definition TVs that were thousands and thousands of dollars for a TV you'd laugh at now.

James: But it did change your relationship with money and how you view money.

Bryan: It made a tremendous difference, and we're kind of progressing through my life narrative. But we'll get to the point where I take a very high-paying job and watch the people around me falling into some of the same traps I fell into so many years ago, and me being able to sit back and go, "I don't think you should do that right now. Trust me, I know how this story ends, you really don't need that Gucci shirt, you're going to feel very stupid about this in a few years."

James: How long did this poker thing last for you?

Bryan: I was going hard for about two years. The extracurriculars, the partying, the other stuff very much caught up with me. I always say I don't think I ever had a drug or an alcohol problem, but I definitely had a partying problem. I partied way too much. Like seven nights a week. I played my hours of poker for the day and it was time to party, every single day. But all that caught up with me, and at the same time, I started to hate playing poker. Just hate it. I hated every second I was playing online poker. Because it gets so mechanical and dehumanizing at some point, and I see so many people go through it. I've seen so many of my friends go through it. But you know how it is, if you're multi-tabling, and all you have to do is check your boxes at the end of the day, your bank account should go up, and you just repeat over and over every day, same thing. Checking your boxes, clicking your folds, clicking your aces, and at the end of the day, there's more money, and it lost all meaning to me, and I hated, hated playing poker. And so I stopped.

James: Just stopped one day?

Bryan: Yeah, people are always like, "Did you go bust?" No, I just stopped, I didn't want to do it anymore. Then eventually I went bust, I spent all the money I had in reserve for-- I was still spending money like I had it coming in when I was playing poker. That didn't last for so long. But it had nothing to do with the games, I just lost interest and wasn't playing anymore.

James: It can get rather mechanical at some point, right?

Bryan: I felt like I was working at the factory, you know? I was working at the poker factory every day, just clicking my boxes, punching my timecard, and that was it. I had no joy, no passion for it, it just went one day.

James: Had you already dropped out of school at that point?

Bryan: Yeah. I remember I had a test-- I don't know what day of the week it was. I had a test coming up and the night before the test, I was in a poker tournament that I started like, mid-day, and I was like, "I'll finish this poker tournament and afterwards, I'll study for this test and go to it." And I ended up winning the tournament for $40,000 or something like that, and I was like, "You know what? I'm not going to this test tomorrow, I'm going out to celebrate." And that was it. I never went to another class after that.

So that had been about two years at that point, once I stopped playing.

James: What happens after that in the life of Bryan Gottlieb?

Bryan: Well, one of the things about partying all the time is that you get to know everyone at all the bars. And by doing that, I was like, "If I'm not going to play poker, I have to do something." I seemed to like being at the bars quite a bit, so maybe I'll be a bartender. And one of the things that came with my conspicuous consumption was that I was a very generous tipper, and so I made a lot of friends in the service industry in my town. And when I came to them and was like, "Hey, I want to start bartending," I found a place pretty quickly and started doing that for a few years.

James: Was it a difficult ramp-up process? Or did you get into it, from a skill set perspective, fairly easily?

Bryan: It was fairly easy. I mean, there's not a lot to it, right? You learn some drinks and it's pretty much a done deal. And the rest of it is just socializing. And I always worked in non-corporate places. At least when I was in Albany. So it was partying, drinking, doing shots the whole night, and hoping you were sober enough to count your money at the end of the night. It was a lot of fun for that era of my life, I really enjoyed it.

James: It sounds like it was a way to continue the social lifestyle that you had without having to rely on poker. You replaced poker with another profession to make a living. Is that right?

Bryan: Right, yeah, I think that's spot-on. Another non-traditional-- I didn't have to wake up early, I worked usually from 10pm to 4am, those were my hours, and it fit with what my lifestyle looked like at the time, and it was the easiest route for me to go down.

James: Did anything interesting ever happen as you were working at the bar? Any interesting clients-- not clients, but customers, just weird stuff happening?

Bryan: A lot. A lot of weird stuff. I had a gun flashed at me because I didn't make a drink strong enough, that was interesting. I had a lot of celebrities come through and drank with them. They're usually not very interesting for the most part.

James: They're just people, right?

Bryan: Yeah, they're always a letdown, that's been my basic experience with celebrities. I'm trying to think if I had any absolute gang buster stories, but nothing is springing into mind. Just typical bartender stuff. There were a lot of long, long nights, a lot of partying. For someone at that age, it was a very fun environment.

James: And what happens after that? After bartending? How long did you bartend for?

Bryan: So I'm doing the bartending thing, and at some point, I was like, "Ok, I like this, but I can't do this forever." I was very aware of the fact that I'm getting older, and one of the things I always said for myself is you can't bartend when you're 30 years old. I made myself promise that I would not bartend at the age of 30 because people in the industry who are around for a long time, once you hit that 30-year-old point, you're going to be bartending for the rest of your life. And I knew I didn't want to do that. Not that there's anything wrong with it, if that's what you love. I have a lot of friends who are still bartending to this day and that's what they really love doing, but it wasn't for me.

I was like, "Ok, I have to go back and get my undergraduate degree." I went back to school while I was still bartending, I was doing both, and finished my undergraduate degree. Not really anything too exciting there, just picked up the credits I needed, moved on, and that was the end of it. And at that point, I had a very special guest come into my bar one night, who would turn out to be my wife. Which changed a lot of the plans that I had going forward. I knew I was going to transition away from the bartending game, but I wasn't exactly sure how to do it at that point. It was a goal of mine, but I hadn't taken any affirmative steps to doing so. And my wife comes into the bar one night, I meet her, and we hit it off immediately, we're talking, and I'm like, "I want to move to Vegas, what do you think about moving out there?" And we'd only known each other three months at that point, and she was like, "Yeah, that sounds good."

We moved to Vegas and I started playing a little poker, which as it turns out, I still hated, and bartending out there. Again, not knowing what I was doing but just being like, "Ok, this is fun for now, and we'll see where it goes." And I bartended on the Strip a little bit, down on Freemont Street, but we went to Vegas at a really bad time. We went in 2007, which was like the peak of the foreclosure crisis, and Vegas was hit hardest by that crisis. Maybe worse than anywhere in the entire country. The economy was in shambles, it was not a good time to be in Vegas. So we moved back to the East Coast and then I was like, "You know what? I think I should go to

law school." And that's really the extent of the decision-making process there.

James: You just woke up one day and you said, "I want to
go to law school."

Bryan: I couldn't even tell you what was going through my
head. I think it was something that I had thought
about before. I mean, after I had this flash of an
idea, I explored a little more, and the thing which
cemented it as the correct approach in my eyes was
that law school was very much a meritocracy. And
basically, I knew if I were to succeed in law school,
I was likely to jumpstart a real career right out the
gate. There would be opportunities immediately.
And I liked that, I didn't want to have to take an
entry-level job and build up for years and years. So
I think maybe that, more than anything, pushed me
in the direction of law school.

James: That's a very good observation. You basically looked
at what was available for someone in his 30s and
thought that was a pretty good bet to make, right?

Bryan: Right, it seemed like there was-- if I did well, there
was the potential to catapult a career right away.
And I knew there was risk involved, I didn't go to
a top-tier law school. I think a lot of people-- this
is getting into some law school inside baseball, so
again, I'm speaking to a very small portion of your
audience.

James: No, it's all good.

Bryan: But a lot of people who go to schools a little bit further down the ranking list don't really know what
they're getting into. But job prospects, when you're
not in an elite law school, are not good. They're

only good at the very top of the class. And my intention was that if I was not in the top 10% of my law school class after my first year, I would drop out, cut my loss at that point, and just stop. But things went well, so I was able to continue on through law school.

James: Absolutely. I have a few friends who are lawyers as well, and it's definitely not the glamorous lifestyle.

Bryan: Yeah. And even when you find success, which I think I did, success can sometimes-- it's not always what it's cracked up to be, let's just say that.

James: When you were in school, I remember you said that you were very engaged, and you felt very excited to go to class and learn something. You were there voluntarily, on your own.

Bryan: For the first time in my life.

James: Exactly. But as you became a lawyer, you maybe realized that things were not as you had originally perceived it to be. I mean, you got what you wanted, which was you got into a profession that you targeted getting into, so that's awesome. But you also mentioned that it's not exactly up to your expectations, right?

Bryan: I think that's a good way of putting it. Ultimately, I graduated law school at the very top of my class and got a job with a prestigious firm in New York City. And I have nothing but good things to say about the opportunities there, and the people there were honestly great people. Almost everyone I encountered was an intelligent, bright, fantastic person, I still stay in touch with a lot of them to this day. But the world of big, New York City law firms, is tough.

It's hellacious hours, incredible demands, great salary. I mean, I don't think anyone will dispute that. But it's your life.

By that point, my wife and I had been married, and we moved to New York City so I could take this job. It was hard on her, it was hard on me. She was working from home, so she was spending a lot of time at home by herself, and we were generally unhappy with the circumstances surrounding the practice at a large law firm.

Beyond that, I had some moral issues with what we were working in service of. And it's tough for a lawyer, right? Because you recognize the fact that everyone does have to have access to representation, it's important. It's the foundation of our system. But that doesn't mean I have to want to play a part in helping who I see as the worst actors in our economic justice system, which primarily, I would define as banks, and that's mostly who the clientele was for New York City, as you could imagine. I wasn't super thrilled with that position, I didn't like that I was spending the vast majority of my waking hours in service of banks.

James: Would you say that there was a level of guilt associated with that, or was it something else?

Bryan: There's definitely some guilt. I think that's a fine way to phrase it. Because you know it's not in line with your values, why you're doing it. And you know, there are justifications for it. Like I said, I do believe everyone deserves access to representation and quite frankly, a lot of the-- I have to be careful with what I say when it comes to the practice of law because, obviously, there's very intense protection on specific things I've done. A lot of the laws and regulations against banks are almost impossible to comply with. They're so dense and so all-encompassing, and so demanding, that they're kind of just there to assign liability.

That's problematic as well, that's not the ideal system for regulation of these entities, but the absence would probably be 10 times more horrifying, letting banks do whatever they want unchecked, that would be super problematic as well. So I see why they need representation to work their way through these regulations, because they are incredibly intense and almost impossible to have full compliance with. But at the same time, I didn't want to be the one doing it anymore, I didn't feel good about it.

James: It sounds like kind of an impossible situation. Someone's got to do it, but it doesn't make it good, acceptable, or maybe value-wise, aligned to what you personally believe in.

Bryan: Right. And ultimately, you have to go home at night feeling good about what you do every day. I don't know how you can go through your day and not be working further into something that you care about at least a little bit. You have to be like, I accomplished something, I moved something forward. I don't think you need to say this is the be-all-end-all of my existence, but you have to say that in general, the world is probably a little bit better because of my participation in it. And I didn't feel like I was saying that at the end of the day.

James: It must have been very tough to step away from that. Because in the back of my mind, at least, I'm always thinking about, how many times can I reinvent myself, right? How many times can I hit the reset button? And if I keep resetting, is it really the job that's the problem or is it me? Did that ever come across in your mind?

Bryan: Just every single day. Literally, every single day, I think about that. Especially when I was leaving that job, because the money was so good. And there's only so many people who get those opportunities. And they're not distributed fairly. I don't think I was more deserving of that opportunity than a ton of other people, but I got it. And there was a level of guilt that I had from walking away from that opportunity that I know a lot of people fight for and want desperately, and here I am--

James: Are you being ungrateful, right?

Bryan: Right. That crossed my mind all the time. All the time, that came up for me. And still does. To this day, I think about it. What if I had stayed, toughed it out? I could have put my family in a very good financial position, only at the cost of my soul. What's a soul worth anyway? Who cares? But yeah, it comes up all the time. And when you're talking about the reset button, I think I stand kind of on the precipice of this again now.

So maybe I should talk about-- I leave this big firm, and I left it to go work for a legal service provider for the poor. Essentially, I helped impoverished people who are in foreclosure situations. And I help them try and keep their homes through legal means as well as various governmental and private programs that are out there to assist people facing foreclosures. Basically, it was kind of my effort at atonement. As opposed to working for the bank, now I was working against the bank. As they try to take people's homes away, I was fighting on behalf of the people so they could keep their homes.

And again, the people I work with, the things they want to accomplish, it's all inspiring. I think the organization and all the attorneys care so much about their clients and these people who, a lot of other people have cast aside and don't care about, there's a huge effort on getting them access to the legal representation that they deserve. But there's also a tremendous amount of challenges that come with working with that segment of the population. Maybe I'm just not strong enough for it, I don't know.

It's hard for me to see these people in super trying circumstances, super unfair circumstances. Their entire lives have worked against them to put them in a position where they aren't able to take care of their finances and they don't understand the consequence of signing a 13% interest loan on their home. They were never put in a position to succeed. The game has been stacked against them from the very beginning. And you fight and fight, and do all you can for them, and a lot of times, they're not able to capitalize on that fight because they don't have the tools to do so. They don't understand the underworking of the banking system and all the things that go into it. It's very trying. You feel good for your successes, but the reality of the situation is, when you're dealing with low-income people, is there's always going to be a lot more failures than successes. That's just the nature of the game. There's no way around it -- the system is stacked against them.

I don't want to get too political, but they're essentially faced with a government who doesn't care about them, who doesn't want to put the effort and take care of them. They're in incredibly difficult spots and it's kind of the opposite problem, where you come home at the end of the day and despite all your efforts on behalf of people who really, really need those efforts, you feel like you didn't accomplish anything. You didn't do anything.

And there's this weird situation, and this is again, some more very specific inside baseball, but a lot of what funds the foreclosure prevention programs, at least in New York State, is money that the banks had to pay in settlement of previous prosecution. Where the banks had previous wrong doings, they were fined billions of dollars, mostly from the mortgage crisis, and New York State set up funds and distributed this money across a bunch of places. And they were using it to help people keep their homes. Which, you think about it, your first thought is, "Oh, this is a nice usage of this money, I'm glad it's being reallocated to let people keep their homes and protect the people as opposed to the banks." But then you stop for a second and you go one step further, and you're realizing what's actually happening is that you're filtering the money that the banks paid in punishment, you're using it to repay loans to them that they would have otherwise never been able to collect on, because these people are too poor to pay off these loans. They're actually just getting the money back.

James: So the banks are still getting rewarded by the system?

Bryan: Well, I think that's a cynical way to look at it, because that ignores the fact that there is still an individual in the midst of all this who would have otherwise lost their home and now gets to stay in their home. You can't ignore that aspect of it. And that's kind of what you're doing by just tracing the money.

James: These are people, not just statistics, they're people.

Bryan: That's exactly right. And that's where the triumph comes from. But ultimately, when you think about it at a larger scale, you see the problem. You're giving the banks their money back, you're making sure that they get paid on their loans that they otherwise would not have gotten paid on. So yeah, there's a lot of systemic problems, and if anything, I was frustrated by how little of an impact I've been having on those problems, and I want to do something that makes people happier instead. Because I think fighting the system leads to a lot of frustration, and they're bigger than one person. It's about changing the collective consciousness. And maybe the best way for me to have an impact on the collective consciousness is by talking about things like this. Maybe-- it's kind of crazy to say this, but maybe it's by doing episodes like the greatness episode and letting people know it's ok to push yourself, chase dreams, and to inspire someone who can go forward and help push the collective consciousness forward. It's kind of grandiose to think about a Magic podcast having that kind of effect, but I feel better about what I do with Magic content creation than I do as a lawyer for the poor. Which is a strange thing to say, but it feels like I'm making more of a difference doing the former rather than the latter. Does that sound crazy to you?

James: No. It's not crazy at all. I feel the same way when I'm doing content like this with you and other people.

Bryan: And one of the big sources of inspiration for me, in that regard, has been Gerry. And I know when Gerry was on with you last, you guys talked a lot about depression. And I think Gerry has taken on that topic, has become a champion of discussion of that topic. And we see people either through our discord or through Twitter who interact with him on that topic all the time. And you think about how many people he's reached with the message of self-care, self-help, and not allowing yourself to be stigmatized for mental issues. I don't know if he discovers that's his passion and he decides to become a therapist, I don't know if that has more impact on the world than him just being who he is as a Magic personality and speaking about depression, speaking about those issues. I think he's probably more apt to have a bigger impact via his podcasting, via his content creation. It's a powerful platform to have.

James: Absolutely. So what is next for you? I mean, there's obviously the podcast, but what are other things that are top of mind in your life?

Bryan: That's a good question. My responses are going to be pretty broad, but I'm cool with that, because quite frankly, I don't know what's going to come next. As a family, we decided we're going to let my wife drive the narrative for a while. She is very successful in what she does, and just by virtue of opportunity, it's been my career driving a lot of the decisions, moving to New York to lawyer, being back up here. So letting her take the lead for a little while. It looks like we're going to be moving from the East Coast sometime soon. The leader in the clubhouse is Seattle right now, but Denver is also in play. Somewhere

where there's appropriate snowboarding and some good urban areas is really where we'd like to go. That's the location part of it.

As far as what I'm going to do, I'm really into the content thing. I'm enjoying what I do so much, I would like to continue to expand what I'm doing. Does this mean launching an additional podcast? Maybe starting to do some video content? Some coaching is something that's on the table for me and it's something that's not super well-done in the Magic world right now, it can be much better than it currently is. I may get involved with that.

And quite frankly, I want to be doing coverage for Magic, and I think I would be damn good at it. I don't know what's going to lead me down that road, I don't know who it will ultimately be with, but I think I can bring a lot to coverage at the game. Not only as an on-air personality, but I want to talk to people about coverage. Because I love Magic so much, I want it to be presented for what I know that it is, and that's the best game on the planet. And I think at times, the presentation has lagged behind the quality of the game. And I want to play a part in helping address that lag and moving Magic forward.

I'm at a place where I'm comfortable exploring some passions right now, and my passion right now is mostly talking about Magic, even more so than playing it. I'm never going to be a week-to-week tournament grinder, you're not going to see me at every single SCG event. I don't like travel all that much. I like traveling to different locales, I don't necessarily like traveling to different convention centers, the way Magic travel often pans out. I'm only taking on that burden if I'm talking about the game. The variance inherent in Magic and that soul-crushing aspect of, "I need this last Pro Point, but I just can't get it." That's not what I'm looking to travel around the country for. I want to travel around the country and be an ambassador for the game, and portray the game, play it at the highest level and point it out for just how special it is.

And I'm exploring other options, as far as teaching goes, too. Like I said, I haven't loved being a lawyer, but I loved law school. And my experiences as a lawyer, despite the fact that I walked away frustrated with it all, I still think it translates into helping make other lawyers very good at their jobs. And being involved at the law school level and maybe teaching a bit might be for me, going forward.

James: That's great. When it comes to the Magic part and being involved in that, have you given some thought as to what your stepping stones would be?

Bryan: No, not specifically. I think that sometimes presenting proof of change is the best way to encourage it. So just doing it, you know what I mean? Just finding the spot to do some coverage and saying, "Look, this is what Magic can be." I don't know where that opportunity is going to come from, but if I have to, I'll create it. I'll find a way to present Magic in new and novel ways that can bring people to the game. Because it shouldn't be hard, this game is too good. This is the best game ever made, I say it every time.

Any gripe I ever have about Magic, any complaint about the state of a metagame, or the state of coverage, or decisions around the players' club... any complaint I've ever made comes from the strongest place of love possible, because I know how good this game is. There's something monumentally special about Magic, and for me, having been alive for 35 years now, nothing has come close to capturing my passions this way. I've been playing since basically late '94, '95-ish. And while Magic has flowed throughout my entire life, it's always been there. And I think it will always be there, I never see it going away. For a game to have that kind of grasp on you, it has to be something intensely special, right? And it needs to be shown as that to a new generation of players. I want tons of young people into the game, I want the game to last forever, to grow, and to be here for as long as I am here. So I'll find a way to play a part in that, be it through podcasting, coaching, ultimately covering Magic tournaments, whatever it is, that's what I'm going to do, going forward.

James: This is one thing I've always heard you say on your podcast, that Magic is amazing. But I don't know if you've ever said why it's a great thing for you. I mean, you obviously believe in it so much, but have you ever verbalized why it is the greatest game ever and what it's done for you?

Bryan: That's a tough topic to be brief on, and as you may have noticed, brevity is not always my strong suit, but I will try. There's two parts to it. One is so ethereal it's almost meaningless, but there's this *feel* to Magic. Everything feels right, everything feels perfect to me. It's like it intertwines with my soul. And I know that's almost a nonsense statement that means nothing, but like, sometimes I feel experiences as Magic experiences. Like, some things to me will feel like expending my mana appropriately, or lightning bolting a three-toughness creature. Those experiences happen throughout my day because the mechanics and the essence of Magic gameplay is so beautiful and so perfect. And like I said, I recognize that doesn't mean a whole lot, but it's something that I feel and have never really perfectly verbalized before. Someday, I'll figure out exactly how to put it into words.

But beyond that, there's also the fact that Magic is a different game every single day of the week. Magic, right now, is not the same game that it is going to be tomorrow. Someone will have figured out something new or explored something new. Or there'll be new cards, at least. Or there'll be a new format. Magic changes all the time - it's always interesting, it's always fresh, there's always something new to explore. There's very few times where we come to record a podcast and we're like, "Oh man, what are we going to talk about today?" Because there's so many layers to Magic, there's so many aspects of it, both surface and sub-surface. There's the mental aspect of it, there's the collection aspect of it, which is something that we don't really get into, but it means a lot to a lot of people. There's the art aspect of it, the cosplay aspect of it. It's so many things to so many people, and I think that is a large portion of why it has been and continues to be the best game ever created.

I don't know that I've ever perfectly verbalized it. I've never talked about it and been, "Yes, finally, I got it out." But I'll keep trying and one day someone will be like, "Now I understand what he's talking about."

James: To close the interview, I have two final rapid-fire questions to ask you.

Bryan: Let's do it.

James: If you could go back in time five years and tell your-self something, what would you say to the younger Bryan?

Bryan: Be a better person. It's that simple. I liked being edgy for a long time. I think a lot of us who came up with the Internet fell into that trap along the way. I mistook edginess for cleverness, and I didn't always have the best attitude about Magic. Losing is not something that comes easy to me, it's something that I've had to work at doing gracefully. And even still to this day, sometimes it's hard. I hate to admit that, I want to be the most gracious loser all the time, but I've had blips on my radar over the past five years where I haven't been. For the most part, I think I am, but I'm not perfect.

If I were able to go back five years and just be like, "Look, think about how you're presenting yourself to people, think about how your actions affect them, think about how just a small thing, like saying, 'thanks for the game,' or not being salty in the aftermath of a bad loss will affect your oppo-nent's enjoyment, and really focus on those things and use those to push you to grow as a person." I hope that five years ago me would listen to that. Because five years ago, there was starting to be this burgeoning sense of, "I want to make my commu-nity a better place."

Ten years ago, I probably would have punched myself in the face or something horrible. I was a crappy person ten years ago. But if you don't look back at yourself ten years ago and don't have at least some shame and some disappointment in who you were, then you haven't grown as a person. And I embrace the fact that I wasn't the person I am now, and that I had a lot of crappy aspects about my personality. And I hope that ten years from now I listen to this interview and I'm like, "Wow, that guy was an idiot, I'm so glad that I'm not him anymore and I have now evolved to be this person." It's this process of continuous growth that I would like to have pushed along a little bit faster going back five years.

James: That's awesome. Next question. If you were talking to someone who was getting into content creation, whether Magic or other, for the first time, what advice would you give him or her?

Bryan: You have to believe in yourself, because if you don't, no one else will either. If you leave yourself room to be doubted and to fail, then you will be doubted, and you will fail. And you have reason to believe in yourself, too. You have something to say. If you are able to sit down and record an entire podcast, or write an entire article, or just have a conversation with someone, you have something worth saying. It's there, it's within you. And the world will be a better place for you having shared it with a bunch of people. And believe that, embrace that, and go forward and make whatever content you want to make. You don't have to please everyone, but that content might mean a lot to one person, to ten people, or maybe thousands of people, you never know. So make it, do it, be brave and proud of yourself.

"My dad understood why I would fly all over the country playing these Grand Prix to earn $250. Because it wasn't about the money, it wasn't even about the Pro Points, it was about proving something. And he got that."

—Andrew Elenbogen

Chapter 11

Andrew Elenbogen

Andrew's story says something about the way we look at success in today's society. He won Pro Tour Guilds of Ravnica in 2018, and a lot of the narratives I read centered around Andrew being some sort of unknown Magic player who achieved *overnight success*.

But the idea of *overnight success*, at least in Andrew's case, is a falsehood. The reality is that Andrew worked for years on his Magic game to be in a position to win a Pro Tour. He made tremendous sacrifices and traveled to an unbelievable amount of tournaments.

Of course he had to get lucky within the confines of a single tournament, but that's how the structure of the game goes. More importantly, Andrew worked his tail off to be in a position to get lucky.

I wanted to highlight Andrew's story because he represents the hundreds of thousands of grinders who are looking for a significant finish to break through.

It's a challenging road, and Andrew's certainly had to overcome his share of personal problems to reach the finish line. There are similarities between him and the highly competitive players you see every week at the local gaming store.

Andrew has a good head on his shoulders. He is grateful for all the success that he's accumulated. As Andrew will readily admit, winning at the highest level of Magic competition changed his life in more ways than one. He hasn't forgotten that.

Never one to take things for granted, Andrew still plays Grand Prix events all over the United States because he loves the game. He doesn't need to qualify this season, but he's still going out there and having fun, and supporting his fellow players. It's where he belongs.

The circumstances in which I connected with Andrew were fortuitous. My startup company, CardBoard Live, is building a livestreaming platform to help gaming content creators tell great stories to their fans. We sponsored a number of players at Pro Tour Guilds of Ravnica. Andrew happened to be one of them.

What first looked like a great two-day run for him transformed into a historic finish for Team CardBoard Live, as Andrew made the prestigious top eight. For CardBoard Live, it felt like winning the lottery.

I could not remember the last time I was so invested in any one player. I was glued to coverage all weekend, willing Andrew to victory. When he was finally crowned the winner with a decisive victory over Luis Scott-Vargas, I literally jumped out of my seat.

But the fact of the matter is – Andrew is great, regardless of who's sponsoring him. I'm glad for the opportunity to talk to him, and for having a platform to share his journey with others.

This young man is just getting started, and the road looks bright for him. He is no overnight success, and he is certainly no one-hit wonder.

Recorded in November 2018.

James: How has life changed for you after winning the Pro Tour?

Andrew: That's a good question. Quite a bit has changed. Prior to winning the Pro Tour, I would say that some of the other pros, or players who play in a lot of Grand Prix events, knew who I was. But winning the Pro Tour has produced an overnight change.

Overnight, I gained 1,000 Twitter followers. And that's insane. I'm getting all these congratulations from millions of people, some of whom I don't really know that well, or that I met one time and we fell out of touch.

I'm getting all of these requests to do Magic type things, like this podcast. I wrote an article for Star City Games. It's been a big change in terms of the percent of my time that I spend doing Magic-related things.

And that's a trade-off. It's a trade-off in that I left work early this week because I had to do some of these things I talked about. I am a full-time software engineer, but I've always been a weekend warrior, traveling to tournaments. Now I'm trying to re-evaluate what this means going forward. Am I going to try to work less hours in general, so that I can do more with Magic?

James: Mostly good things to consider, I hope?

Andrew: Oh yeah. Honestly, it's been awesome. I was kind of worried when I top-eighted, because Twitch chat is often not kind to people who are on the stream, especially when you're playing against a fan-favorite like LSV [Luis Scott-Vargas], and especially when LSV is getting very unlucky. But honestly, I re-watched the finals and I read the Twitch chat comments and people seemed to react pretty positively. I'm not entirely sure why, but whatever it is that I'm doing, I appear to be doing it right. So overall, I can't complain, it's been completely amazing.

James: For many of us watching you on Twitch, you represent the "everyperson" Magic player. We can put ourselves in your shoes and see the quest or the journey that you've been taking all the way to the very top. As well, you seemed so genuinely happy, excited, and humbled to be there, which was cool to see.

Andrew: I appreciate the compliment. I certainly was incredibly happy, it was the happiest I'd been in a very long time, it would be difficult for me to say exactly how long it's been since I've been this happy, but a very long time, I was ecstatic. And I try to be accurate about how I view myself—at least in the areas of abilities at Magic, I think I am pretty decently self-aware, although perhaps everyone says that about themselves, it's hard for me to say. But I think it's fair for me to say that I did not, in my life, think I would ever top-eight a Pro Tour. I did not in my life think I would ever *win* a Pro Tour. I think I was very unlikely to do so. I still think I'm very unlikely to do so.

I don't think you're going to see me top-eight the next Pro Tour, I don't think that I'm going to make the Magic Hall of Fame or anything. I just think that on this weekend, I played pretty well, I got pretty lucky, I had a pretty good deck choice, and the stars aligned. And that happens in Magic. And it's great when it happens in your favor, even though it's pretty unfortunate when it does not happen in your favor—sorry, LSV...I still don't feel that I am good enough at Magic to have top-eighted a Pro Tour, even though I factually have done so. Which is kind of a weird place to be, but that is how I feel about Magic right now.

382

James: You have a good mindset because it's about staying hungry. Even though you've accomplished something that hundreds, thousands, tens of thousands of players dream about, at the same time, it seems like you are self-aware that you have lots of room to improve before you could become a Hall of Fame player.

Andrew: Yes, I certainly feel that. And I hope that I'm not at my peak in terms of skill level. I hope that I will continue to improve. And I will admit that I have felt for a while—for the last year or so—I have felt that I was playing the best Magic I have ever played. Which is not necessarily saying Pro Tour top eight caliber Magic or Hall of Fame caliber Magic. But I could tell I was playing better. And that certainly felt great, even though I didn't have this big finish. And now I do, and hopefully the rest of the world knows that I'm a lot better than I used to be as well.

James: That's awesome.

Andrew: Yeah. And to be clear about my relationship with the game, because I think people are probably not super aware of this—I play a lot of GPs [Grand Prix], by anyone's standards. I fly all over the US playing GPs, and I drive pretty long distances to get to them. I'm not saying that I play the most GPs of anyone, but as far as people who you've never heard of, I play a lot of GPs. And I do that mostly because GPs are awesome...I have a lot of friends who play a lot of GPs and I see them every time I do this, it's a big reunion of people that I like. And I also really like playing Magic. If I didn't like it, I wouldn't do this, it's a lot of time, money, and effort to invest. But this means that—I don't know how to phrase it...

James: I think what you're trying to say is that it was no overnight success. You have grinded hard on the professional competitive circuit for quite some time.

Andrew: Yes, that's exactly what I'm saying. I played at least 10 or 15 GPs this year, I played at least 10 or 15 GPs the previous year, I'm playing a GP a month, at least, plus some SCGs, typically, plus RTPQs. Ultimately, I'm playing Magic tournaments for the last several years multiple times every month, I'm driving long distances, I'm flying. I put in a lot of hours, and that has, to some extent, paid off, although I still could be better.

But I feel that my story—ok, let's talk a little about this. My friend, Sam Ihlenfeldt, who is also a great player who I've known for many years, when Sam top-eighted the Pro Tour, it was his literal first Pro Tour. Sam literally went from zero to hero in no time flat, that's what happened.

My story is a little different than that, perhaps it's a small distinction. But...my first GP was ten years ago now. I have been playing competitive Magic for many years. I have been grinding, I have been getting those 11-4 [results], those cashes [prizes], those 10-5 [results] for a single Pro Point. Prior to winning the Pro Tour and becoming Platinum, I was a Silver Level Pro, mostly on two [Pro] Point finishes, mostly on every GP I showed up, I 6-2ed into day two, I would have another—whatever finish, hit 11-4, get my two points, get $250, which doesn't even pay for my flight, and then fly to another one the next weekend. That was my life, and probably still will be my life but with more benefits. And so I do think that my story is more of a culmination of a long grind than a literal everyman's.

James: I want get inside your mind a little bit regarding the events of the Pro Tour. Maybe start from day one, where you finished 7-1.

Andrew: Let me talk about it a little bit...I will state that I'm pretty good under pressure. That's something that has been true for me for many years. I actually had the reverse problem growing up–my problem was that I was so confident I would succeed at tests and stuff, that I would have trouble making myself prepare because I had zero nervousness or stress whatsoever about it. But after day one, I was honestly totally fine, I didn't have any trouble. We all went out to dinner. I had a pretty reasonable burger—I'm a big fan of burgers—and I went to bed. I didn't think much of the 7-1. I mean, obviously 7-1 is an amazing record, but my goal for this tournament was 11-5. I knew if I [got] 11-5, you get instant qualification for the next PT, you get 10 Pro Points, and I was already Silver, so that put me very close to being Gold. I suspected if I [hit] 11-5 it would mean a lot of Pro Tours in a row...It's a tough field and I still need[ed] to play well, but I didn't have any big dreams...[F]unnily enough, a friend asked me, "If you had the option to lock in 10-6, exactly the record 10-6, for every Pro Tour you ever played for the rest of your life, would you accept?" And I immediately accepted. Yes, I certainly would.

James: Stay on the train, right?

Andrew: It means you'd be Gold for life and on the PT forever. That would be awesome, that's all I want. Maybe I'll do better occasionally, but it cannot be that frequent. That's what I felt the night before.

James: So you start day two, and how did the day go for you?

Andrew: Well, the first thing that happened is that my draft deck was really bad. And I knew it was bad. My draft was a disaster. I think *I* screwed it up, I think my pick three is really wrong…the point is, I train-wrecked my own draft, I knew my deck was terrible, and I was like, "Oh god, this is not going to work out. I'm going to 0-3 this draft, I'm going to be 7-4, and then…I'm going to miss 11-5, and I'm going to miss Gold, I would just have wasted this 7-1."

James: Was all this stuff was through your head as soon as you made that pick?

Andrew: Well, more like later in the draft…. But yeah, certainly my thought when I'm picking up my draft and going to register my deck…I managed one win with the deck against Mark Jacobson, a very strong player. But his deck was poorly matched up against mine even though my deck was objectively worse… Everything keeps going my way, round after round. Many absurd and unlikely events happened. I don't know. I win this [round] against Green-Black, where I draw all four Venerated Loxodons. And my opponent literally looks at the Finality in their hand and realizes that it kills none of my creatures because they're all 5/5s…. It was surreal, I was running so hot. And I'm just, wow, this is crazy. Maybe somehow, I can do it.

But then, I lost [one favorable match up]…and that was my fourth loss. Everybody was telling me that this is the largest Pro Tour ever, I was very unlikely to make top eight. They thought X-4 was a long shot. Maybe one would slip in, is what I was told.

I got to my last run against Mark Jacobson, still on the line. I locked up my 11-5 at this point, which is great, anything else is gravy to me. I feel good, but a win would make me instantly Gold as opposed to needing to string up some finishes to make Gold, which is nice. It means $2,000 additional.

I'm playing against Mark Jacobson, and both Mark and I are on the standings, we've done the math, we have friends helping us out with the math. And possibly the same friend, but that's not the point. We both believed that we are dead for top eight. We think we cannot make it, we think we are playing a match for ninth. I play this match against Mark Jacobson, and I honestly think that match was also unfavorable for me. He was playing main deck sweepers, lots of hate. I was pretty scared. But I somehow pulled out the win...and was able to defeat him.

And then I get on the feature match arena and...I could make top eight only if two specific matches broke my way...And when I got to the feature match arena, Ari Lax—another of my old friends, he's from Michigan and that's how I know him—Ari goes, "I believe you just made the top eight." And I'm like, "No way." And Ari is like, "Well, you're up 5% in tie breakers, so I believe the most likely way that you'd miss top eight is that a meteor annihilates the site and we all die."

James: [Laughs]

Andrew: No, I mean, it was a ridiculous statement, but that's legitimately what he said. He thought that my odds of missing were lower than my odds of missing by meteor annihilation....I was overwhelmed at that moment, I was like, holy crap. Somehow, someway, I top-eighted a Pro Tour. Regardless of what happens from here, this is an accomplishment that I will always get to take with me, it's an accomplishment that comes with a lot of fame, money, etc., etc. I still didn't think I was going to do very well in the tournament, I still had no faith in that, honestly.

James: Just happy to be there, it sounds like.

Andrew: Once I reached the top eight, I was certainly just happy to be there...Again, I don't know if I will ever top-eight another Pro Tour. I hope that I will, and I hope that I will have proved a point where I can be someone who people are on the lookout to top-eight every weekend. But I don't know if that will happen.

James: What was going through your mind during the top eight?

Andrew: I guess the first thing I'll talk a little bit about [is] the night before. I mentioned that I'm not nervous in general, but the night before the PT top eight, I was very nervous. It's the first time I'd been nervous in many years. This is my shot to make something happen, to somehow, someway succeed in a Pro Tour top eight. I didn't want to blow it. I had a ton of trouble sleeping, which rarely happens to me before tournaments, and I was tossing and turning, and my friends were loud when they were testing my matchups upstairs. Which I really appreciate they did, but they weren't the quietest. I got maybe five hours sleep, I wasn't feeling so great the morning of.

I was very nervous as I'm shuffling up, but [my opponent] Wilson Mok is a great guy. I didn't know him before this weekend, but I know him now, and he was laughing and joking before the round, and that's how I like to take my matches, too, a pretty casual demeanor even with high stakes, so that kind of put me at ease.

And as soon as we started playing the games, there's this moment in the quarter finals when I suddenly realized it doesn't matter. If I'm playing an FNM, if I'm playing a playtest game, if I'm playing for the fun of it, I'm ultimately very spiky when it comes to Magic, I'm very competitive. I am playing Magic to prove something... [a]nd if that's your goal, then all you have to do is make the right play every turn, every game. Do the best to achieve that. And the right play doesn't change if you're under the feature match lights. The right play doesn't change when you're on the Pro Tour stage. The right play is the right play...Once the cards started being played, I realized it was just another match, and I don't think I got in my head too much after a few turns of that first match.

The worst part is that I know I made mistakes in the quarter finals, and I recognized them in hindsight during game five. I caught multiple errors that I made and I was like, "Oh god, why did I do that?" And that may have caused a snowballing effect. But luckily, I drew well...so I was able to win.

The other thing about being in the Pro Tour top eight that I don't think people realize is how much waiting there is. It sounds weird but what happens is that coverage keeps pausing your match so they can see the start of your [next] game, right? The other match will play for a bit, and if they see the other match is close to finishing whatever game they're on, then they'll pause your match as soon as you finish so they can show the start of your next game while they shuffle up, and you kind of go back and forth like that.

James: That's brutal. Because you lose your momentum. It's like a sports team when they get forced to call time out.

Andrew: It's exactly like that. Because sometimes you're thinking hard about your opening hand, you're like, "Okay, keep." And then you sit there, staring at your keep for minutes at a time, until you finally get told to start. And sometimes that's so stressful because maybe it's a risky keep.

James: You start overthinking it, right?

Andrew: You're like, "Oh god, my hand has one land. What am I doing here? What if this doesn't work out? I know I have Legion's Landing, but maybe I won't get to flip it this game." And you start going insane, and that can be nerve-wrecking, too. But again, I found that as soon as the cards started being played, it didn't matter. None of that mattered. I just had to play. And that was really freeing for me.

James: That's good. And then obviously, the big one was the finals, with LSV, one of the all-time greats. Tell me what was going through your mind as you sat down for that match.

Andrew: The real truth of the matter is that I thought I was going to lose every turn of every game of that entire match for the first four games. I just didn't think there was any way. I thought it was impossible. The mirror is pretty play-draw dependent. I think being on the play is more relevant in the mirror than any other match in Standard.... And LSV is better than I will ever be. He's literally the fourth or fifth best player ever to play the game. Most people think there's [Jon] Finkel, Kai [Budde], Paulo [Vitor Damo Da Rosa], and then it's between LSV and Nassif at number four...

And then to make matters worse, he's playing a build of the [same] deck that I think gives up a lot in other places but it's very favored in the mirror, and that made it feel so insurmountable. It made it feel like there was nothing I could possibly do to win. So when he curved out with this flawless draw, I think in game four, I was like, "Oh yeah, that makes sense. I can't win, and also, I could never win this game." And then we're in game five. I'm just playing each game, and I suddenly realize this is game five of the Pro Tour. I'm like, "Ok, that's nice. When I lose, I can tell everyone that I made it to game five against LSV, he's really good." I showed myself to be good, I proved something. Which is nice, because again, I'm pretty Spiky.

James: You took it as far as you could take it. Game five. With your back against the wall against one of the greatest players ever, in a match up that was not favorable based on the builds of the deck.

Andrew: Yes, exactly. I felt pretty good about what was happening there, even though I thought I was certainly going to lose game five. And then, Luis starts mulliganing. He just mulligans. And I'm like, "Okay, he's on six [cards], but given the match-up and the fact that he's on the play, my expectation is that he's still overall favored, that doesn't mean much." I'm still pretty calm at that point. And then he goes to five [cards] pretty quickly. LSV doesn't think about his six very long, I think his six was very bad when

I watched the coverage later. And I'm like, "This is insane."

And there's a moment on coverage that you can literally see that I put my head in my hands. And I'm doing that because, suddenly, things are real to me. I'm contemplating the fact that I might win the Pro Tour. I'm like, "What the heck is happening? What is going on? Why is LSV mulliganing to five [cards]? I have no idea what is occurring right now."

James: I think it was your friend Max [McVety], because he told me that he was chanting "Six, six, six," and then LSV started mulling to six. And then he started chanting "Five, five, five, five." It didn't work when he started chanting three, but it is what it is, right? [Laughs]

Andrew: Yeah, I heard that. And I heard a similar thing from my friends on-site, where they were going, "Go to five, go to five, go to five." [Laughs] Apparently, all my friends were trying to send me their energy, in so far that is a concept, and I guess it worked. LSV kept mulliganing and I thought I might win. And I was even more stressed, because I looked at my hand, and the seven I kept, I think it's a clear keep, but it was not that great. I had a lot of one-drops and three lands. I was like, "Oh man? What if I just draw a bunch of lands and I flood out? I'll lose this match where my opponent mulled to four, I'll feel so bad."

But that didn't happen, I did pretty well from that point. And suddenly, there's this moment where I drop Venerated Loxodon. When I cast it, I knew I was going to win the game. I knew that nothing mattered, it didn't matter what else he had. If he had Settle [the Wreckage], none of that was important.

The Loxodon was not going to be beat. I could play around anything. I was going to win.

And at that moment, I was so happy, when I cast the Loxodon, because the thing is, this is one of the best moments in Magic that I think a lot of people don't get to experience. I understand it's pretty negative for LSV, and I apologize to him for that, but the situation for me is, I know I'm going to win the game, the game is over, but I still get to keep playing it, there's still a few more turns, where I can just revel in the fact that I am about to win the Pro Tour.

I'm there, with these Loxodons on the board, attacking, and I don't know, the next turn or maybe the turn after, I cast Pride of the Conquerers for lethal, I put it down, I know it's lethal and there aren't any outs he can possibly have. And LSV extends the hand and I find myself winning the Pro Tour.

I can't even describe how it felt, I just-- I could not believe it. I get up and I put my hands on my head but I'm even in shock about what happened. I thought I was going to lose for so much of the match. For 95% of it or whatever. And suddenly, I just won it. And it meant everything. I cannot describe how much winning the Pro Tour meant to me.

James: I think when people experience the happiest moments of their lives, people have different things going through their minds. For some people, it might be memories flashing back. And for other people, they lose all sense of time and space. How would you describe your situation at that point in time?

Andrew: Definitely closer to the latter. It wasn't a matter of-- I don't know, I didn't start thinking about all the things that got me there, or what the future would hold, or the fact that I was Platinum. It was more just, I was overwhelmed by, to some extent, emotion. I was overwhelmed by how I was feeling at that moment. I was just lost at the moment, I think. That's the best way I can describe it. And it was a good and weird experience for me, because I am not a very emotional person. I have self-identified as a robot more than once. And I don't typically experience strong emotions. And I understand it's a cliché, but a reason that I play Magic-- certainly not *the* reason, is that I want to feel something. And let me tell you, winning the Pro Tour, I sure felt something. So that was surreal. It was amazing.

James: Just feeling like you're on cloud nine.

Andrew: I was overwhelmed. I felt like I had achieved a dream that I never thought I would.

James: I talked to your friends who watched you play on this Pro Tour and they said that you took your game to a whole new level during the Top Eight, that you were playing better as the tournament went on. Did you feel like you were making crisper and sharper plays?

Andrew: I definitely don't think that's crazy. I do think I played poorly, specifically in the quarter finals. But I think that has a lot to do with the fact that I was more nervous and sleepier. But I think in the semis and the finals, I played very, very well. Some of the better Magic that I've played, if I'm allowed to say that. Obviously, it might be that I'm not good enough to notice the mistakes that I'm making or what have you. And I can think of at least one error I made during that time. But overall, I played very well in both those matches.

I mentioned before that one of my big problems when I was growing up is that I didn't do well when I was not under pressure, when I felt like I didn't need to study for a test, I wouldn't. I didn't feel enough pressure. And some people play their best when they're playtesting, when nothing is on the line. I'm very much the reverse. In playtesting, I have a hard time playing well because I feel like, "Who the hell cares if I lose this game?" The flipside of that, which is pretty positive, is that I typically play my best Magic when it counts. I'm a good person to have in the clutch, you might say. And that meant that somehow, when the pressure was ratcheted up so high, I was tuned in.

James: The other thing I noticed is that you looked very nervous. And I talked one of your friends, and he clarified that that's how you always look when you play competitively.

Andrew: That's absolutely correct. There's several things about this. One is that I do this rocking thing when I play Magic competitively. I do it every time, I've done it for years, it has nothing to do with my mental state, it's just something that happens to me. It might be a symptom of ADHD.

James: So you can be playing in an FNM and you would do the same thing?

Andrew: Absolutely. I'm not entirely sure. Just to fully clarify, I also have been-- some experts believe that I'm slightly on the spectrum, but it's debatable. The point is, maybe it's a syndrome or something like that. But I do it every time, it's who I am. And the way I look when I play-- I never realized this about myself, but my friend Paul Dean pointed out once, I tend to look concerned or unhappy, even when I'm crushing my opponent and going to win. I don't think people should take those reactions as nervousness, it's just who I am. It's not to say that I was not nervous, it's just that my behavior in the top eight was not an expression of nervousness.

James: It's good to know that. Switching gears, we always want to know a little bit about our guests, their backgrounds, and where they're from. I know that you are currently in Ann Arbor, Michigan. Is that where you grew up?

Andrew: Yes. I lived in Ann Arbor all through high school. I grew up here. I was born here. When I went to college, I decided that I did not want to be in Ann Arbor anymore... I wanted to change. So I ended up going to college in Minnesota. I went to Carleton College, which is in a small town called Northville, about an hour from Twin Cities. And I kind of didn't like it. I'm not saying the college itself was a problem, but I didn't like being where I was. I liked Ann Arbor a lot more. And I didn't realize how much I liked Ann Arbor until I was no longer there. I graduated... [as] a software engineer, and I knew that I could work anywhere I wanted because there's pretty good opportunities to work remotely. I decided the place I most wanted to live, in the world, was back where I started.

I have good friends in Minnesota, and I don't want to say that I don't, and I don't want to say that those friends aren't awesome, because they are. But at the time, I had a lot more friends back here, I had my family here, and I'm pretty close to my family. I know that many people don't have that great of a relationship with their parents, I always had a great relationship with them. I was lucky enough for that, too, obviously, because I had no control over it, no one picks their parents.

And there were other things. I really like the size of Ann Arbor. It's small enough where parking downtown is never a problem, you're not required to take public transit, driving everywhere is totally reasonable. But it's large enough that everything is here. If I want to go to a movie, there's three the-atres in town, there's a wide array of restaurants that I like. I felt that it was large enough to be com-plete as a city, but small enough to not have big city problems.

James: That's a good balance. Sounds like I should visit.

Andrew: I think it's an amazing city. I think I'm pretty biased, and I haven't lived in that many places, so I don't know how much my word should be weighed.

James: Can you tell me a bit about your family? It sounds like you're rather close to them.

Andrew: My family growing up was me, my mom, my dad, and my brother. My brother is younger than I am. And my brother and I have had a rocky relationship, but I think that we get along well these days. When we were younger, it was problematic. I think we have some issues in areas that we are similar, actually, but that's not the point. My parents-- I have basically gotten along very well since day one. I know many people fight with their parents in their teenage years, I never had that. My parents are awesome. Well, yeah, so the thing is-- I should mention this here because speaking about this is awkward if I don't. This year, about six months ago, I lost my father to a brain aneurism. It was extremely sudden. My father was 64. He was not that old. Not young, but not that old either.

James: No, that's very young and I'm very sorry to hear that.

Andrew: It's one of the worst things that has happened to me. I was definitely not OK for a long time after that, and I did poorly at Magic as a result. I guess that may be small potatoes when it comes to tragedies of this nature, but it certainly is true. But a major reason why I wanted to come back to Ann Arbor was honestly to spend time with my parents. I still get dinner with my mom once a week. For a long time, I ate dinner with my parents once a week.

My dad, when he was alive, played on my trivia team every week. I was pretty close to my dad, and I am pretty close to my mom. And the thing is they're very different, but I share different traits with each of them. My dad is in this space where he's unbelievably competitive. He was just as competitive as I am. And when I was growing up, we used to play chess. I played competitive chess before Magic. And my father and I would sometimes have shouting matches after chess games. That's not a joke.

James: Intense.

Andrew: We both really wanted it, that's what you have to understand. And the point in which I started beating him consistently is the point we stopped playing chess.

James: He wasn't taking it easy on you.

Andrew: No. He would give me a handicap. When I was a little kid, he gave me a queen, and as I got older, he gave me a rook, and then a knight. And then, eventually, we were playing on even terms. But at no point did he not try hard to win. He would give himself a handicap and go all out. That was his way.

James: It sounded like he was a pretty good player.

Andrew: Without getting too much into chess, he was around 1500 in rating at his peak, probably more like 1100 strength by the time he was an adult and semi-retired from chess. Not amazing, but a competitive chess player. I grew up doing that, and my dad used to drive me to chess tournaments all the time. When you're a competitive chess player and you're in middle school, your parents drive you all around every weekend, it's a ton of work. And my dad did all of that, and he was amazing at it. He would bring us food, he would give us encouragement, he would make sure everyone showed up to the tournament, he would literally call people's parents up and say, "Are you sending your son to this tournament? If not, why not?" He was nicer than that, but that's the gist of what he was saying. And he was my biggest supporter in competitive endeavors.

I'm not saying my mom wasn't also great. My mom is amazing and she's an incredibly kind person. But I think my mom does not precisely understand why I want to win so badly. My mom used to lose games to me and my brother when we were kids intentionally, because she wanted to see us happy.

And my dad, he got it. My dad understood why I would fly all over the country playing these Grand Prix to earn $250. Because it wasn't about the money, it wasn't even about the Pro Points, it was about proving something. And he got that. When I would tweet out updates or post updates to my Facebook page, he would refresh it nonstop. He knew exactly what my Pro Point status was in any given time, he knew what my Pro Level was, and he would ask me what decks, what I was known for, what was my favorite deck. He tried to keep up with it as much as he possibly could. That was a lot to lose. And in some sense, I wish he'd been around to see this Pro Tour win because it would have meant everything to him, just like it means everything to me. But life doesn't always work out that way, I guess.

James: Sounds like you guys were cut from the same cloth. You had a lot of similarities with him, at least in that sense.

Andrew: Well, I think that like most people, I'm a composition of my parents. I will say that my dad, unlike me, had crippling issues with nervousness. And when I would play chess tournaments, he used to tell me that he couldn't watch my games because he thought they were too nerve-wracking.

James: Whereas you were actually OK in the moment?

Andrew: Yeah, I'm pretty good with that kind of thing. I think I get that from my mom, is my guess. And so, it's difficult to describe how much he did for me, and how much the little things add up, like the trivia-- he used to drive me to the airport a lot, he really liked doing that, and I was flying all the time, so I appreciated the free rides. And it hit me the first time I asked a friend to drive me to the airport, I was like, "Wait, why am I doing this?" And I'm like, "Oh yeah, my father is dead." It was a big shock, as weird as that small moment sounds. But that's the story of my relationship with my parents. Both of them have always been unbelievably supportive, regardless of the fact that I did unusual things between competitive chess and competitive Magic. Not exactly the beaten path. I didn't play any sports in high school, I was the captain of the chess team. That's who I am.

James: Tell me a little bit more about how you transitioned from chess into Magic?

Andrew: The first time I played Magic, my parents randomly brought me some Magic cards, I'm not exactly sure why.

James: That's unusual.

Andrew: But they did. It was the seventh edition box set, that came with this CD that you could play against the computer. And just pre-made decks, you had no control on decks, the cards were all locked in, and the decks also had incredibly good hate cards in them against each other, which I think is probably poor game design. But they did. So I started playing on that, and what happened is I went to chess camp, I went to the Emerson Chess Camp, which I would subsequently go to many times. Great place for learning chess. And at recess, there was a group of people that would gather under the gazebo and play Magic, instead of running around or getting any physical activity. And I fell in with that crowd and I quickly learned to play. I would bring with me some of the cards that I had from this initial purchase that my parents made. And that's how it started. I then played Magic casually for years. To give you a sense of this, this Emerson Chess Camp that I'm describing occurred in 3rd grade, I'm a kid.

James: Yeah. Seventh edition was a long time ago.

Andrew: All this time, I'm playing chess competitively, all throughout elementary school, all throughout high school, all throughout middle school too, and I'm still playing Magic. In fact, I'm typically playing Magic between rounds of chess. My friends, who I would go to chess tournaments with, all play to varying levels. And I'm literally playing Magic with them between rounds. My dad coached the chess team for my high school, and I remember we had to institute a rule called "No Magic at Chess Club." That was a real rule that we had because it was too much of a problem when people needed to prepare for the tournaments.

James: It started to take over.

Andrew: Yeah. I graduate high school, and I'm playing with my high school chess team. We're very good. We won two state championships. And when I graduated high school, I realized I didn't have that team anymore, I was going to a new place. And the Carleton Chess Club didn't seem that interested in playing tournaments. Not that they weren't good, that just wasn't their scene.

I realized that I needed another outlet. I'm the sort of person that I cannot exist without a competitive outlet, I'd go insane. I need something to strive for, to compete at, to crush my opponents at, whatever you want to describe it. That's necessary to my functioning as a person.

I looked around and realized that I like playing Magic so much that I literally do it for fun when I'm supposed to be playing chess to prepare for tournaments. And chess preparation can feel like a grind a lot of the time, even though I like playing chess tournaments. I also realized there was this SCG coming up, SCG Cincinnati was open. This was the summer I graduated high school. And so me and a couple of friends got on Magic Online, we got on screen share, and we all started preparing for this tournament together. We worked together a deck, we tested a lot, we tried to do our best. And we go to the tournament, we got crushed, we did really, really poorly. I think one of us made day two and didn't cash, the other two of us finished 5-5 each. I was like, okay, maybe this isn't for me.

But what happened is on day two, there's a draft open...And the thing is that I've been playing a lot of Limited at this point in my life. I draft every week at my local store, and I'm pretty good...It's not a big accomplishment, but I'm usually pulling a top eight in FNM every time, and top four usually splits, so that's as far as it goes. And this draft open-- first of all, my friends crush it. This group of eight random kids from Ann Arbor, four of us in the top eight. And I win the draft open. And in a top four split, I end up with exactly $250, which is perhaps not that much money, but felt like a lot to me at the time because I never had a real job and that kind of thing. And at that point, I was hooked...That was the start of this journey that hopefully has not ended, but just had a major peak.

James: Would you say that you saw success early on?

Andrew: Yeah...that took about three years, to clarify. My first FNM was in ninth grade, and then I won the draft open the summer after high school, so I guess it's four years, whatever. And the thing is that I have to talk about the way my group of friends played casual because I think it's a very weird thing. The thing is that when we played casual, it was pretty intense. My group was pretty Spiky, we all wanted to win. Card availability was a huge problem, we had all Limited cards, but we would build decks and we would tune them to the metagame of our casual metagame. Our decks were mostly-- it's not that all of them were great, it's that all of them did the thing they were trying to do to their utmost, given the cards available. And by the end of it, by the time I won this draft open, the casual decks that we were playing with were really, really good, by an objective standard. The cards we were playing with would crush any Standard deck, that's what I mean.

James: It wasn't an 80-card deck. It was very finely-tuned, efficient, and you guys were playing to win.

Andrew: Yes, exactly. That's precisely correct. So honestly, at the time I played my first FNM, I was already a pretty reasonable Magic player. It took me a while to understand drafting, I didn't just walk in and knew how to draft. But as far as my actual in-game plays, I sort of think from day one I was pretty good, relative to the people at the store I was playing at. Not the best in the store or anything, but certainly not the worst either.

Honestly, even before chess and even before Magic, I was always good at strategy games, almost any game. I was a strong Stratego player as a kid. I understand that sounds weird, but it's true. It is definitely true that I am gifted in the area of playing turn-based strategy games, for whatever reason.

James: Ok. So you win the draft open and you start getting on to the GP train, right?

Andrew: Yes. That's exactly right. I'm playing all these GPs, and I'm grinding, and I'm grinding, and I'm driving. I'm not flying to any Grand Prix, but I am driving pretty far distances. At this point in time, in my early college, I don't have a group of people at my college who will drive to tournaments with me. I have a group of Magic friends who I play with, but we're mostly cubing, or drafting. They're not driving five hours to play in a constructed Grand Prix. So this one Grand Prix, GP Boston, what happens is I drive 14 hours to Boston, and I play this Grand Prix. I'm playing a lot of Modern. My first PTQ top eight was in Modern around this time. And I pretty much play exclusively Tron at this point. Which means I'm one of those people, but yeah.

James: [Laughs] Yeah.

Andrew: And what happens at Boston is that the metagame that weekend is perfect for Tron. Tron at this time is not very respected, I think it was underestimated for a long time, and everyone at this GP is playing Jund or Pod as far as the eye can see. And both of those are very favorable match-ups for Tron. So I played this GP that I had literally driven 14 hours to, and I don't top-eight because it's a 2,000 player GP, but I have a 13-2 record. And 13-2 is good for a Pro Tour invite. They don't pay for the flight at this point in time - they do now - but at this time, if you 13-2'd, you paid your own way.

But my parents are very generous. My mom immediately agrees to pay, when I ask her about this, and I go to PT Hawaii. And that's the story of my first breakthrough moment, I guess. I had cashed a few GPs before that, all in Modern and Limited. I had never cashed a Standard GP. I'm not a Standard player at all, I play mostly only Modern and Limited. But yeah, that's the beginning for me.

These days, I play quite a bit of Standard. But when I was growing up, I certainly didn't. GP Minneapolis, which was my second GP top eight and my third qualification, it was the first Standard GP that I cashed.

James: I've also heard that you seem to be a huge force in organizing the Ann Arbor Magic logistics scene, in the sense that you help make sure that people get rides, find the right places to stay. It's a lot of things and, honestly, it's a lot of hassle. I've even heard that you booked flights for some of your friends. It sounds like you're very integral to this whole thing. What made you decide to take it on for your group?

Andrew: I'll answer that, but to do that, I need to take a step back for a moment.

Right after my first Pro Tour, I got invited, in Minneapolis, to an invite-only playtesting group. The goal was, we're going to grind PTQs, we're going to get on the PT. Most people on this group had played at least one PTQ already and that was the qualification to get in.

This group was organized by Matthias Hunt, who I consider to be my Magic mentor. And Matthias took the best players he knew, none of whom knew each other, and invited them all to this playgroup. Including me. I met Matthias at a random Minnesota PTQ. And he had beaten me, but he was impressed by my play.... And in this play group, I got a lot better. I got a lot better very quickly because I was playing with people at my own level, for the first time in a while.

And the thing is that in this group, the role that I play in the Ann Arbor group was Matthias' role. Matthias invited me to the playtesting, and he said, "We will meet at this time, in this place, we're going to playtest for this tournament, which we are all going to, everyone shows up for practice." And he would book all the hotels, organize logistics like what the cars are, who's picking up whom, which was complicated because I was an hour away in Carleton. So sometimes someone had to drive down to me, or I drove to them. And Matthias just ran that. He just made it happen.

I learned to do the thing that I do for the Ann Arbor community from Matthias. Because then what happened is, I graduated college, right? And I knew I wanted to move back to Ann Arbor, there was no question in my mind, I moved home, and I was like, "You know what I should do? I should do exactly that thing that he did." And so I organized the playtest group. The playtest group has fallen apart for various reasons. But for a long time we were meeting once a week in my house to test for whatever our next tournament was. I booked all the hotels, I made all the car arrangements, I did all the logistics things.

One trick I use a lot is I used unpublished fare hotel sites, stuff like Hotwire, Priceline Express Deals, Expedia unpublished fares, there's a bunch of them. You book hotels last-minute for lower rates.

And Matthias showed me that. And he showed me how to be a logistics manager, in addition to running a Magic playtest group. And most of what I do in Ann Arbor is replicating that very successful group. Many of the people in that group who qualified for the PT, I would claim, as a direct result of that group. I was not one of them, but I think the group as a whole is very successful. Out of the eight of us, I think three qualified for that Pro Tour.

James: That's amazing, the fact that your group had those results, but also the fact that you took Matthias' framework and you not only paid it forward, but you were able to keep that going, to a lot of success. I'm really happy to hear that.

Andrew: It's definitely true that now—it's kind of weird. When we go to a tournament, the Ann Arbor guys and me, everybody expects that I will book a hotel…And it just occurs, and everyone knows, if they message me, I will send them the information. Typically, the day before, I send out some messages that are like, "Ok, here is the carpool. This car has these people in it, this car has these people in it. This car will pick up this person this time, this person that time, this person at that time," and I plan it all out. The thing is I'm into that, logistical organization. Questions like, "Ok, so this car needs to get these three people who are available at three different times. What's the right ordering? Should one of them switch to the other car so one car can leave earlier?" Just trying to make things work out such that everyone is happiest. I like the subgame that is logistics.

James: Very nice. Sounds like you've always been quite organized.

Andrew: Kind of. It depends on what you're talking about. For instance, organizing my room doesn't feel like a subgame. So I'm not good at it.

But this does feel like a subgame that I can win. I was super into my college schedule when I was in college. Sometime in my sophomore year, I planned out every class I was going to take until I graduated because it sounded like fun. Because that felt the same way, I was trying to check off all my distribution requirements, make sure I took all the classes I wanted to, make sure I got all the requirements for my major, do a whole bunch of different things at once, and everything depended on everything. "It turns out there's electives I want to take at these time slots these next three years, so I have to take algorithms at this time right now, because I will never be able to take it again because other things will conflict with it." That kind of thing.

James: While we're on the topic of talking about teams and groups, what can you tell me about Team Delta Flyers and the origin story behind that?

Andrew: That's a pretty funny story. For Team Limited Grand Prix, I always team with the same team every time, and I don't think it's going to change anytime soon. That team is me, Max McVety and Tyler Hill.

At some point in time, Matt Sperling was making a power ranking of teams, which he does regularly. I mean, power ratings for team tournaments, for whatever reason, have become a thing in the community. He made a Facebook post and the deal was: anyone can post here. You would just post, state your team, and he would rank them in power rankings, although many teams got, "Not good enough to be great." But that's fine.

I posted, and the thing is, at the time that I posted this, Tyler was a Gold Level Pro, Max McVety was a Silver Level Pro, and I'm not at a Pro Level, it wasn't a good year for me, but that's ok. And I know that Matt Sperling doesn't know who any of us are, he's going to be, "Who the hell are these randos?" So when he posted it, and I commented, I put our Pro Levels in because I wanted Matt Sperling to get that this team is not three guys in a local store, this is a Gold Pro, a Silver Pro, and some guy.

James: [Laughs] "We're legit."

Andrew: Yeah, basically. So I did that, and Sperling comments, "No need to include your Delta flight status."

James: Oh, savage beats. [Laughs]

Andrew: Yeah. Then his article, when listing our team, he didn't give us a rank in the top 25 or whatever, he just pasted a photo of that comment.

James: Nice.

Andrew: Roasting us mercilessly, which was pretty hilarious, I admit. Honestly, every interaction I've had with Sperling has been awesome, I think he likes daggering people because it's funny, but he's a very good-natured person in real life.

James: He can dish it, and he can also take it.

Andrew: Yeah. But then what happened at this tournament, which is great-- so my team does well at this tournament. I think we come in 11th or something. Anyway, we have a good cash finish. And when this happens, Sperling's team, the Scottsdale Foundation, which is him, David Williams, and Paul Reitzel, finished four places below us, they came in 15th. My team is obviously ecstatic about this fact given the article. I take a picture of the standings and I tweet at Sperling, "Sucks to suck #DeltaFlyers." And from that point forward, my team has been named Delta Flyers. We made it our own, we referred to ourselves as that. That's who we are now.

James: I hear you have this ritual of doing something on day two of a tournament, right?

Andrew: Yeah, yeah. I decided to play the joke to the maximum extent possible, so I purchased a Delta polo shirt for $15 or something, and I now wear this gray polo shirt with a little Delta symbol on it, and it says Delta, which is the logo, on every day two of team GPs. And usually, no one gets it. My opponents don't understand what the heck I'm doing.

James: Does this guy work for Delta Airlines or something? [Laughs]

Andrew: I've gotten that question a lot of times, but honestly, I don't care. I find it hilarious.

James: It *is* hilarious.

Andrew: So I keep wearing it. Every team event, on day two, I'm wearing this Delta Flyer shirt. But I might purchase Max one, and he has to wear it. But we'll see.

James: It's the new team uniform.

Andrew: Yeah. I mean, it's tricky, because everyone on Delta Flyers is sponsored. I'm sponsored by CardBoard Live, they're sponsored by RIW Hobbies. And so I'm not sure if we could actually do this, but it is definitely entertaining to me.

James: You have to find a way. You have to all wear it, maybe Delta caps or something. Find something you can stich on to the shirt, you know?

Andrew: Yeah. I guess that's what we'll have to do. The Delta Flyers is a team that works really well together, our strengths are super complementary. I think team synergy, specifically in team Limited is super important, because you have an hour to accomplish this really hard task of deck building and it's important that you get everything done and that no one is overlapping, and that you're on the same page. You don't have time to endlessly debate how good cards are. In the abstract, you have to know where people are on all things, so you can have a higher-level discussion.

My team gets along super well, and the breakdown of our team is straightforward. I am the strongest deck builder in my team. I carry on the deck building projects, I run the show, call the shots for that portion.

While I'm doing that, what happens is T-Hill, Tyler Hill, is a mad scientist, he's like a madman. Think Sam Black, he's just crazy idea after crazy idea. Literally ten insane ideas every build, and I have to shoot them down but recognize them when they're great, that's what I have to do.

And while this is happening, Max McVety is an aggro-savant. He only plays aggro, but he plays it very, very well. Max, we hand him aggro cards and all he does is tell us whether the cards we are currently staring at are better or worse than the previous set, and he endlessly analyzes and fine-tunes his aggressive deck for that tournament, his 40 cards he's going to play.

That's our dynamic, and honestly, it's great. Because the trade-off of me having to carry this portion is that I think I have the weakest technical play on my team, or at least, that's been true historically. I'm pretty good right now, but when the actual games came, I would often have the worst record, the worst technical play, but my contribution was done. If we all had great decks, then I had done my part. It didn't matter if I had 2-6 day one, which happened once, because our team [got] 6-2. But that's the story of the Delta Flyers.

James: It sounds like a good combination. That's always what you want in a team, you want people with different skill sets and you're willing to work together to synthesize them together.

Andrew: Precisely. I think we do that pretty well.

James: That's awesome. And switching gears again, I've heard you can be very opinionated on food. What can you tell me about your food power rankings?

Andrew: That's very fair. I do a thing a lot of people do, which is that I state my opinions as fact. I will acknowledge I do this, it's not a secret. And when it comes to food, I will make statements like, "This place is better than that place, this is the right place to go for this in the city." And obviously, the city I know the best is Ann Arbor. My lifestyle is that I eat out pretty much every meal. I don't really cook. I go to restaurants all the time, and I'm pretty opinionated about the best ones in any given category.

Probably the category that I have the most expertise on is burgers, and the reason is that when I was a kid, I was a picky eater. I grew out of it, but as a result, I didn't eat many foods growing up. And one of the foods I was willing to eat as a kid was burgers. I ate very large numbers of them, from many different places. Wherever we were, I think my family goes out to a restaurant, and no matter what was on the menu, I'd order a burger. It's a steakhouse, seafood, none of that mattered, I would get a burger. And so, that meant that I had a large set of examples to draw from.

At some point, I was like, well, if burgers are my thing, I should do it right. So I found lists of places that were highly rated by food critics, that were burger places like, best burgers in Ann Arbor, or I'd travel somewhere, and I'd look up the best burger in that city. I have a pretty refined burger palate, I guess is what I'm saying, and I can say that in Ann Arbor, I think the best burger is unequivocally, unarguably, and beyond debate, Frita Batidos, which is an amazing Cuban-inspired burger place in the city.

James: Tell me why they have the best burgers.

Andrew: Ok. So it has a lot to do with the fixings. They put egg on it, sunny side-up, and they cook it just right for the burger. And they have mustard cheese, which I think is a great complement with the egg, you've got to get mustard cheese with the egg because it blends the egg's flavor. I guess it's nice from a texture perspective, the egg is running, and the mustard is smooth, it all works. And they obviously cook a great patty, to medium-rare, by default, of course. They will go medium rare if you don't say anything, which is the right answer. And yeah, it's awesome. I'm not the only one who thinks this, I don't want to make this sound like it's my secret place, they have won national awards for their burgers, they have a

million trophies for burger competitions in the restaurant. They are amazing, and I think anyone who
is in Ann Arbor should eat at Frita Batidos for sure.
It's great.

James: That is an awesome, awesome endorsement of Frida.
Have you thought about becoming a burger food
critic?

Andrew: Yeah, I mean—that does sound fun...I'm not sure
what that would look like, but it definitely is the
sort of thing I would be interested in doing. I know
David Ochoa has carved a niche for himself where
he's the Magic food guy, that's his thing, and he
would write these articles that briefly mention
Magic but are really about food, and maybe I can
move into a kind of space like that, as long as the
food is only burgers. I'm worried that's too niche,
my audience is Magic players who like burgers and
specifically high-quality pricy burgers. I don't know
how many views that would get, which ultimately, is
the point of Magic articles for the most part.

James: I like the fact that you talk openly about it so that
others can benefit from your insights.

Andrew: I try to get recommendations for food whenever I
go somewhere now. When I was in Atlanta for the
Pro Tour, I had a co-worker who used to work in
Atlanta, and I asked her, "What are five good places
near the convention center that you would recom-
mend?" —[When] you're on a Magic trip...[y]ou're
somewhere in the world, and you're not going to
get to do much fun stuff because you're playing
Magic all the time. But what you do get to do is you
have these dinners, and every dinner, a big group of

Magic players, it's really fun, and it's probably one of my favorite portions of every Magic trip. You all sit on a table and you're going to eat, and so, I want to make those dinners great because they're the most tourist-y thing I get to do on these Magic trips. So I try to research restaurants every time I go somewhere now, even though I definitely order a burger a lot, still.

James: You're right, eating with our friends is one of the best things that we can do.

Andrew: Yeah, that's how I feel. And part of it is when you travel for Magic-- maybe everyone does this, but at least because my group of friends are mostly people with full-time jobs traveling on the weekends, we're not going to be in that city extra days to do fun stuff, most of the time. The meals are all you get, so you better make the most of them.

James: So Andrew, looking forward, can you share with me some of your Magic-related goals?

Andrew: That's a good question. Now I'm Platinum, I won the Pro Tour, and that makes you instantly Platinum, which is surreal, I never thought I would be Platinum in my life, but here I am, a Platinum Pro. The thing is I was flying to GPs to play them when I had no Pro Points. GPs are fun for me. If they weren't fun for me, I wouldn't play them. I would never have done all the things that I did to keep this point, if GPs were not fun in of themselves. I think that your odds of qualifying for the Pro Tour through GPs are not that great -- I say that even though I've done it four times. So much has to go right in a weekend to top-eight a tournament that size.

But I still have a lot of friends playing GPs, none of my friends are going to stop playing GPs, and most of my friends are not in this position of being Platinum with regards to their Pro Points, so they have a good reason to play GPs. And, in addition to that, as a Platinum Pro, I get paid appearance fees for a certain number of GPs per cycle. And that's additional incentive to go. I feel I'm not going to change very much with respects to my GPs. I'm still going to play a lot of GPs, try to keep doing well, even if it doesn't really matter because I'm Platinum anyway. But I'm sure that when that automatic Platinum stops, I will be grateful that current me has played a lot of GPs and won a buffer of Pro Points and that kind of thing.

And honestly, what I'm looking to accomplish is that I want to stay on the train, I want to play all the Pro Tours for the next several years, I would like to not embarrass myself at Worlds, I don't expect to have good results, but I would like to win some matches. And yeah, having another good Pro Tour finish wouldn't hurt. I will mention that I had never cashed a Pro Tour prior to this one. It is a fact that I have either failed to cash or won all Pro Tours that I have played. I would like to cash more Pro Tours, I would like to prove that this isn't a fluke event that even if I'm not someone who is good enough to top-eight Pro Tours regularly, I am someone who is good enough to cash them, which I think is potentially true. I think that's most of my goals, maintain Pro status, keep playing GPs. Maybe that's not a goal, but it's a thing. And show that I'm good enough to cash Pro Tours on a consistent basis.

James: Have you thought about doing more in terms of outside of playing the game? Because I know that more opportunities are likely to have come to you now and I know a lot of the really good all-time players also have content jobs. I'm curious if you're interested in that.

Andrew: I am. I definitely am. It's kind of tricky, and the reason I think is tricky is, I think the best way, from a promotion perspective, to promote oneself as a Magic player is to stream. I think streaming is the method of the future, it's what everybody is moving towards, which is good news for CardBoard Live. But that's not the point.

James: Yeah.

Andrew: The point is, I'm not well set up for streaming. I think that I am very analytical, that I'm pretty insightful, that I have a lot of theory, which means that my analysis of Magic play is pretty on-point. But what I think I am not is particularly entertaining. I don't think I'm good at being happy, upbeat-- I mean, I'm a very happy person but I'm not an outwardly happy person.

Matthias, who does commentary, he does this as his day job, he'll tell you that you have to show four times the emotion that you want the audience to see when you're performing. It takes so much more to get them to understand how you feel than it does for you to actually feel it, and I just don't do that at all, I'm not a very emotive person. And that means I think I'm very poorly set up for stream, which is unfortunate, because I think it's the right way to go.

For the same reasons I'm a bad fit for streaming, I think I am a good fit for writing. That is why

I immediately reached out to Cedric [Phillips] and wrote this SCG article following the Pro Tour win. I would be willing to [do a] regular writing thing if I had the opportunity. It's tricky though, because you're always in the spot where there are a lot of smaller sites, and you could write for one of them, and they won't pay you that well, and you don't get any views, but you can build up your chops, improve your craft. I don't think I'm that great of a writer yet, simply because I have not done it that much. I don't think I'm naturally deficient or anything, but I don't have—

James: Yeah, you need to put in the reps, like anything.

Andrew: Exactly, and I haven't. And I freely admit that. This article was maybe the fourth or fifth Magic article I've ever written in my life, it's not a thing I've done a huge amount of, but that's definitely the content production path I see myself going down. But that comes with a whole lot of other questions. Let's say the best-case scenario happens. Let's say a major site like CFB, SCG, even a smaller site, offered me a regular writing position tomorrow. They came up to me and said, "Hey Andrew, we would like you to write articles regularly and we will pay you a decent amount," whatever that means. Now the question is, what does that mean for my day job? Does that mean I'm going to work less hours? Does that mean I'm going to quit my job and try to have Magic full-time? I don't know if I want to do those things. That's a lot to lose. I'm a software engineer, I'm fairly well-paid. It's a lot of money to give up; but Magic is amazing. Maybe I would feel a lot happier if I tried to play Magic full-time. I'm just not sure, honestly. I would state that I am interested in writing but I'm not sure what it would mean if I started writing regularly. I guess your guess is as good as mine. [Laughs] We'll have to see how things play out.

James: I think life is one of those things where sometimes you don't know how things will play out, but you're along for the journey and just see what happens. You have the Star City Games article now, you might learn something from the feedback. You might have an opportunity come to you tomorrow. Just keep your options open. I like the fact that you're being very self-aware too, of what you're good at, and what you need to improve on. And that's really refreshing to hear in this day and age.

Andrew: I think that one of my strengths is that I'm pretty self-aware. I don't believe that I'm good at everything. That's not to say I'm not good at some things, I think there are things I'm excellent at. But I don't think that I'm some sort of superhero who's good at everything.

James: Because you're talking about being self-aware and trying to look at things critically—if you could go back in time five years, is there something you would tell the younger Andrew?

Andrew: That's a good question. I'm not too sure. The thing is-- five years ago, just think about where my life was at, I was a junior in college, I think. I was 20. I am not sure whether or not I was working with Matthias' test group at that point. I'd either just started working with him or just before I had started working with them, I think... And I had played my first Pro Tour, or I was soon to play it. See? I don't know.

My general approach to Magic isn't that different than it was then, honestly. I always tried to be self-aware and I always tried to know who is better than me, know where I stand, and know what I'm good and bad at, that kind of thing. And I don't think I've gotten noticeably better in that time. I had gotten better at Magic, but I'm not sure there's any single piece of advice I can give myself that would-- it's not like there's some epiphany I had...It was just playing a lot, getting my 1,000 hours or whatever. A lot of small improvements here and there, no single defining moment-- I just don't know if I really have one.

As far as a person, that's a different question. I think that college me was not always the best at maintaining non-Magic relationships with people. Not necessarily in the romantic sense, although not necessarily in that sense either. Just keeping in touch with people. I tried, but I should have tried harder. Ultimately, one thing I'm grateful for Magic is that I have friends all over the world that I see regularly, and I think I would have a few more friends if I was willing to go a little farther to make it happen. That's about the wisest thing I have to tell myself. I don't think I could really make past me's life that much easier.

James: [Laughs] Yeah, that's a good well-reasoned answer. Do you have any shout outs that you want to give to anybody at all?

Andrew: Max, my mom, and Matthias were all integral to every part of my Magic career. And I mentioned them in my Pro Tour speech, and I'll mention them again here just because they're awesome. Max has always been my partner in crime. We prepare for every tournament together, Max is amazing. Matthias is a major reason I'm where I am today, it's because of him.

And my mom, I said I'm very close to. She's incredibly supportive. She paid my ticket for my first Pro Tour, which means a lot for me. And I guess I'll just also say that-- I'm not sure at which extent do I believe in any sort of afterlife or anything like that, but I'll say that I miss my dad and he would be very proud to see this moment. I'll shout out his deceased self, if that makes any sense. [Laughs]

James: I think he would be very proud. I'm getting a little bit emotional here as well. If there is something after him passing away in terms of a place in the world, I think he would be very proud looking down on you right now and seeing what you have achieved.

Andrew: Yeah. I think so as well. He really got the competition thing and he more than most people that I interact with regularly would understand what the Pro Tour means to me.

"You shouldn't hold back on doing the things you want to do because you're worried about what other people think. A younger me spent way too much time worrying about that. Even five years ago, I was a lot better at that compared to in the past. And I'm still getting better at it."

—*Luis Scott-Vargas*

Chapter 12

Luis Scott-Vargas

Luis Scott-Vargas, or LSV, wears so many hats that it's a miracle they all stay on his head. But he manages to do it all, and then some.

Luis is a professional Magic player, Vice President of Marketing at ChannelFireball.com, game designer at Dire Wolf Games, commentator at Magic events, and co-host of the *Limited Resources* podcast.

He is also a member of the Magic Hall of Fame and widely considered to be one of the game's greatest players. What's incredible is that Luis currently has ten (ten!) Pro Tour top eights to his name, and this number will likely grow as he continues to actively play the game. He shows no signs of stopping or slowing down.

Perhaps most importantly, Luis is a self-professed master troll. In the trolling department, Luis locks up "greatest of all time" status – no debate there. Over the decades, he's trolled a wide swath of the Magic community in hilarious, merciless and savage ways. One of the recipients, his best friend Paul Cheon, happens to be an exceedingly good sport about it.

As one of the founding members of ChannelFireball.com – the first site to provide high-quality Magic video content – Luis is uniquely qualified as both a world-class player and top-notch content producer. The work ethic that Luis exhibits on a weekly basis to produce timely and relevant content is unbelievable.

I could probably list five more pages of Luis's achievements, but what really stands out for me is his willingness to help others in the community.

After I wrote my first book, I looked for folks in the Magic community to endorse it. On a long shot, I cold-emailed Luis my book manuscript and asked for a "blurb."

Despite knowing absolutely *nothing* about me or my background, Luis took the time to read the whole thing. He not only read my book – he proceeded to write a glowing endorsement for me.

That was insanely generous of him, and I was massively floored. This small gesture was *the* driving force that made me believe that maybe – *just maybe* – I had a future as a content creator. Getting one of the game's greats to recognize my work was a tremendous vote of confidence.

Luis, to this day, doesn't know how grateful I am for what he did. I'm a strong believer that things happen for a reason. His gesture certainly altered the trajectory of my relationship with Magic, and with content creation.

Fast forward a few years later, and Luis and I finally met at a ChannelFireball-hosted Grand Prix event in 2019. I had tried to convince Luis to do a podcast with me for *years*. After meeting face-to-face and having a dialogue about the details of the interview, Luis finally said yes.

And just like that, we recorded this conversation. I wanted to leave the best for last, not only because of Luis's personal significance to me as a content creator, but because he shares his thoughts about the future of Magic.

Given all that's happened in 2019 with regards to the game, Luis's musings felt like the right way to conclude the book.

Recorded in April 2019.

James: Whereabouts are you located today, Luis?

Luis: I'm back home in Denver. I just got back yesterday from Boston for the Mythic Invitational.

James: You must be quite the experienced traveler by this point and have accumulated quite a lot of air miles. Is there a particular airline that you tend to go with?

Luis: I think Southwest is the best airline. It doesn't go internationally, so when I go to tournaments a little further away, I can't use them. I've spent a lot of time thinking about this—it's funny—but Southwest has a lot of things that no other airline does. And that I believe gives it a pretty significant competitive advantage.

James: What kind of stuff?

Luis: You don't have a seat assignment, you board by groups. So it's a lot more efficient because everyone boards and you just take whatever available seat you want. If you're in group A, you board before group B, and they board before group C. It's a fast boarding process. They don't charge for checked bags, which a lot of airlines do. So when you buy a flight on Southwest, you know that the flight charge that you're paying is what you're paying. There's no add-ons, they're not trying to upsell you on a bunch of other stuff.

They also—and this is a really big one for me, because I travel a lot—they let you cancel any flight at any point and get a full refund. The refund is in Southwest credits. It's money saved on their system, so you can only use it to buy their flights. But since I fly with them so much, it means I have full confidence that I will always get my money back if my plans change.

[Laughs] What me and Ben Stark started to do for Grand Prix is we would book our flights with Southwest and then we'd book returning flights on Sunday morning, Sunday night, and Monday morning. Because based on how the tournament went, we could fly back at different times. You can just cancel the ones you don't use and use that credit to book your next set of flights.

That gives me so much confidence that if I'm thinking about going to an event and I'm not sure, I will always book on Southwest. Which means they eventually get that money at some point, but because I feel like there's no risk incurred, it's so much different. And yeah, they do a lot of stuff like that. It's kind of weird that no other airline does. And I think there's a reason why Southwest is the most profitable domestic airline.

James: That's amazing. And as someone who has never lived in the United States, this is brand new to me. I should keep this in mind for the future when I'm booking domestic flights.

Luis: As someone who likes seeing efficiencies and optimization, I find it interesting to see what their business strategy is and how I believe it has helped them quite a bit.

Here's the other thing they do. It's changing a little now, but they used to not have any of their flights displayed on any of the flight aggregator websites. In order to look for Southwest flights, you had to go to Southwest.com. And it's funny because you'd think that showing up on more places makes you better, but I think that's another thing that sets them apart and it trains people to go to Southwest first. And if the flights are good enough, they'll never go anywhere else. So it's not compared as often. It's really interesting.

James: You've got to believe that's intentional.

Luis: I would hope so. [Laughs]

James: You're one of the most well-known players, if not one of the *greatest* players ever in Magic. There's almost nothing that hasn't been written or covered about you. Your achievements are...I think I'll run out of time listing all of your achievements. But let me ask—what is one thing that most people do not know about you?

Luis: I've got two younger brothers, Antonio and Miguel, and they both play Magic. And I had them come out to where I was in LA so we could have a bit of a family-type vacation, and it was funny introducing them to people. They play Magic locally—my brother Antonio goes to FNM every week—he's often had the experience of someone looking at the pairing slip and asking if he's related to me. And he says, "I am, but don't worry, I'm bad at Magic." Let's just say I'm the best Scott-Vargas by *a lot*. [Laughs]

James: I think that's a pretty objective and fair claim.

Luis: My brother Miguel is way less connected to Magic— he plays Commander every now and then. Seeing this whole spectacle and seeing how people interact with me and all that, he thought it was pretty funny to watch.

James: Do you guys look physically similar?

Luis: Me and Antonio look somewhat alike, for sure. Miguel looks very different. He's also 11 years younger than me, so you would not have guessed that we're related just based on looking at us now.

James: I'm only asking because you're well-known online for being a master troll. Maybe I'll say humorist—

Luis: [Laughs] No, no, troll is definitely accurate.

James: [Laughs] Ok, I wasn't sure if I was going to offend you. But I was curious if Antonio ever followed in your footsteps and maybe *posed* as Luis Scott-Vargas at some point in time.

Luis: [Laughs] No, he hasn't done that. Though our family, especially on my dad's side, it's where it [the trolling behavior] comes from. We are all very much like that. The trolling genes do run pretty deep. I remember my dad's brother, my uncle, got me a box of cereal for Christmas. There's a toy inside it. I opened it, and it was a box of Cheerios. And as a seven-year-old kid, I didn't find that very amusing.

James: Oh my gosh, that must have been very traumatic. [Laughs]

Luis: [Laughs] Yeah, Christmas is a big deal when you're seven years old. And Antonio had been singing the song, "All I want for Christmas is my two front teeth." Just some Christmas jingle, so he received two teeth on a keychain. It was just like... [Laughs]

James: Oh my gosh. Was there also a note in there that said, "Santa Claus is not real?"

Luis: There wasn't. But I think at that point we knew Santa wasn't real. I don't remember which Christmas this was, but all I know is that we got enough of this growing up that I think me and Antonio are on the trolling side. My youngest brother, Miguel, is not really, though.

James: So Miguel is a little bit more serious, as far as this stuff is concerned?

Luis: He's not even more serious. He just doesn't troll people. He's a lot more outgoing. We would go back to the hotel. We had dinner, we'd hang out. It was midnight, and Miguel would go out. I guess he's 24 or whatever, 25, he's interested in seeing Boston's nightlife, leaving at midnight and hanging out until 4 a.m. doing who knows what. [Laughs] But it's a little different than the two of us.

James: Let's go right back to the beginning. I would love for you to tell me a little bit about your family situation, and your parents. You told me a bit about your siblings already, but I'd love to know more about your family and where you grew up.

Luis: I grew up in Oakland. I lived in Oakland until I went to college, so I lived in California nearly my whole life. I ended up moving to Denver seven years ago now, but other than that, I lived in various parts of California. My parents are not gamers and did not like me playing Magic very much. I'm sure you have experience with how gamers can be, and the obsession that comes with it. And I got really obsessed with Magic.

I learned how to play Magic when I was 11. As a kid, especially in high school, I spent so much time on Magic that my grades were suffering, and my parents were pretty unhappy about that. They were very much not the kind of parents that would tell me what to do or direct my life. They're not helicopter parents. They did a very good job of showing me and my brothers that we can do what we want to do, with some limits, and Magic went past that for them because it was to the exclusion of other things that I was doing.

I actually stopped playing Magic in high school because my parents wouldn't let me. And it's funny looking back on that because they're now very supportive of my Magic endeavors, but it's now my career, so it means a lot to me and has a lot of opportunity there. But when I was a kid getting bad grades in high school, they were like, "You're spending too much time playing Magic. You need to focus on school."

James: Tell me about your parents in more detail. What are their personalities like, and what were their occupations?

Luis: My mom's side of the family is from Minnesota, and that's where my parents met. And my mom has three younger brothers, my uncles. I have a lot of uncles, I guess six uncles, because my mom has three brothers and my dad has two brothers. Five uncles, I did not do the math right.

But my mom was very much like—she's a hippie. She's very empathetic, she's very conscious when it comes to social justice and the environment, a lot of that kind of thing. And she is very open and, as we were kids, she tried to expose us to a lot of different situations and different ways to be. I remember my parents would go to protests when I was a kid and I would go with them—because I had to, I'm a kid.

And I remember that being part of— I realize that's not what most people did. And Magic is not the sort of thing she would— it wasn't the sort of thing she would want to do. She understands that I love it, but being inside playing a game, especially one that's expensive and takes a lot of time, she's a lot more connected to nature, she lives on a working farm now, she raises chickens and stuff like that. So it's a very different experience than what she's used to, but she also always did a very good job of teaching us to keep an open mind.

And she recently retired, but she was a nurse for 25 years. Which is funny because she knows the things that any bump or illness could be, she over-identifies them [Laughs]. She's almost on the other side of, "This could be bad, we're going to get it checked out."

But my dad is pretty different. He's definitely a troll, he does have a lot of that, I've gotten a lot of that humor from him. He also is very much in favor of learning, coming to your own conclusions and keeping an open mind. He was a chemist and then he was a teacher for quite a while, then he ran science workshops to teach teachers how to teach. He gave them tools to teach science. He's super into all that.

I think one of the first games of Magic I ever played was against my dad. Although he didn't play after that, he was just doing that because I needed someone to play against. But he is more on the side of— he always loved computers and technology. We always had computers, even back when I was a kid, and it was not something that was super common.

I think that the biggest thing I got from my parents was understanding what truly mattered. My dad quit a job that paid a lot of money, as a chemist, to be a teacher, which does not pay a lot of money. He made the transition because he didn't like what he was doing, and he wasn't passionate about it.

That's one of the biggest things I've learned, is following what you're passionate about. I mean, within reason. I hate when people are like, "Just follow your dreams and it will all work out." It won't, it doesn't always work out. Often it does not work out. To be successful, you have to be very lucky.

But I think another good part of that too is— try to follow what you're passionate about. Or, don't make decisions based on just money. Don't get bribed to do something. And that comes with a healthy dose of privilege that you're in a financial situation where you can pick and choose what you want to do. Or you can take a job that pays less because you're still making enough money to get by.

Obviously, people have to do what they have to do. But I think if you can afford to do so, it's good to not make decisions solely based on what is the most financially lucrative, because there's a lot more that goes into life and what you do other than that, and I think that's something that came through very strongly in my upbringing.

Neither of my parents ever cared about money intrinsically very much. They made sure me and my brothers were fed and clothed, and we never wanted for anything. But my parents, more than that, didn't care about accumulating wealth and didn't make a lot of decisions based on that. And I found that to be a pretty valuable perspective. Because there's a lot of things that it takes to live a successful, happy, and well-balanced life, and money is one of those things, but it's not the only thing.

James: It's something that I realize, too, as I get older. The reason why I ask a lot of people about their backgrounds is that I think that your upbringing and your parents specifically guide so much of what you end up becoming, or a lot of the values that you have. You just can't help but be aligned to that.

Luis: Where you come from and how you're raised obviously impacts you quite a bit. At some point, you realize your parents aren't omnipotent, they make mistakes, they're human and all those things. But that still doesn't mean you can't look back and realize how much who you are now is shaped by what you learned growing up.

James: What kind of things did you enjoy doing as a kid before you found Magic?

Luis: I was pretty young. I was 11 when I first started to play, but I was in the Boy Scouts. My friend Seth and I, we bought a starter deck of Revised and two packs of The Dark at the same time, and we were both in the same Boy Scouts troop, we were best friends in elementary and middle school. I liked rock climbing, water rafting, and hiking. I still love hiking and being outside, that's one of the things that I love about being in Colorado, I frequently go hike in the mountains because you can drive for 20 minutes and you're there.

And I played some sports, I was encouraged by my parents to try these things out, so I remember I played basketball and football in middle school, and I did cross-country in high school. But I was never passionate about it. I liked those things, I still try to do various things like that, but I was nowhere near as passionate about sports as I am about Magic.

James: You're obviously very competitive when it comes to Magic and that's led to a lot of your success. Were you competitive in all these other things as well before you found Magic?

Luis: Not quite in the same way. Part of it was I was never near the best at them. And that didn't light a fire in me to try to become the best because I didn't care about it that much. But later, I would become a lot more competitive, and I think I did need a competitive outlet. For a while that was chess, I was in the chess club in high school, and I would play a lot of chess. And in college, before I picked up Magic again, I was a competitive Street Fighter player. I played in tournaments. I represented my college in an inter-college tournament. And I was really into that. But then I dropped that when I started playing Magic again, it clicked that this is what I should be doing.

James: So at first it was you and your friend Seth who got introduced to Magic?

Luis: Yeah. The two of us played, we started going to our local shop, which we could walk to, Dragon's Den, which has long since passed. I ended up meeting other folks who played Magic and becoming a part of the community a little bit there. At this point, I played Magic at a very consistent level for over the last 15 years. But the first half of the time I spent playing Magic, I was very on-and-off, because I wasn't as connected. I was not connected to the tournament scene at all, but even just the local community, it wasn't always Magic that I would play, I would take breaks, and stuff like that. So it was spotty the first couple of years just because you're a casual player and you have a bunch of cards, if you don't go play for a while, you don't really feel it because you're not quite as enmeshed with it. Whereas right now, if I took two months off playing Magic now, it would be crazy. I can't even imagine doing that.

James: Was there a particular point when you realized you were pretty good at Magic? Was there some achievement, or something that someone said to you that signified that?

Luis: I didn't know it until much later, when I started playing Magic again in college, where I would go to The End Zone, our local shop. The End Zone has also long been shut down. And I would do the drafts on Wednesdays and then I would do the drafts on Wednesdays and Fridays, as I started playing more, and at some point the guys there said, "Hey, you should come to this PTQ." And I went to the PTQ and lost playing for top eight.

James: Wait, so that was your first PTQ?

Luis: Uh-huh.

James: Wow. Walk me through that. Which event was that and what was the era?

Luis: It was Onslaught Block Constructed, so this is late 2003, beginning of 2004, something like that. I qualified for PT New Orleans. There used to be 3 PTQs in Northern California for every Pro Tour. And there would be two in the Bay Area and one in Sacramento. I drove down to the Bay Area, played in the PTQ, lost to David Ochoa, actually, for top eight. David and I have been friends for a very long time, and he ended up playing professionally for a number of years.

The next PTQ, I made top eight and played against a friend who wanted to go to the tournament a lot more than I did. I didn't have any aspirations of flying to a Magic tournament, it sounded insane to me at the time. I conceded in the top eight so my friend could maybe win. He ended up winning the PTQ.

And the third PTQ, I top-eighted and then lost, too [Laughs]. It used to be that you could mana burn, and they're also— I don't even know if this was the rule, but it's what the judge said, is I tapped seven lands and then went to untap one of them and he was like, "No, you tapped it, you can't undo it." So I had to play my six mana spell and mana burn, and then die next turn because of that extra point in damage. That was pretty frustrating. But at that point I felt, "Oh, I am pretty good at this." I didn't have a point of reference before, except that I would win a lot at the local shop. But going to a PTQ and top-eighting two of the first three I played, it was like, "I think I know what I'm doing."

James: What led you to start playing again in college? Was it that you felt so bad that your parents didn't allow you to play in high school that you had to get back into it?

Luis: [Laughs] It wasn't that. I never had a big chip on my shoulder because of that or anything. Because I agreed with them, I needed to do better in high school or else I wouldn't even end up going to college. I was working at the dining hall on campus over the summer and— I was a dumb kid. I agreed to a schedule that was horrendous. There was no way I would ever agree to this now. I would work the breakfast rush or whatever, I would work from 7 a.m. to noon, and then I would be off from noon to four, and then I would work from 4 to 8, or 4 to 9. And it's a horrendous schedule because you have four hours in the day when you can't do anything. Obviously, I shouldn't have done that, but I didn't know any better.

But what I did with those four hours is, I remember walking around downtown and just like, "What am I going to do?" And then going into this Magic shop and they were running a Sealed League, where you got a sealed deck, I think a starter, and then two boosters or something. And then you would play, and you would keep track of your wins and losses, you'd play against other people in the league, and at the end of the month, the four people with the best record would have a play-off. It was a great way to kill a couple of hours. So that is what got me back into it.

James: It's very practical. To spend the time between your insane work shifts.

Luis: [Laughs] Let's just say that those hours— the fact that I was getting paid $7.50 an hour did not go a long way to make me feel good about doing those hours.

James: And also depending on how much you spent on Magic, you'd probably end up spending all the money you earned, right?

Luis: Yeah. But yes, it was mostly, I had to do something and— oh yeah, Magic, I remember Magic. I never forgot Magic, but it was more like, "I guess I could try playing this again," and then I got into it really quickly. Turns out I am quite into Magic.

James: Was it during those PTQs that you started to get "the fire"?

Luis: It wasn't until the next year when there was a Pro Tour in California, in San Diego, that I decided, "Hey, I would really like to play in this Pro Tour." And look, again, I say this not realizing back then how difficult this path was. But in my head, I'm like, "I want to win a PTQ because I want to play in this PT because it's in California." So then I won a PTQ. [Laughs] That's not normally how it goes, but things were different back then. The formats were much harder, and the tournaments weren't quite as big.

I don't know, I felt like I had a pretty good edge on the field, and I ended up winning a PTQ for Pro Tour San Diego 2004, driving down to the Pro Tour. Going 8-7 or whatever but making day two and feeling like I would like to play in more of these, which I ended up doing.

James: That's awesome. And during this very pivotal period in your Magic life, who were the people that you had met that you think really helped you?

Luis: The guys that I lived with had a big part on this. I ended up moving in with guys I met from the local card shop. Ryan, Eirik and Matt. And I still am good friends with Eirik and Matt. I don't see Ryan as often, we lost touch. But for example, at GP LA...Eirik was there, and he was rooming with me for that. Because we still keep in touch, he plays Magic and goes to tournaments every now and then,

I think we're going to hang out in London at the end of the month. But living with those guys and all of us wanting to play in tournaments and go to these things really did help. I mean, yes, I think we probably could have stood to diversify what we were doing with our time a little bit more, but I don't know, we were a bunch of 20-year-olds who were really into— "Let's do this Magic thing." All of us were going to school at the time, at UC Davis, but we all spent a lot of time playing Magic at the card store. In fact, we would meet at the card store between class and after class. If you went there, we would be there, probably.

James: Just obsessing about Magic, right?

Luis: Oh, yeah. Then David Ochoa, who I mentioned, I played with him, we had been playing— since we played in the Bay Area, we knew each other from there, and he's one of my oldest friends at this point. I just got to see him recently, it's awesome, even though he doesn't play Magic anymore. But we would always go to tournaments and talk about decks and stuff like that.

James: And the friends that you played Magic with a lot in school, did they ever expect that you would become the player that you are today?

Luis: No, not at all. They knew me before that, and then we all played Magic and went to these tournaments, and then as time happened, my career took the course it did, and they all think it's really funny to look back on that. Because both Matt and Eirik have played in Pro Tours. In fact, I played Matt in one of the Pro Tours I won, that was his first Pro Tour. And

Eirik played PT Paris, he had the Caw-Blade deck, because that's what our team came up with. They had some experience with Magic at a higher level there, too. Magic is not a footnote, but a smaller part of their life, even though it was a huge part of our lives back then, it has continued that way for me and it's kind of funny for them to see that as they go through their lives as well.

James: I know that you're also very good friends with Paul Cheon, who currently works at Wizards. When did you guys meet? How did that happen?

Luis: That's kind of connected. Paul and I were on the same clan on Magic Online—Dragon Quest. And Paul's first Pro Tour was my second Pro Tour, which was Pro Tour Philadelphia in 2005. We both busted out of the PT and we started money drafting. This is back when people used to do that. So you'd do 2-on-2 or 3-on-3 drafts for $20 or $50, or whatever. And again, it's been a long time since I've ever seen anyone do this, but this is back when we were young, hungry grinders. We cared about the money and it was a cool way to test our skills against these famous PT players that we'd heard of and whatnot. Actually, Paul and I bonded over beating Cedric Phillips, in a money draft 15 years ago. [Laughs] We beat Cedric badly, three drafts in a row, it was really satisfying.

Paul was in Southern California, he was in L.A., and I was in Northern California. And he'd come hang out when we would go to PTQs, he would come stay with us, and then he ended up moving in with us. So the next year, it was me, Paul, Eirik, and Matt, and we all lived together. Paul was bumming our couch, he wasn't paying rent or anything, but he wasn't in a position to be able to do that. He lived with us for— I don't know, almost two years, solid year and a half, with the three of us, plus Paul.

James: Wow, on the couch, huh? [Laughs]

Luis: Yeah, that was where he was at. And we lived, breathed, and ate Magic. And too much food. But mostly Magic. We played a ton of Magic Online, we became feared Magic Online grinders back when no one really knew who we were and we didn't have any accomplishments, but a lot of the people who were good, especially in the US, thought we were good because we played all these drafts and because we would play online all the time. And it was funny when we first started seeing some tournament success, that kind of transition.

James: It's almost a parallel to poker. The way that you described the money drafts reminds me of the movie *Rounders*, where you're going to do underground games, try to make money, and win off the rich, experienced players. Actually, I don't want to say rich. Just experienced players.

Luis: [Laughs] Yeah, no one was really rich at that point.

James: Yeah, Magic is not one of those things like poker, for that. And then you're talking about the grinding online, making a name for yourself so that when you start to get more accomplished, you start spiking paper Magic or paper tournaments, right?

Luis: Yeah. That's kind of how it ended up happening. It's funny how we, at some point, remembering this, we were the great unknowns of the future of American Magic or whatever.

James: Obviously, you and Paul go way back, and what is something that people may not know about Paul?

Luis: Paul started college at UCLA when he was 13, which is—yeah, not typical. And also, I don't think it's a very good thing to do. I don't think a 13-year-old kid needs to be thrown into that and I think Paul has some pretty mixed feelings about that as well. But Paul is one of those genius kids or whatever. Paul is a really smart dude and I remember talking to him about this many, many times.

James: Yeah, I mean, it must not be easy to associate with people that are way older than you, when you're 13-years-old, right?

Luis: Also, what do they think when they see a 13-year-old on the class? "Wow, that kid is pretty smart, he's probably pretty cool." It's more like, "Does that kid think he's smarter than me? He's 13 and in my class." You know? There's no way the kids reacted well to that.

James: Yeah. Do you guys still hang out quite often?

Luis: Yeah, I saw Paul a couple of days ago, he was doing commentary at the Invitational, and doing it very well. I think Paul might just be the best commentator right now. And I even say this putting myself in the mix. I think Paul is awesome. He's hitting a stride, and I think we're lucky to have him working on Magic and we're lucky that he's doing the other things he does. Though it is sad that he doesn't stream anymore.

James: What do you think is your biggest moment as a Magic player?

Luis: It's hard to answer that because biggest moment can mean a lot of different things. I think one of the moments—winning the Pro Tour was honestly the first time I felt like, maybe I can do this, maybe this is a thing. You know? Because I had a lot of near-misses in terms of—I had a lot of exit opportunities when it comes to Magic. Here's what's funny. Everyone's life—you know the movie *Sliding Doors*?

James: The Gwyneth Paltrow movie, right?

Luis: Yeah, where she misses a subway door in the beginning of the movie and then the rest of the movie is about the two different tracks her life takes based on that, right? Every person has a lot of these *Sliding Doors* moments in their life, and you're not aware of most of them. You don't have a movie crew trying to replicate what would happen. All of us have missed a bus, missed a flight, or left early for something, and probably had our lives meaningfully changed as a result, and it's hard to track down those moments.

But when you're a Magic professional, where Magic is part of your life, those moments are much more clear to you. Because you can look back and say, "Wow, if my tie-breakers were worse, I wouldn't have top-eighted that Pro Tour and won the Pro Tour. And if that happened, who knows where I would have been."

Or, "If I drew a card..." Andrea Mengucci beat Matt Nass at the Invitational in one of the games that I watched, where if Matt Nass actually went one card higher, he would have won. And that would have knocked Andrea out of the tournament. And now Andrea has $250,000. Right? Had the cards been in a slightly different order, maybe Matt Nass— or maybe neither of them would have had that money. And that money is going to change Andrea's life dramatically. Both in terms of the actual money and the opportunities now that he's an Invitational winner.

All of us have stories like that, and Magic has given me a lot of those where I've seen times where had I not made top sixteen at the tournament to qualify for the next tournament, I may not have been a professional Magic player. Had "x" happened, "y" would have happened. But I think PT Berlin is a big one. Honestly, being on the *Spellslingers* show with Day9 was a pretty big one, because this was a couple of years ago. And the Magic landscape is changing, I know we are going to talk about that later because there's a lot to talk about there, but this is back when Magic wasn't even close to being a huge deal and I was on the set of a show that was a very big production, I was definitely not used to that. And even years later, people still talk to me about *Spellslingers*. So I think it's something that has impacted or touched a lot of people or gotten to a lot of people that don't normally play, that aren't the same audiences. And this was one of the first times it felt like it had crossed over into being something that people who aren't super invested in Magic might watch. I think those were two of the biggest things.

James: You have had a lot of success, overall, when it comes to playing Magic. What is something important that you've learned that's not the stereotypical "take it one match at a time" sort of advice?

Luis: The biggest thing that Magic can teach you is how to lose. Is how to deal with things not going your way. And it can be hard, trust me. I did not feel good when I got knocked out of the Invitational last week, when I went 0-2. It's the worst record you could have. But I think Magic really does teach you— it's a two-prong thing, it's like, how do you deal when something bad happens to you, and how do you learn from it, and what can you do differently? And it's important to realize when you can and can't. I mean, the old saying, what is it? "Grant me the serenity to accept the things I can't change, the courage to change the ones I can, and the wisdom to tell the difference." People say that, obviously it's an important concept, but Magic really drills it into you.

I've lost more games of Magic than almost anyone, right? I've played so much Magic. And it makes it so that when I get a flat tire, I don't get really mad. Yeah, I'm not happy about it, but I know it's just going to happen. You're going to run over a nail sometimes. Sometimes you're going to be late or your flight is going to get cancelled. Sometimes you're going to drop your ice cream. All these things happen. And what Magic does is, it pounds that into you. Because most people don't have to confront losing quite so many times, quite as often, as much as when you play Magic. And you care when you lose at Magic. I mean, I still care. And I think it's valuable because people don't— you're not born learning how to deal with frustration.

And having Magic helps give you tools to deal with that, both in terms of accepting when a bad thing happened, what's next? And also, how am I going to learn from this? What can I do to prevent this in the future? The second part of that being, I made the right decision, a bad thing happened anyway, I'm going to make the same decision next time, not being result-oriented.

This is another key part of it. Results are clearly a way to get data out of what happened, right? It makes sense that you would want to do that. But I think if you really think about things and you look at them, you can realize that if you're going to drive to work and there's two different ways you can take, and one way takes 15 minutes and one way takes 10 minutes, and you take the way that takes 10 minutes, and there's an accident, and it takes you an hour, that doesn't mean that the next day you should take the longer route, because that doesn't make any sense. You could have an accident there. You should just take the shorter route.

And a lot of people do badly with this where they make a bad decision and it turns out well, they're [thinking], "Wow, I made a good decision." Or they make a good decision that turns out badly and they're like, "That was a terrible decision, I shouldn't do that." And the answer isn't those things, the answer is, make the best decision given the information you have. Maybe learn and adjust from that, maybe after the third time, there's an accident and you realize, "Wow, this route is never a good route because there's a bunch of potholes that always cause accidents." But most of the time, if you're making the right decision, you should be able to separate that from the outcome and continue to make the right decision as these things go on.

James: Is there something that players can do to have more clarity over those decisions? Because I think everything that you just said— anyone hearing this will agree 100%. But in the heat of the moment, or even after the heat of the moment, they may miss the forest for the trees and not actually think about it that way.

Luis: I think that part of it is— if you look for what you could be doing better, you'll end up, I think, in a better place. Because the answer is, sometimes, "I couldn't have done anything better, I was going to lose no matter what." And I feel that way about the Invitational, right? I got run over in a bunch of games, and I don't feel like I had any close decisions.

But most games of Magic aren't like that. Most games of Magic, or any other complicated thing you'll do, you often have options. And when you know the outcomes you don't like, I think it's valuable to look at what you could have done differently. And sometimes, you'll study it and come to the conclusion, "No, I made the right decision, it just ended badly." And that's fine. But you do need to put in that due diligence of, "Let's take stock of what I did and let's see what I could do differently next time." Because it's important to try to figure that out so that you can improve.

James: What's the best match of Magic you've ever played, and why?

Luis: The finals match in Pro Tour Kyoto 2009 against Gabriel Nassif is one of my all-time great matches of Magic. I mean, it was the final of the Pro Tour, game four was just absurd, and we actually— me and Marshall [Sutcliffe], actually, went back and re-recorded commentary over game four 10 years later, because it was that good of a game.

James: Right. I recall you asking the community for a copy of the original video.

Luis: Yeah. We couldn't find the original video. Luckily, someone had uploaded it and they got in touch with me over Twitter. It was a wild match. And you can find both the original and our commentary version on YouTube,[18] I think.

Another match which unfortunately wasn't recorded...was a written feature match, when I played against Tomi Walamies for top eight at PT London, which was my third Pro Tour. And I was pretty excited to even be in that position. But we played this insane match of Limited where, at different points, I thought I couldn't win, then I thought I couldn't lose, then I thought I couldn't win.

I ended up getting decked because there's a card called Hinder, which is counter target spell and put it on the top or bottom of its owner's library. During his upkeep with no cards in deck, [Tomi] played an instant and Hindered it to the top so he wouldn't run out of cards. And I knew he was going to do that, but I had to keep just playing anyway. It was a wild game.

James: I want to talk to you a little about Channel Fireball. You had an instrumental hand in the founding of it, and it's a story that people don't often know much about. Channel Fireball is a collective, it's a company, it's one of the most influential Magic organizations today. Maybe you can start off by telling me how you were involved in this thing with Jon and Mashi.

---

[18] https://youtu.be/OmYVlfb7xJE

Luis: This was at the end of 2008. Jon Saso, the owner of Superstars and Sports—a long-standing comic/cards/memorabilia store in Cupertino, San Jose—approached me about wanting to start a new website and launch a whole new Magic website. His dad, Gary Saso, actually founded Superstars. It's funny because when I was younger, me and David Ochoa, we would go to Jon's store and trade in cards and this is how we got our first set of Power Nine. We would trade in a bunch of Standard cards for Power Nine, because Jon always had a good buy list, he was very aggressive about buying cards. I remember trading for a Black Lotus and a Mox Jet and all these things.

Jon and Mashi Scanlan—he's in the Magic TV segments, and he's ThaGuyOnTheLeft on Twitter—they approached me about wanting to start a website that they wanted to call ChannelFireball.com. See, there's two meanings there. One is, Channel Fireball, like the Magic combo, Channel plus Fireball, it's a combo from Alpha. Mountain, Black Lotus, Channel, Fireball—turn one win. And the other is that the whole genesis of the idea was that we would offer channels, like TV channels of Magic content. Because at this point, no one was really doing Magic videos, that just wasn't a thing. And their idea, that they had thought up in Jon's garage, as they were sitting around drinking—Mashi and Jon, Alex Alepin and some of these other guys who still actually work at Channel Fireball—their idea was, what if we offered videos? What if we offered TV channels of content? And this would fill a need that no one is really filling now, and it would be awesome.

At this point, I was working for Adventures Cards and Comics, also known as BlackBorder. com. The owner Avrom had sponsored me and Paul Cheon. And I owe a lot to Avrom, he took a chance on us when we were nobodies, we had never done any sort of Magic content. His sponsorship was what let us pursue our Magic dreams. And it was a tough decision, to decide whether to go with Jon, Mashi, and their goal of making a whole new website and a completely new thing or stay at the place I already was.

And I ended up— after much back and forth and really having a tough decision, deciding that I wanted to try and start this new thing. The idea of creating something new was just so appealing to me. And we ended up launching Channel Fireball after trials and tribulations with the website, which continue to this day. You know, it's hard to have a good website [Laughs].

James: [Laughs] Behind the scenes at Channel Fireball, yeah.

Luis: Yeah. A robust website that sells 10,000 different individual products and has all this kind of content, it is hard to—the architecture for that is difficult. But anyway, we ended up launching Channel Fireball, and it was cool that kicking off the launch, I got second at the Pro Tour in Kyoto, so that was our way of announcing to the whole Magic world that we were going to do this thing.

James: That's awesome. And as I heard from you and others, it wasn't exactly a smooth ride. In the early years of Channel Fireball, what were some of the challenges you guys faced?

Luis: Part of it was...it was a pretty intensive project when it came to both labor and costs. And Jon and I didn't take a salary for a while. Because this wasn't exactly a startup in that Superstars did exist, and we had this inventory, and we had a lot of the physical stuff. But the website was completely new. And we did not have unlimited resources. That was difficult for a while, Mashi ended up taking some years off, working as an attorney instead, because we couldn't afford to keep everything going the way we wanted to. And that was not easy.

James: It must have been tough. What was going through your mind at the time?

Luis: Well, this is the part where there is some survivorship bias. I don't want to say something like, "If you believe in yourself and stick with it, things will be alright," because often, they're not alright. Often, things don't work out. Most things fail. Most businesses, most restaurants, most new ideas have a hard time getting off the ground because it is difficult. And depending on what level of success you're looking for, it can be hard to hit.

That said, we really believed in what we were doing, and for that reason, we decided to continue doing it, and we thought that it was worth pursuing. I don't know how long we could have pursued it if things didn't start to pick up, but they did. Honestly, I think offering draft videos was—it's not even a hard concept, so it's not like we're a bunch of geniuses or whatever, but we were [the] only people offering draft videos initially. Just videos of Magic gameplay.

And I remember Jon telling me right before Alara Reborn came out, "Hey, you've got to do set reviews. Zvi [Mowshowitz] used to do set reviews, no one really does card-by-card reviews, you've got to do them." And now the set reviews, I think, are the most popular piece of content that I do. Most of the people who talk to me about content mention the set reviews, and they are a lot of people's initial entry into Magic content. Just, "Hey, how can I get better at Magic?" And they say, "Read LSV's set reviews." Just doing that. These things weren't complicated, but we just did them. And sometimes that's all it takes.

James: It makes sense, because a lot of players, their first experience with organized Magic is pre-releases. People get hyped when a new set comes out, so they want to read things around the new set in a way that doesn't seem intimidating. I think the set reviews dovetail into that.

Luis: Yeah. We are very invested Magic players, right? I am, you are, I read your book. [Laughs]

James: [Laughs] Thank you. Thank you for doing that.

Luis: No, I enjoyed it quite a bit. It can be easy for us to forget how intimidating evaluating new cards is. And I try to keep that in mind. When I'm talking about a card in a set review, I talk about it as if the person reading it knows not a whole lot about Magic. And hopefully, there's still value for the people who do, I think there is, but I want to explain why this thing is good. What makes this card good, bad, or in-between, or under what circumstances is it good? And that can be a really comforting tool.

One of the peculiarities of the schedule is my Green review, because I always do it in color order, comes out last. Frequently, people have told me that if you live in Australia or in APAC countries that's very, very far ahead of my time zone, they don't get to the last set review before the pre-release, and some people just aren't comfortable playing with the cards until they've had a chance to read what I've written about them, because that gives them a lot more understanding of them.

James: It just shows you how global the game is, and also how much of a readership there is, right?

Luis: [Laughs] Yeah, it is funny. Magic is certainly a huge global game at this point.

James: What are some things about starting a Magic-related business that people may not necessarily know?

Luis: One is, what are you doing to differentiate yourself? Because it's all well and good for me to say, "Yeah, we did draft videos and set reviews." Yeah, ten years ago, there weren't those things, or there weren't enough of them. That's not true now. If Channel Fireball were to launch now, it would not succeed, right? Because what would we be offering that's not offered by dozens of places at this point? So you want to be bringing something new to the table.

Another is, you have to have follow-up, consistency. One of the biggest things that we always hear as podcasters, because I also have a podcast, *Limited Resources*, and we talked about a lot of aspiring podcasters who have this great idea. A great idea doesn't matter as much as showing up and doing the thing. It does when you're talking about a business, because a business is trying to fill a particular niche. But when you're doing something like a podcast, showing up and doing it, and being consistent, is way more important. Because anyone can have an idea and do two episodes. The question is, do you do seven episodes, ten episodes, twenty episodes, and at that point, have you hit a groove, have you started building an audience? It's the same as streaming. Yes, you do need something to differentiate yourself because there's so many streamers these days, but showing up and being consistent is one of the ways to help build an audience.

James: I love that because that's something that I try to apply to my life as well. Over half of the battle is showing up. And ideas are free, execution of ideas are not, right?

Luis: [Laughs] Exactly, execution is where a lot of people stumble.

James: And I think it applies to Magic, too. People have all these great theories, and some Magic players are super well-read. They probably memorized PV's latest article, your article, or whatever. But at the end of the day, there's something to be said for having a foundation and grinding Magic. Not to say that you want to grind Magic all your life, but if you don't go and do it, it doesn't really matter what ideas are in your head.

Luis: Yeah, exactly. It is very easy to have great plans and great ideas, but just showing up is another part of that equation that you have to apply. You could be the best Magic player in the world, if you go to one tournament, you're not necessarily going to do well. You have to go to a bunch of tournaments in order to leverage that.

James: Walk me though how you continued on the trajectory with Channel Fireball.

Luis: When we started Channel Fireball, I was the editor-in-chief, and I did a lot of the article editing, posting articles, contacted authors, we had an original slate of authors that we launched with— I don't think any of them still write for us, though. But they were instrumental in launching the website. I'm going to give them a shout out. Jeremy Fuentes, Zaiem Beg, Jon Loucks, David Ochoa, Gerry Thompson. They were the original contributing members and getting it off the ground like that was really important. I think that part of it is Channel Fireball let me—because it was such a Magic-related line of work, and it gave me flexibility—it let me pursue my career in Magic, which also helped Channel Fireball, a nice symbiotic relationship there, and that's what allowed me to form the Team Channel Fireball and, really, our team did dominate for a number of years.

           We were, by far, the best team. I'm not making that claim now, though we are number one of the team series rankings, but mostly, back then, we were bringing something to the table that a lot of people didn't. And we came up with a lot of good decks and had a lot of good finishes as a result. In fact, it's kind of a beat for the people who didn't get there, but almost every member of the original Team Channel Fireball is now in the Hall of Fame. And I think a lot of us owe it to that team. This is myself, Brian Kibler, Josh Utter-Leyton, Owen Turtenwald, Ben Stark, Martin Juza, Shuhei Nakamura, Paulo Vitor Damo Da Rosa, and Eric Froehlich. These are people who were in the original team. To have that

457

many Hall of Famers, I think does show that we know what we're doing.

But I think that the success of Team Channel Fireball and myself was very interwoven with the website Channel Fireball, even though a lot of work got done on the website that wasn't directly related to me. It needed to grow and eventually— we have a lot of employees now, and I don't know all of them, which is very different from when we had five people. [Laughs]

James: You have had other roles or gigs outside of Channel Fireball. Can you talk me through some of those as well?

Luis: The reason I moved to Denver in the first place was to work for Dire Wolf Digital, which is a game studio here. And back then, it was to work on a project that never came into fruition, which is very typical when it comes to game development. But it soon transitioned into working on Eternal, which is a digital card game that you can play also on mobile, on PC, Steam, iOS. I'm a senior game designer at Dire Wolf. I've been more focused on doing event coverage, I cover our qualifying tournaments leading up to Worlds this year and do some design work as well. But that's one of the reasons that— one of the paths that my career has taken, which I didn't anticipate, is I've done a lot of game design work, which I enjoy greatly. And it's funny how it all ties back in, because a lot of what you're doing when you're playing Magic is trying to optimize what you're doing in-game and have tactics and strategy. When you're doing game design, it's a lot of very similar kind of work, even if it's trying to come to different results. You're not trying to optimize or win as much as trying to optimize what is a good user experience? How does a good game flow? What is a good system? What are pleasing gameplay experiences? What kind of players does this appeal to? It has helped me understand Magic a lot better.

James: The way you described it, there seems to be a good synergy or relationship between playing the game at a high level and designing a game. When you started in that role, was it difficult to ramp up as a game designer?

Luis: Definitely. It's a hard job. It's an awesome and rewarding job, but it's the kind of job where you are tasked with— you're trying to answer a bunch of questions and you're trying to make a bunch of decisions, and you very rarely know whether you answered them right. It's hard to get the feedback. Some things are more obvious than others, right? To put on my game designer hat, Nexus of Fate, the Buy-A-Box promo, not a good card.

James: [Laughs] Yeah.

Luis: It doesn't take a professional game designer to tell you that, right? But on the flip side, which cards are good? You don't know when you make a set of 300 cards, how much each individual card impacts things or what effects they have. Because I can tell you pretty confidently that printing Baneslayer Angel made Magic tons of money. You know, Baneslayer Angel changed the paradigm, it was a big creature that looked appealing that was also good.

James: Yes. It was a Spike card, and it was also a Johnny card. It fit many demographics.

Luis: It's the sort of thing where you can look at some cards like that, but when you're trying to dive even deeper, it's hard to know whether you made good or bad decisions in a lot of cases, because there's a lot of confounding factors where— The Mythic Invitational last weekend was an unparalleled success on tons of metrics. Does that mean that all tournaments should be best of one? I don't think so and I sure hope not. But that was part and parcel of what went down, and part of your job as a game designer, or as a marketer, or as anyone who is making decisions and trying to gauge reactions is try to parse out what was successful, what wasn't, and what made those things be that way.

So game design is really hard. I learned a ton from Matt Place, he used to work at Wizards, and he is certainly the most influential person when it comes to game design for me.

James: It is interesting what you said because I work in software, or building software products, and I think there's an art to listening to the data and listening to the feedback, and also doing things out of your own convictions because you feel that in your gut. It sounds to me that, designing a game, you have to balance that as well, right?

Luis: Definitely. You need to get the right conclusions from the data you have, and you also need to—you don't want to be too biased. Yes, your deck matters and part of the reason you're in a position to make these decisions is because you've presumably made good ones in the past. But you also have to be willing to change that if the data really does indicate that you're doing something wrong. I don't know, it's really hard.

James: And in a parallel universe, because we're talking about *Sliding Doors*, in a parallel universe where you are not working on Eternal and you are not working on Channel Fireball, had you considered working for Wizards at some point? Because I assume the door was probably open for you at some point, in terms of being a designer for them. I know lots of amazing people have walked through those doors.

Luis: It's been hard. I've never seriously considered it because playing professional Magic is such a big part of what I enjoy doing, and I think it would be hard to give that up. And that's part of the reason I never have pursued it. There's a lot that would appeal to me about it. If you told me as a kid, I could maybe work for Wizards someday, I would be over the moon, because it sounds awesome. And it still does sound awesome, it's not that it doesn't, it's just that I get to have my cake and eat it too, working on the things I get to work on while still playing Magic, and it would be hard to give up part of that. And also, it would be hard to give up streaming and being the public-facing figure that I am, being on LR [the *Limited Resources* podcast].

Paul [Cheon] is happy at Wizards and I'm glad he's there, I think Paul is incredible, he does a great job. Paul did have to give up streaming. And he does the Wizards stream every week or every other week, but it's not quite the same, still. It's awesome that he does that, I think it's cool, but giving up a big part of your autonomy when it comes to how you relate to the public is something that would be hard for me to do.

James: If you're a super-competitive player and you get those highs from competition and playing with the best, it must be hard to almost force a mandatory retirement on yourself, right?

Luis: Yeah, that is how I would have seen it a lot of the time. My relationship to competitive play is very wild, I took a year off to do coverage, right? My tournament attendance goes up and down depending on how I'm feeling. That said, cutting that off completely is not something that I would come too close to doing.

James: You don't have to name any names, but have you had conversations with people about this type of decision? I imagine it must not be easy for them to make that choice, to walk through the doors of Wizards of the Coast.

Luis: Yeah, it is hard. It is hard to be on the other side of things. I mean, I kind of get that experience with Eternal as a game designer, of getting to watch people play with your cards, react to what you make, and complain about the obviously over-powered or under-powered decisions. [Laughs] Cards you make, or whatever.

James: [Laughs] Yeah.

Luis: And there's a satisfaction there, there really is. It's just a different thing. You don't feel the same kind of rush that, at least, I get from playing. I'm not alone in that, there's a lot of people who feel that way. So it's a much more level-headed experience. I have also felt that on the coverage side where—look, when you go do coverage of a Pro Tour, it's a lot of work, there is variance in how you do, right? You can have a good tournament, a bad tournament, or what have you. But when you do it, it's a pretty flat experience.

There's not huge highs or low lows, it's more like, I'm doing this job, it's a fun job, but there's a lot of cool stuff going on, it's exciting. But it's still, at the end of the weekend, you're going to get paid the same amount you knew you were going to get paid going in, that's just how jobs work.

And when you go play at a Pro Tour as a player, it's huge. The difference between a Pro Tour where you do well and top-eight, and you're on top of the world, and a Pro Tour where you go 0-5, is really big. You don't have those highs and lows when it comes to coverage, and the same is true when you're designing games. You're not going to experience quite as high highs or low lows, and that probably works better for some people. Maybe I'm an action junkie, it would be hard for me to give that up.

James: I've talked to a couple of people on the show and they didn't exactly articulate it, but I would imagine for someone like Jon Finkel as an example, there's probably still a reason why they're going to these events, right? It's the camaraderie—

Luis: It's not about the money [Laughs].

James: It's not about the money, that's for sure. Jon probably doesn't need it at this point. I don't want to put words in his mouth, but I think it's about the community and also about the high-level competition, right?

Luis: Yeah. I care about those things a lot more than anything else. Look, I'm not out here— and I don't think Jon feels this way either. We don't have something to prove. Paulo [Vitor] doesn't have anything to prove. But it doesn't mean it doesn't feel good to do well at a tournament and feel that rush of success.

James: And let me switch gears into Magic's future. Because we've been talking on this and touching on it for the past little while, you just talked about coming back from the Mythic Invitational. So how do you feel about Arena, and its impact on the landscape of Magic?

Luis: It's opening the door to a lot of people to reduce the barrier to entry. The number of people who now stream Magic, who it turns out, always did play, like Savjz, right? Who made top four at the Mythic Invitational, is a very successful Hearthstone streamer and tournament player. He now plays Magic. And it's not that he didn't play Magic before, he always did, but Arena now gives him the ability to play Magic on stream, so it's a lot more visible. It also is clearly giving a lot of people the ability to play and the desire to play when they wouldn't necessarily have done so earlier.

So look, I actually do like Magic Online, I play a lot of Magic Online, it's what got me started as a competitive player or professional player, I still play it, I played some today. But it's a way to play Vintage online now, which is awesome. But I don't think that Magic Online is what you would use if you wanted to expose new people to Magic, and in fact, it has consistently not done a good job in that, just because it looks like a videogame from the 90s, right? It doesn't work like a modern videogame.

James: [Laughs] It's still stuck there, yes.

Luis: Yeah. And Arena is clearly designed for looks as well as playability, and it shows.

James: I know I'm only a datapoint of one, but I started playing Arena recently as part of work research.[19] That's how I justified it. I never played Magic Online, despite all these years, I've only played paper. And the first day I played Arena, six hours passed by, and I played the next day to try and get the free deck that they said they would promise me for the next day. And it's just this dopamine rush, and I had no idea that I would enjoy playing the pre-constructed decks so much. But here I am, playing Arena. And I hope, above all else, that they never, ever release a mobile version, or else my life will just be over.

Luis: [Laughs] Oh yeah. So yes, it is a game-changer, it really is.

James: You talked about how streaming plus Arena—that's how it brings more personalities into the mix, folks who've always played Magic but didn't stream. How about streaming as a whole? You guys at Channel Fireball are the forefathers of video content. But streaming adds a whole new dimension now. Every day I visit Twitch, I can see all these Magic streamers on my front page. How do you see that evolving, in terms of the streaming experience? Both for viewers and also for streamers.

Luis: I think Magic—there were Magic streamers before Arena. You had Paul Cheon as one of the earlier ones, Kenji NumotTheNummy is still very successful, Gaby Spartz—

---

[19] As part of our efforts with CardBoard Live to enable better storytelling experiences for Magic play.

James: Yeah. I mean, all-time streamers, absolutely. They're legends in my mind.

Luis: Yeah. Not Paul. But the other two, definitely.

James: [Laughs]

Luis: But it's a game-changer now in terms of the kind of viewership numbers you can expect and what people are watching for. And now you have this injection of tons of new people into the streaming ecosystem. Because first of all, you had the people like Savjz, or any of the people who've come over from Hearthstone...all these pretty big streamers from other games. Day9 does some streaming, Kibler is now back streaming Magic.

And then you also have the MPL, which is something that we haven't talked about yet, and the fact that all those streamers have a contract to stream 10 hours a week. Almost all of them are streaming more than that, but that was just to get their foot in the door. The number of streamers has gone up dramatically and now you have a lot of different options when it comes to what kinds of streams you want to watch. Do you want to watch someone talk about Limited and explain every single turn in excruciating detail? Marshall Sutcliffe will do that.

If you want to watch someone play a bunch of wacky decks, a bunch of streamers will do that. If you want to just watch someone who is going to play competitive, best of three rank, you have a lot of MPL members who will do that. It means that streaming is now— honestly, the whole Channel Fireball TV channel thing, streaming is that, Twitch is that, where you can find almost any kind of Magic you want available there pretty easily.

James: There's something for everyone, right?

Luis: Yeah, both in terms of what kind of energy level you want. Do you want someone who is really energetic and is going for big moments? Do you want someone who is a little more laid back and relaxed? What do you want to watch? What format do you want to watch? There's all of it there. And there's going to be, and there has been, some overlap between streaming and competitive play, what does it mean to be a Pro Magic player, what are the metrics for success? I think there's a lot of uncertainty as to how exactly it's going to go, but I do think it is positive for Magic and the people involved.

James: What about competitive play as a whole? I mean, it's one event, but it was the biggest, that being the Mythic Invitational. What do you see that foreshadowing in terms of things to come from Wizards of the Coast and Magic esports?

Luis: Definitely that Arena tournaments are going to be the headliners. I know a lot of people have seen the success here of Arena, where the emphasis— they see that as paper Magic being at risk. I don't see it that way at all. I think both these things complement each other really well. But when it comes to tournaments and viewership, the Mythic Invitational blew everything else out of the water, and there's a lot of different reasons for that. But I think Arena is a big part of that, and that's one that I expect us to see more in the future in terms of where the focus is, where the emphasis is.

James: What are some other things, other than Arena itself, that impressed you about the Mythic Invitational?

Luis: I think that the coverage team did a very good job. It was a good mix of people like Marshall [Sutcliffe] and Paul [Cheon], who are coverage mainstays at this point, and then new folks who bring a different vibe and energy. You had Becca Scott as the floor reporter, you had AliasV as a play-by-play, and then you had [Brian] Kibler and Day9 as hosts. That's a different lineup than what we normally see. And I think that definitely helped— again, it's not that there's any one thing— I think the biggest takeaway for me is that Arena is a very good way to showcase Magic tournaments. As a viewing experience, as a coverage experience, as a playing experience, all those things, it's very good. I think that anytime you say you're going to give away a million dollars and you have a huge stage, that also helps. So that's not necessarily something that could be replicated. I think that there's a lot of things you can do to make tournaments more successful and this had a good mix of those. Part of what would worry me going forward is if the conclusion was "best of one is the best." [Laughs]

James: [Laughs] Something tells me that they're going to experiment with different formats.

Luis: Yeah, I believe so. Because what we talked about earlier, you have to parse what was good and what was bad out of all these various things, and in this particular case, I think that this tournament was successful despite the format, not because of it. I don't think that the best of one standard format showcased Magic in a way that Magic needs to be showcased. The deck diversity was low and the overall quality of games was somewhat lower than a lot of Magic that we could play here.

The other thing is you had a mix of— the invite list of this tournament was unique, and I don't think we're going to see another tournament this year with quite the same list. Because this tournament had 30 MPL members and 26 invited people. So these are streamers, this is the invite I got, you had a mix of— mostly streamers, but a couple of other content-type folks. And then the top eight Arena people on the ladder. And if you did a normal best two-out-of-three tournament, I suspect that the MPL would have cleaned up. Because the skill gap between the most skilled people in the tournament and the less experienced people in the tournament is way bigger than a normal tournament.

And a lot of these streamers were quite skillful and are quite skillful, but [even though Andrea Mengucci won the tournament] I don't think [he's] better than William Jensen or Reid Duke, you know? That's not a knock on them, these are the 30— the MPL is the 32 most successful professional Magic players of the current time. So it makes sense that if you have a tournament that's a mix of personalities, that's part of why I think the tournament was successful.

It's awesome that you get to watch Amy the Amazonian play Magic against Luis Salvatto or whatever. But also, I think, having a high variance format does make it so that everyone is on a slightly more even playing field because you're just increasing— you're increasing the luck and making it more likely that someone can punch above their weight class, which I think is totally fine for what the tournament was supposed to be.

James: Some of the best moments were seeing the professional streamers. They did an excellent job of presenting their brand. And that's something that I think Magic players and MPL Pros need to step up their game on, in this new world.

Luis: Totally. I've been on that side for so long, and that's one of the things they definitely need to learn from these streamers is—be entertaining. You're an entertainer. And I get that that's part of what— it goes into the uncertainty of what is going to happen with professional Magic. Because there are professional Magic players, I know, I've talked to them, who want to be professional Magic players. They want to show up and have the best chance of winning the tournament, and that's what they're focused on.

That's never been where I'm at. I've always considered myself an entertainer primarily. That's my first job. And I think that that's a cool way to go about things because I think that's the world we're in, and that helps Wizards get their goals too, which is more people watching. But I can't blame people for wanting to be the best at this, and deciding that's what they're going to focus [on]. I just think that, if we're in a landscape where you're judged on how many eyeballs you can bring to the table, you should put a thought towards how entertaining you want to be.

I understand that can be a cause for unease if you're not sure what metrics are the most important and how you're going to get there if you're like, "Look, I want to play 60 hours of Magic a week and just be the best at Magic I possibly can, I'm not interested in playing it up for the crowd." And if what we're seeing is being entertaining as part of your job as a professional Magic player, there might be some growing pains there.

James: Yeah, and it's tough if you're not LSV, you're not handsome, top five all-time in Magic and an entertainer, first and foremost. [Laughs]

Luis: I don't know if I would describe myself in all those ways, but I do think that I know how to be a buffoon. So I'll settle for that. I mean, look at me and Cedric Phillips, right? The match itself was not good. It just, objectively, was low quality.

James: [Laughs] I know, but the drama leading up to that was great.

Luis: Yeah, yeah. Cedric beat me in ten minutes with two white weenie decks. But that is secondary to the point, which is me and Cedric spent weeks talking trash to each other. In fact, we still did post-tournament, somehow. And I think that is what gets people hyped about this. And not everyone is going to want to do this, nor should they. You have to make your own decision as to what you value. But I love this kind of stuff, and I think this is the path forward. It is where I would spend time and energy if I were someone looking to succeed at Magic. Don't just focus on how good you are, focus on the entertainment value. There's a reason that a lot of these people were invited to this tournament, it was not a list of who's the best players in Magic, because I think that would have led to a less entertaining tournament.

James: Yeah, and hey, I could not be happier at the top two players at this event. I mean, Andrea Mengucci, he's been doing Legacy videos forever on CFB, mind you. He's super entertaining. I don't think he's the best player in the world, but he has a certain brand and

471

he knows how to build his audience. He's a delight to watch. So it was really good to see him at the top.

Luis: Oh yeah, I'm a big Mengucci fan. I love interacting with him on Twitter and talking to him, and we like a lot of the same things, which is good food and beta Magic cards. He's an awesome winner, he is very enthusiastic, he fits this mold very well, he's very entertaining, and I think he's one of the better people that they could have had win the tournament.

James: Yeah. And I didn't know the second-place finisher, Piotr, all that well. But I was impressed, too, for two reasons. He was humorous in a dry way, and he also had that propeller hat.

Luis: Oh, the hat, yes.

James: It was so awesome. He's also from Poland, which means he's representing Magic at a sort of global stage. I thought it was really cool to see him there, too. It was just really fun to see personalities like that, you know?

Luis: Yeah. I think that he did a good job representing that as well.

And I think that leaves a ton of optimism going forward of like, Magic can achieve these great things, and it might take some time to figure out exactly what the best balance of all this is, because— look, you don't want to have— it's not fun to watch a "rock-paper-scissors" contest, right? We're just going to show up and flip coins and act entertaining while doing so. But it's also— I don't think Magic necessarily needs to be this intricate chess match where people sit there and think for two minutes before making a play, because that's not fun to watch either. Let's find a way to make it exciting, have the strategy, have depth, and accomplish all these things at the same time. And I firmly believe that is possible.

James: I'm wondering, Luis, what the future holds for you. If you were to project a year to three years into the future, what do you see as your goals as a Magic professional or as a content professional?

Luis: That's a good question. A lot of my focus is on the projects I work on. Making sure Eternal has the best chance to succeed, I poured my heart and soul into that. Making sure Channel Fireball is equipped to face the future, whatever that future may look like. We have some exciting stuff... They're working on a lot of cool stuff in that regard as well, so I'm kind of— if I got to choose where to put my luck, assuming everyone has a finite supply of luck— I know that's not how it works. But assuming they did, I would put my luck on the projects I'm working on, rather than my tournament successes. And maybe this is me speaking from a position of privilege, but I don't have a ton I feel like I need to prove.

My biggest—the biggest thing for me going into every tournament is, I want to play up to the level I believe I can play at. I want to not embarrass myself. I don't want to do a bad job by my own metrics. I'm not that worried about needing to hit any certain levels in terms of finishes to prove that I'm good at Magic. I think I've done mine already. It would be hard to argue with that. It's more on the things that I'm working on because that is stuff that takes a lot of my time and attention, and my hopes and dreams.

That said, I'm going to be making Magic content in three years. I would be shocked if I were not. And what that content will look like? I don't know. It might have more of a streaming emphasis, it might have less. It might be more on Channel Fireball. It might take some other form - I don't know. But it's going to be— I'm still going to be part of it. I'm very connected to this game, it's a big part of my life, it is something that I don't see changing in the foreseeable future. I know at some point it might, at some point I might take a step back, but now is the opposite, I'm putting my foot on the gas pedal now, because there's just so much going on.

James: What's something that you would tell the younger LSV from five years ago, if you could go back in time?

Luis: This has gotten better almost every year of my life, but I am still not where I'd want to be on this. I would tell him to not care about what other people think.

One of the biggest level-ups I ever got was when I realized people just don't care about what you do. They're not paying as much attention at all the little things you think they're caring about. You wore mismatched socks, or you spilled something on your shirt? People don't even care or notice.

You shouldn't hold back on doing the things you want to do because you're worried about what other people think. A younger me spent way too much time worrying about that. Even five years ago, I was a lot better at that compared to in the past. And I'm still getting better at it. Just be more assertive and confident.

And always ask. Honestly, the worst that can happen in most cases when you ask, is that someone says no. I mean, you're a good example of this. How many times have you asked me to go on the podcast?

James: [Laughs] How long has it been? Two years or something like that?

Luis: It's been three years. I think you probably asked me like, ten times or something. And I kept saying, "No, but keep asking me." Because I didn't have the time, inclination, or whatever. But now we're here, we're doing it, and if you had just taken that first "no" and never asked again, it wouldn't have happened.

But you're persistent, which is really good. And I think not being afraid to put yourself out there is such a big thing when it comes to basically any facet of life, and it's hard to do. And that's one of the things I feel you generally get better at the older you get.

And I don't know that there's a way to shortcut that, but maybe me saying this can help someone listening realize that going for the things you want to go for is so much better than just sitting there and watching things pass you by. Or not knowing what would happen.

Because if you ask and get told no about a job, a date, anything like that, at least you know. At least you know and maybe you can learn from that. If you don't say anything, all you're going to worry about five years later is: "I really wonder if I should have tried harder to get that internship," or whatever.

James: Yeah, what's the saying? You miss all the shots you don't take, or something like that?

Luis: Yeah, I think Michael Scott said that.

James: [Laughs] Yeah, Michael Scott was the original innovator before Patrick Chapin.

Luis: Exactly. [Laughs] Yeah, I mean, it's something I've gotten a lot better on. I try to encourage people to do so when I can. It's hard because our natural inclination is to be unassuming, to be cowardly, and to not rock the boat. The boat could stand to rocking in most cases. In most cases, no one is going to make you do things outside of your comfort zone and you have to do that yourself.

James: What advice would you give to a player who is playing in their first Magic tournament?

Luis: I think not putting too much of an emphasis on results. Try to have fun and don't focus on winning as being the goal. Because if you go and winning is the only way you're going to be happy, if you don't top-eight, you're going to be unhappy, you're going to be unhappy at almost every tournament you go to. And that's a set-up for failure.

I think that having realistic expectations or even no expectations—I don't have expectations when I go to a tournament. I don't go to a tournament like, "Yeah, I'm going to top-eight this one." I just go and play, and when I top-eight, I'm happy. And when I don't, yeah, sometimes I'm pretty sad, but at least I wasn't putting it all on making top eight. I know that's one of the outcomes, in fact, the most likely outcome. So don't worry too much about trying to finish any particular place to prove to you or other people that you're worthy or valid, or your preparation was good, or you're good at Magic, or whatever. Just go and play and try to get as much as you can out of the experience.

James: Would you say that for your Magic career, you were mostly happy or unhappy?

Luis: Mostly happy. I'm lucky enough to have had a lot of success in that— it's easy to be happy when you're doing well. I've had a couple of pretty big droughts when it comes to Pro Level success. I hit Silver one year— for those of you who don't know, the Pro Club, Silver was the lowest level, Platinum was the highest, and given the amount of tournaments I went to, I would hit Silver just based on the minimum Points. So when I say I hit Silver, it means I did not win much more than the minimum, I lost at every tournament. And I had a pretty solid drought there, and it didn't feel good, I was pretty unhappy. But having gone through that, I think makes me better in the future when dealing with that. Because now, when I have a losing streak, I know those things are possible.

Paulo Vitor Damo da Rosa, one of the best players of all time, he was Silver two years in a row, and if he can— if that can happen to him, it can happen to literally anyone. So it's hard to get too bogged down on that, even when it is hard to deal with it in the moment.

I think I hit one of my lowest lows in Magic when I lost in the Invitational last week. It was hard to deal with because it was a combination of having the worst possible finish, which is 0-2, it being really short, because most tournaments, if you go to a Pro Tour, you have to pick up five losses before you're out. So minimum, you're playing five best two-out-of-three matches. Here, I lost two best-of-one Dual Standard matches. I played five games of Magic. [Laughs] I think I played Magic for 20 minutes. And it felt unbelievable that I'd tested for two months for this tournament where I was out in 20 minutes.

I never had an experience like that. So it was pretty rough. Especially with the amount of money at stake, and how little I liked playing the format, it was really hard to deal with. I'm okay now, but it was a pretty rough day.

James: When you had those lowlights—not this past weekend, but from before, when you were in the drought—what was it that kept you going?

Luis: Probably that I still knew and believed I was great at Magic. And that can be hard too, because I know this advice isn't as applicable to everyone who is listening because if you haven't experienced success, you might not have much to fall back on. But I already won a Pro Tour, I had a bunch of Pro Tour top eights. I knew I was good at Magic. And even though my confidence took a hit there, and I started to doubt that, I still, at the baseline, was like, you know what? I know I'm good at Magic, I know I understand this. And I was able to help myself put it in perspective and realize I was having a bad run.

It can be harder when you don't know that about yourself. I remember a funny anecdote. Jared Boettcher was experiencing a lot of tournament success at this point. He had top-sixteened two PTs in a row, he was Platinum, and I remember watching him play, and he was playing so bad, and I remember thinking, this guy is winning it all and I'm losing it all? And he's playing like this? Do I not understand Magic anymore? Seriously, is there something that I'm not getting? How can this guy be winning so much? Turns out he was cheating and got banned for it.

James: Right, he was stacking the lands with the shuffles and stuff, right?

Luis: He was rigging the deck shuffling. That made me feel so much better. [Laughs]

James: That was your rock bottom. Like, what's happening here, right?

Luis: If this guy is winning and I'm losing, there's got to be something that I don't understand going on. The part I didn't understand is he was literally cheating. But you know, at the time, I didn't know that, so it was rough to handle.

Glossary
(A to Z)

Affinity deck. A deck archetype that consists almost entirely of synergistic artifact creatures and the Affinity mechanic. The marquee card of this deck is Arcbound Ravager.

Aggro. Short for "aggression." Refers to a strategy of aggressively attacking and dealing damage to the opponent as the way to victory, often trading long-term stability for speed and explosiveness. See also: Control, Midrange.

Apprentice. The original "unofficial" online program for Magic that allows players to play the game over the Internet.

Arena. An updated official online program for Magic, released in 2018. The program is streamlined for faster pace of play and stronger visual appeal compared to its predecessor Magic Online. See also: Magic Online.

Block format. A group of connected, in-sequence Magic expansion sets with common themes and backstory shared between them. For competitive Magic purposes, "Block Constructed" tournaments refer to special events where only cards from a certain Block can be used in deckbuilding.

Block PTQ (Pro Tour Qualifier). A Pro Tour Qualifier where only cards from a specific Block can be used. See also: Block, Pro Tour Qualifier, Pro Tour.

Blue-White Control deck. A deck archetype that uses the blue and white colors of Magic to control the state of the game. See also: Control.

Breakers. When players have the same record (wins-losses-draws) in a tournament, tiebreakers (or "breakers") are established by examining the players with superior win percentages against the top players in that event. This determines who has the higher seeding in the final standings.

Caw-Blade deck. A Standard deck that features Squadron Hawk, Stoneforge Mystic, counter-magic, Jace, The Mind Sculptor, and equipment cards such as Batterskull. A strong Control deck for its time that created a stranglehold in competitive Magic. Some have claimed Caw-Blade as one of the strongest decks in Magic's existence, relative to the other deck options at the time. See also: Control.

ChannelFireball (CFB). An online retailer for Magic cards and related gaming accessories based out of Santa Clara, California. Also one of the biggest Magic strategy content sites on the Internet today, with a strong emphasis on video.

Cockatrice. An open source, multiplatform program for playing card games over the Internet. Can be used to "unofficially" play Magic, as well as other collectible trading card games.

Combo. A "combination" deck leverages the unique interaction between a few key cards to win the game with minimum interaction from the opponent. Unlike traditional Magic strategies like Aggro or Control, the goal of a Combo deck is typically to do something powerful and win as quickly as possible, on one key turn of the game.

Control. A strategy of regulating the game and stifling what the opponent is trying to do. Do they have creatures? Kill the creatures. Do they have key spells? Counter those spells. Control means establishing dominance over the game state, and then winning at one's leisure once the opponent is powerless. See also: Aggro, Midrange.

Counter, or counter-magic. A general concept that refers to playing a spell to "counter," or neutralize, the opponent's spell. A reactive strategy that is often employed in Control and Midrange decks. See also: Control, Midrange.

Coverage. The broadcast coverage, typically via video stream, of a competitive Magic tournament. Coverage includes the logistics of presenting gameplay, as well as play-by-play commentary.

Cube, Cube draft, or Cubing. A specialized format of Magic that is similar to a Draft, only with "packs" of cards curated based on a specialized, fixed pool of cards. This allows the creator of the Cube to design interesting interactions of cards that are drafted together. See also: Draft.

Czech Pile deck. A Control deck in the Legacy format popularized by Czech player Tomas Mar. It uses cards in the black, blue, red, and green colors. Key cards include Deathrite Shaman, Baleful Strix, Jace, the Mind Sculptor, and Kolaghan's Command. See also: Control, Legacy format.

"The Deck." A deck and concept popularized by Brian Weissman. It relies on gradually accumulating card advantage and controlling what the opponent is trying to do, via powerful spells. The thesis of the deck was to slowly but surely establish an iron grip over the game, and then use a singular win condition to close the match. "The Deck" had a profound effect on the way the game was played; prior to its rise, Magic decks tended to lean towards other archetypes such as Aggro (aggression) and creature-based strategies. See also: Aggro.

Death and Taxes deck. A white Control deck in the Legacy and Modern formats. Typically uses creatures to stifle the opponent's development. See also: Control.

Decked, or getting decked. Losing a match by running out of cards to draw in one's deck.

Delver, or Delver deck. Refers to both the card Delver of Secrets, as well as the deck that contains the namesake card. Delver decks tend to contain cheap and low-cost threats, backed by counter-magic and methods to disrupt the opponent's mana development. It can play both the Aggro and Control roles. See also: Aggro, Control.

Draft format, draft, or drafting. A competitive format of Magic where decks are not constructed beforehand. Rather, players in a group (or "pod") open new packs of Magic cards, draft one card, and then pass the remaining cards to the player next to them. After all the cards are drafted, players build a deck with their cards and a tournament is run with the newly-constructed decks. See also: Limited format, Sealed format.

Duelists' Convocation International (DCI). The official sanctioning body for Magic competitive play. Provides guidelines for logistics, rules, and judging within tournaments.

Elf-ball deck. A green Elves-based Combo deck. Wins by attacking with an insurmountable force of Elves. See also: Combo.

Expected Value (EV). Refers to the typical predicted financial outcome of a Magic endeavor, whether it be opening a box of cards or participating in a tournament. "Positive EV" refers to recouping one's cost and profiting, when comparing the cost of admission versus the reward.

Extended format. An earlier non-rotating Magic format that allowed cards from a wide range of Blocks to be played. Later replaced by the Modern format. See also: Block format, Modern format.

Faeries deck. A deck that consists of Faeries cards.

Friday Night Magic (FNM). Officially sanctioned Magic tournaments, held on Friday nights in participating gaming stores. FNMs serve as the entry point to competitive tournaments.

Gold status. A status used to denote a Magic player who has earned a certain threshold of points in a given season of competitive play. In increasingly beneficial order, the levels are Bronze, Silver, Gold, Platinum. See also: Pro Points.

Grand Prix (GP). Competitive Magic tournaments that award prizes and invitations to Mythic Invitational events. Held at different cities around the world, GPs create a fun atmosphere for players to play high-level Magic and live out the "Gathering" part of the game. As of 2019, GPs are held as events within a "MagicFest" weekend.

Grixis. Refers to a Magic deck that plays black, blue and red cards.

High Tide-Time Spiral deck. A Combo deck that abuses synergies between cards like High Tide and Time Spiral to generate a lot of mana. As the *coup de grace*, the deck forces the opponent to draw more cards than they have in their library. In Magic, when you draw a card and there are no more cards left in your deck to draw, you lose. See also: Combo.

Illusions-Donate deck. A Combo deck that relies on combining two cards to win: Illusions of Grandeur and Donate. The basic idea is to play Illusions of Grandeur, which causes its controller to lose twenty life when it leaves play. The next step is to use the Donate spell to give control of the card over to the opponent. Conceptually similar to lighting up a ticking time bomb and then throwing it over to the opponent. See also: Combo.

Invitational Qualifier (IQ). Qualifying tournaments for Star City Games Invitational tournaments. See also: Star City Games.

Jeskai. Refers to a Magic deck that plays blue, white and red cards.

Johnny. A demographic of Magic player who enjoys the flavor of the game. To quote Mark Rosewater, lead designer for Magic: "Johnny is the creative gamer to whom Magic is a form of self-expression. Johnny likes to win, but he wants to win with style. It's very important to Johnny that he win on his own terms. As such, it's important to Johnny that he's using his own deck. Playing Magic is an opportunity for Johnny to show off his creativity." See also: Spike, Timmy.

Jund. Refers to a Magic deck that plays black, red and green cards.

Junior Super Series (JSS). A series of local tournaments for players 16 years and younger. Discontinued in 2008.

Lands deck. A Prison-Control deck that uses primarily land cards with specialized effects to win the game. The Prison element refers to restricting the opponent's primary game plan by locking down the effectiveness of their cards. See also: Control.

Legacy format. A format of competitive Magic play in which cards from all sets are legal. With the exception of certain cards being too powerful to play – there is a "ban list" – Legacy allows players to use cards from Magic's 25-year history. See also: Vintage format.

Lethal. Dealing enough damage to kill the opponent. "Attack for lethal" means to deal enough damage to lower the opponent's life total to zero.

Limited format. Format of competitive play in which decks are constructed from opening packs of cards. A generic umbrella term that refers to both the Draft and Sealed formats. See also: Draft format, Sealed format.

LoadingReadyRun. A Canadian sketch comedy collective, known for producing Magic-related videos.

Magic League. Magic League was one of the original online leagues for competitive players, run through Magic Online. Many notable players have cut their teeth playing this league. See also: Magic Online.

486

Magic Online. The official online program for Magic that allows players to play the game over the Internet. Also referred to as MODO (Magic Online Digital Objects).

Magic Pro League (MPL). An exclusive competitive league and membership given to the top players in the game, introduced in 2019. MPL members draw a salary provided by Wizards of the Coast and are encouraged to stream themselves playing Magic. See also: Mythic Championships.

Maindeck. In a competitive match of Magic, players construct decks with maindeck and sideboard components. Maindeck refers to the cards that are already in the deck by default, whereas sideboard refers to cards from "the bench" that can be swapped in after game one in a best-of-three match. Constructed format is 60 card maindeck and 15 card sideboard. Limited is 40 card minimum maindeck and rest of the card pool is sideboard. See also: Sideboard.

Mana burn. An old rule in Magic in which mana that is not used will "burn" or damage the player. One point of damage per mana not utilized.

Midrange. A Midrange strategy is a spectrum-based strategy that oscillates between Aggro (kill the opponent quickly) vs. Control (regulate the game). An effective Midrange strategy shifts gears based on understanding the opponent's game plan and adapting as a result. See also: Aggro, Control.

Miracles deck. A Control deck in the Legacy and Modern formats that uses the best cards in the blue and white colors. The namesake card is Terminus, which is activated via the Miracle mechanic. See also: Control.

Modern format. A non-rotating Magic constructed format that allows card sets from Eighth Edition and beyond to be used. Contains a "ban list" of cards that are deemed inappropriate for being too powerful or unfun. Replaced the previous Extended format. See also: Extended format.

MODO. The alternative name for Magic Online. See also: Magic Online.

Money draft. A team-based Draft competition with financial wagers on the line. Not officially endorsed by Wizards of the Coast, but popular amongst high-level players. See also: Draft.

MTG Arena. See: Arena.

Mulligan, mull, or taking a mulligan. When a tournament game of Magic begins, players draw an initial opening hand of seven cards at random. If they do not like their opening seven, they have the option of shuffling the cards back and re-drawing an opening hand – this is called taking a mulligan. There is a minor penalty for taking a mulligan that negatively affects the player's chances to win the game.

Mythic Championships (MC). The highest level of Magic competition. Mythic Championships are invite-only tournaments for players who have qualified through winning past MC events, winning MC Qualifiers, being a member of the Magic Pro League, or via special invite. The hallmark of an all-time Magic player is how well they perform at MCs. Top-eighting an MC, or outright winning one, changes a Magic player's life forever. Before 2019, Mythic Championships were called Pro Tours. See also: Pro Tour, Top eight, Magic Pro League.

Mythic Championships Qualifier (MCQ). A qualification tournament to enter a Mythic Championships event. See also: Mythic Championships.

Naya. Refers to a Magic deck that plays green, white and red cards.

New World Order. A deliberate decision by Magic Research & Development to design cards with reduced complexity as a way to make the game more accessible to newer players.

On the draw. Going second in a game of Magic. As there is a benefit to going first, the player going second gets to draw a card.

On the play. Going first in a game of Magic. Benefit is you get to play cards first, but do not draw a card for the first draw phase.

Parallax Wave deck. A Combo-Control deck that combines the cards Opalescence and Parallax Wave to invalidate all of the opponent's creatures. See also: Combo, Control.

Planeswalker. Characters created in the Magic storyline to represent the most powerful beings in the conceptual multiverse. They walk between different planes of the multiverse – hence, planeswalker. In the game, players summon planeswalker cards to fight on the player's behalf.

Platinum status. A status used to denote a Magic player who has earned a certain threshold of points in a given season of competitive play. In increasingly beneficial order, the levels are Bronze, Silver, Gold, Platinum. See also: Pro Points.

Pod. A group of players who are drafting together. Usually refers to the organization of groups for the Limited portion of a Mythic Championship or Pro Tour. Typical pod is eight players. See also: Draft.

Power Nine. Nine iconic cards printed at the beginning of Magic's existence. The cards are: Black Lotus, Ancestral Recall, Time Walk, Mox Pearl, Mox Sapphire, Mox Jet, Mox Ruby, Mox Emerald, and Timetwister. See also: Vintage format.

Pro Points. In the Pro Tour era prior to 2019, finishing well at notable Magic tournaments meant that one could accumulate Pro Points. Depending on how many Pro Points were accumulated, a player could qualify for the following status (in increasingly beneficial order): Bronze, Silver, Gold, Platinum. Reaching a certain status conferred benefits and privileges to the player, such as qualification towards upcoming Pro Tour events. In 2019, this system has been phased out with the rebranding of the Pro Tour to Mythic Championships. See also: Pro Tour.

Pro Tour (PT). The highest level of Magic competition. Pro Tours are invite-only tournaments for players who have qualified through earning Pro Points, winning Pro Tour Qualifiers, or other difficult-to-achieve criteria. The hallmark of an all-time Magic player is how well they perform at Pro Tours. Top-eighting a Pro Tour, or outright winning one, changes a Magic player's life forever. Since 2019, Pro Tours have been renamed to Mythic Championships. See also: Mythic Championships, Top eight.

Pro Tour Qualifier (PTQ). A qualification tournament to enter a Pro Tour event. See also: Pro Tour.

Prowess. A special mechanic in Magic that makes creatures larger when certain spells are cast in a game.

Preliminary Pro Tour Qualifier (PPTQ). A qualification tournament in which the winner is allowed to participate in a Pro Tour Qualifier. See also: Pro Tour Qualifier, Pro Tour.

Psychatog Upheaval deck. A blue and black Control deck that uses Psychatog and Upheaval as its key cards. See also: Control.

Regional Pro Tour Qualifier (RPTQ). A Pro Tour Qualifier that is based in a particular region in the world. See also: Pro Tour Qualifier.

Scoop. To concede. To literally scoop up one's cards, signifying that the game is over.

Scry rule. After a player mulligans using the Vancouver (pre-2019) mulligan rules, they can peek at the top card of their deck and determine whether to keep it on top or place it on the bottom. This "top or bottom" methodology is called the Scry rule. See also: Mulligan.

Sealed format. A competitive format in which players are given six booster packs of Magic, and given license to build a deck from any of the cards opened. Players then play a tournament with the decks they built. Deck must be minimum of 40 cards. See also: Draft format, Limited format.

Show and Tell deck. A Combo deck that uses the namesake card Show and Tell to "cheat out" overpowered creatures and effects. "Cheat out" refers to paying much less mana than what is printed on the card, due to Show and Tell allowing this action. See also: Combo.

Sideboard. In a competitive match of Magic, players construct decks with maindeck and sideboard components. Maindeck refers to the cards that are already in the deck by default, whereas sideboard refers to cards from "the bench" that can be swapped in after game one in a best-of-three match. Constructed format is 60 card maindeck and 15 card sideboard. Limited is 40 card minimum maindeck and rest of the card pool is sideboard. See also: Maindeck.

Silver status. A status used to denote a Magic player who has earned a certain threshold of points in a given season of competitive play. In increasingly beneficial order, the levels are Bronze, Silver, Gold, Platinum. See also: Pro Points.

Sneak and Show deck. A Combo deck that uses Sneak Attack and Show and Tell. Often used interchangeably with "Show and Tell deck." See also: Show and Tell deck.

Spike. A demographic of Magic player whose enjoyment of the game is derived primarily from winning in competition. To quote Mark Rosewater, lead designer for Magic: "Spike plays to win. Spike enjoys winning. To accomplish this, Spike will play whatever the best deck is....To Spike, the thrill of

Magic is the adrenalin rush of competition. Spike enjoys the stimulation of outplaying the opponent and the glory of victory." See also: Johnny, Timmy.

Splinter Twin deck. A Combo deck that uses the Splinter Twin card. See also: Combo.

Standard format. One of the most popular contemporary Magic formats, in which only cards from recent sets are permissible for play.

Star City Games (SCG). An online retailer for Magic cards and related gaming accessories based out of Roanoke, Virginia. Star City Games is well known for holding high-quality regional Magic tournaments called the Star City Games Open Series, or "SCGs" for short. It is also known for hosting some of the finest Magic strategy content on the Internet.

Storm deck. A Combo deck that uses the Storm mechanic to replicate card effects to kill the opponent as quickly as possible. A hallmark card of the deck is Tendrils of Agony. Magic Research & Development has stated on the record that the Storm mechanic was a "mistake," and is not likely to be a major theme in future designs.

Sweepers. A Magic effect that wipes out, or "sweeps," several groups of creatures all at once.

TCGPlayer. An online retailer for collectible cards and related gaming accessories based out of Syracuse, New York.

Tempo. Tempo is a general concept that refers to the pace in which a Magic player presents their threats and develops the board, relative to the opponent.

Timmy. A demographic of Magic player who enjoys winning in big splashy ways. To quote Mark Rosewater, lead designer for Magic: "Timmy is what we in R&D call the 'power gamer.' Timmy likes to win big. He doesn't want to eke out a last minute victory. Timmy wants to smash his opponents. He likes his cards to be impressive, and he enjoys playing big creatures and big spells." See also: Johnny, Spike.

Top eight, or top-eighted. Refers to finishing in the top eight in the standings of a Magic tournament, which typically cuts to a playoff structure and contains significant prizes. The concept of a top eight is shorthand for denoting a significant finish. It follows that the number of lifetime top eights that professional players hold in Pro Tour (and to a lesser extent, Grand Prix) events becomes a litmus test for their dominance in the game. Variations of this term exist in the form of top-X, where X = 16, 32, 64, and so forth.

Tron deck. A Combo-Control deck that accelerates its resources by combining Urza's Mine, Urza's Power Plant, and Urza's Tower – the three conceptual pieces of "Tron." See also: Combo, Control.

Valakut deck. A Combo deck that uses Valakut, the Molten Pinnacle to deal a lot of damage to the opponent. See also: Combo.

Vintage format. A non-rotating format where almost all cards in Magic's existence are allowed for play, including the iconic Power Nine. The difference between the Vintage and Legacy formats is that Vintage is even more powerful, and the Power Nine are not permitted in Legacy play. See also: Power Nine, Legacy format.

Wizards of the Coast, or Wizards (WOTC). The company that makes the *Magic: The Gathering* game. A subsidiary of Hasbro, Inc.

World Magic Cup Qualifier (WMCQ). A qualification tournament for Worlds. See also: Worlds.

Worlds. Shorthand for World Championships. An annual Magic tournament in which players compete by representing their home countries.

Closing Words

I want to thank the people interviewed in this book for being gracious with their time and entrusting me with their experiences.

Thanks to Julian Knab for being highly supportive of the project since Day One. Julian, you're the best.

A heartfelt thank-you to my editors, Jesse Scoble and Devinder Thiara, for devoting endless hours to making the content readable, on-point, and fit for publication.

Much gratitude to Arzu Fallahi, who took this project on short notice and created the fabulous illustrations and cover art.

To Jeremy Edwards, who provided comprehensive feedback and suggestions as the book reached the finish line.

To my friends who helped proof-read the book: Brian Anderson, Sean Brown, Spencer Huang, Victor Legros, Tayelor Martin, Brenden McBain, Ian McKeown, Ethan Nam, Travis Pendleton, Stephen Tang, and Noah Weil.

About the Project Team

James Hsu is the creator of the *Humans of Magic* project and the co-founder of CardBoard Live. He is the author of *Magic: The Addiction*.

James currently lives in Beijing, China.

Jesse Scoble is a writer, game designer, and story editor. Jesse currently works at Ubisoft Montreal, and wrote for Assassin's Creed: Odyssey, Far Cry 5, Assassin's Creed: Origins, and Watch Dogs 2.

Previously he was Creative Design Lead on Wizard101; a designer at Webkinz; a community writer for City of Heroes; and has also contributed to more than 30 RPG books and related anthologies. He co-wrote and directed a comedic web series about working in the video game industry (Project 23A).

Devinder Thiara is a writer, editor and business analyst. His writing credits include Modiphius' Conan RPG Line and John Carter of Mars: Prince of Helium. These days he spends his time on freelance writing/editing projects and working on a book about personal finance between gigs as a business analyst.

Arzu Fallahi is a concept artist and illustrator. She has created concept art for Destiny 2, Skylanders Swap Force and Skylanders Super Chargers. Currently she is freelancing, contributing to a new IP and painting street art.

Made in the
USA
Columbia, SC